the salad garden

—

joy larkcom

To Don, soulmate for half a century

Frances Lincoln Limited
A subsidiary of Quarto Publishing Group UK
74–77 White Lion Street
London N1 9PF

The Salad Garden
Copyright © Frances Lincoln Limited 2017
First Frances Lincoln edition © 2001
Text copyright © Joy Larkcom 2017
Photographs copyright see page 279

British Library Cataloguing in Publication Data
A catalogue record for this book is available
from the British Library

ISBN 978-0-7112-3870-1

Printed in China

9 8 7 6 5 4 3 2 1

Quarto is the authority on a wide range of topics.

Quarto educates, entertains and enriches the
lives of our readers – enthusiasts and lovers of
hands-on living.

www.QuartoKnows.com

the salad garden

—

joy larkcom

FRANCES
LINCOLN

contents

—

Author's note

I would never have imagined, when working on the first edition of *The Salad Garden* in the early 1980s, that I would be revising it again in 2016, in my eighties. What a thrill to find so many people, young and old, not just eating more salads, but discovering the joy and satisfaction of growing their own, marvelling at the taste of freshness and the diverse flavours and colours that can emerge from even a flower pot on a patio. And almost invariably, growing organically.

In the introduction to the 2001 edition (pp. 9–15) I outlined the journey salad growing has taken our family on, from an allotment plot to an experimental market garden with several little potagers in Suffolk. And now a new chapter has opened. In 2002 we uprooted ourselves to retire to County Cork in the south-west corner of Ireland. In the years since, our energies have been channelled into converting a windswept field into a fan-shaped potager. The final project – I promised my husband Don it would be the final project – was to make a small raised bed potager near the house. This has become our new salad garden.

Its core is two pairs of rectangular raised beds built from recycled plastic, 1¼m/4ft wide, 3m/10ft long and 75cm/30in high, so easily reached without bending down or kneeling. At either end two semi-circular, stone walled beds gently round off the area, with an irresistible stone seat set in each. All the beds are linked with rebar arches covered with sheep wire, where sweet peas, honeysuckle, climbing beans, pumpkins, blackberries and other fruit clamber. This is the setting for our salads. I love it.

We also grow salads in the small greenhouse attached to the house, mainly tomatoes in summer, and in winter seedling salads, oriental and Texsel greens, spinach and endives. It is always full.

The past thirty years have seen many changes in varieties available to home gardeners. In this new edition I've drawn on advice from knowledgeable specialists, and the trials carried out by the Royal Horticultural Society, to suggest the best of what is available for today's salad growers. Where possible, I've included compact varieties bred for smaller gardens and containers, as well as varieties with decorative qualities. After all, salad plants have to feed the body and the spirit.

Introduction

It is almost impossible to believe, from the viewpoint of the twenty-first century, how my garden and gardening ideas have changed since I first started growing vegetables seriously in the 1970s. Then my garden was a very plain plot (an allotment in fact), whereas today our Suffolk kitchen garden includes several picturesque little 'potagers' – each carefully designed to have shape, colour and form all year round. Way back then the salad plants we grew could be counted on the fingers of one hand; lettuce, tomatoes, cucumbers, radish... Today, during the course of two or three seasons, we grow well over 150 salad plants.

Finding these plants and learning how to grow them has been a long and wonderful voyage of discovery. Its first 'leg' was what we fondly called our 'Grand Vegetable Tour'. In August 1976, my husband Don Pollard and I, with our children Brendan and Kirsten, who were then seven and five years old, left Montrose Farm for a year to travel around Europe in a caravan. Our main purpose was to learn about traditional and modern methods of vegetable growing, and to collect the seed of local varieties of vegetables, which, as a handful of far-sighted people had begun to appreciate, were an invaluable genetic heritage that was vanishing fast.

Moving in a southward arc, we travelled from Holland to Hungary, through Belgium, France, Spain, Portugal, Italy and Yugoslavia. We gleaned information from seedsmen, seed catalogues and the backs of seed packets; from research stations and markets; from market gardeners, peasants, cooks, botanists and housewives. We managed to collect seed of quite a number of old local varieties (over 100 samples were safely housed in the seed bank later established at Wellesbourne in the UK), and we learnt a great deal about cultivation methods. But we were totally unprepared for the many new salad plants we found, especially plants that could be grown in the colder months of the year. In Holland, Belgium, France and Italy we found beautiful varieties of lettuce, chicory and endive that were previously unknown to us; in Belgium we 'discovered' sparkling iceplant (*Mesembryanthemum crystallinum*) and winter purslane or claytonia (*Montia perfoliata*), that pretty escapee from the American continent; and in Italy, in early spring, we saw people parking their cars on motorways to scour the fields for young leaves of wild plants – our first inkling of that vast neglected heritage of wild plants that can be used raw. Coupled with these new plants were new ideas on how to grow salad plants, above all the 'cut-and-come-again' concept (see p. 234). This extends from cutting broadcast patches of seedlings up to five times, to cutting mature heads of chicory, endive and lettuce and leaving the stumps to resprout for further pickings.

We returned home eager to try out these new plants and ideas.

Shortly afterwards I was asked to take part in an exhibition on the history of English gardening at the Victoria & Albert Museum in London, and this led me to old English gardening books, a hitherto unknown world to me. I discovered John Evelyn's *Acetaria: a Discourse of Sallets*, written in 1699, and his *Directions for the Gardiner at Says Court*, compiled a few years earlier; I also discovered Batty Langley's *New Principles of Gardening* (1728) and other seventeenth- and eighteenth-century classics. One day in the British Museum I tracked down a frail, handwritten, fifteenth-century cookery book, with one of the earliest known lists of 'herbes for a salade'. These books were a revelation, for here were lists, written hundreds of years ago, of the sort of salad plants we had found still being cultivated on the Continent, along with instructions for growing seedling crops, for forcing and blanching salad plants for winter use, for gathering plants from the wild, and even for using flowers, flower buds and shoot tips in salads, either fresh or pickled for winter.

At about the same time, suspecting another untapped treasure trove of useful salad plants, I began to try out some of the Chinese and Japanese vegetables that were becoming available through enterprising seed catalogues. This proved to be the start of a ten-year odyssey, taking me to China, Taiwan, Japan and later to the USA and Canada, unravelling the mysteries of Asian vegetables. The fast-growing leafy greens, above all, came to play a key role in our own salad making.

On our return from our European travels, we turned our garden into a small, experimental market garden run on organic principles. We supplied unusual vegetables to wholefood and health shops, our speciality being bags of mixed fresh salads, which we called 'saladini'. Even though our winter temperatures were often as low as -10°C/14°F, we found that it was quite possible, using unheated polythene tunnels, to grow fresh salads all year round. We usually managed to produce at least twenty different types of plant for each bag.

Growing salads for sale and researching oriental vegetables ran in parallel for several years. All the while I was becoming increasingly aware of how on one hand many people had only tiny areas in which to grow vegetables, but on the other there was a reluctance to grow vegetables in the typical small front garden, as they were deemed 'ugly' or at best 'inappropriate'. Yet what was more beautiful than the 'Purple Giant' mustard, feathery fennel, deeply curled red Lollo lettuce or the glossy, serrated leaves of mizuna greens? What could be more productive and vibrant-looking than a small patch of pak choi, dill or golden purslane?

Vegetable plots, I was convinced, can feed the soul as well as the body.

The happy marriage of beauty and productivity lies at the heart of the modern 'potager'. Although 'potager' is no more than the ordinary French word for a kitchen garden (the place where vegetables are grown for 'potage', or soup) it has been hijacked to mean any vegetable plot which has been artistically designed, making it a place of intrinsic beauty. So a potager may be enclosed by a hedge, fence, wall or trained fruit; there may be arches and seats to add a structural element; the beds may be of varying shapes and sizes and grouped to form patterns; and thought will have been given to the paths between the beds and edging materials. Above all, the vegetables will be chosen and grown to enhance their natural beauty. They offer a palette with which a living painting can be created. I began to use that palette, and have been using it ever since.

By the 1980s we had reorganized our kitchen garden and laid it out in parallel narrow beds – a practical, efficient, centuries-old system, enabling the gardener to develop a high state of fertility in the beds. My first steps in 'painting' with vegetables were making 'patchwork quilts' in these narrow beds. Initially I simply interplanted red and green lettuces; then I sowed cut-and-come-again lettuce in parallel drills in small patches. I would have, say, green Salad Bowl lettuce in the first patch, sown in one direction, and red Salad Bowl in the next, the rows at right angles to the first patch. I got such a kick out of watching the seedlings emerge; neat little bands at first, within a week or so merging into a solid, colourful patchwork.

Not long afterwards I made my first Little Potager, an area no more than 6½ by 4½m/20 by 15 ft. It was later enclosed in an undulating woven willow fence. Then followed a Winter Potager, primarily for edible plants which retain leaf, stem or flower colour in winter; these include leeks, hardy Chinese mustards, purple-flowering pak choi, hardy chicories, Swiss chard, kales, corn salad, 'Parcel' celery and winter pansies. Partially edged with low, stepover apples, the Winter Potager is surrounded on three sides by a trellis of vines, clematis and honeysuckle. With luck it remains colourful and decorative even in mid-winter. The full story is told in my book *Creative Vegetable Gardening*, but what is relevant here is the decorative potential of so many salad plants.

Here are some of the ways I use salad plants to create visual effects. To get height, a key element in potagers, I train tomatoes up attractive spiral steel supports, sometimes intermingling them with ornamental climbers like *Ipomoea lobata* (previously *Mina lobata*) or canary creeper (*Tropaeolum peregrinum*). Red orache and

OPPOSITE The patterns in this narrow bed are outlined with a zigzag of multi-sown leeks. The right-hand triangles are planted with gold-leaved purslane, the left with mixed red lettuce.
ABOVE Lettuces of different types and colours can be used to create delightful effects. Clockwise from left: green butterhead, red Salad Bowl, red Lollo, green crisphead.

the purple-hued giant spinach *Chenopodium giganteum* 'Magentaspreen' are plants that reach theatrical heights, both being useful additions to salads in their early stages. I always leave a few clumps of chicory to run to seed in their second season – they too grow over 2m/7ft high, producing fresh flushes of sky-blue (edible) flowers every morning over many weeks. The giant winter radishes will do the same, making glorious pink- or white-flowered clumps in their second spring, and a seemingly endless crop of delectable, edible seed pods.

To make the most impact with colourful plants, I almost always plant in groups at equidistant spacing rather than in traditional rows. Favourites are 'Bull's Blood' beetroot, with its scarlet leaves, red cabbage, ornamental cabbages and kales, and the many bright red lettuces now available. For textured effects I value the ground-hugging iceplant, glossy-leaved purslanes, dill and fennel. And every year I succumb to the temptation to make patterns with the many salad plants grown as cut-and-come-again seedlings. I sow them in circles, waves, triangles, zigzags – whatever takes my fancy, often outlining the patterns with leeks. Exceptionally pretty, in the ground and in salads, are the purplish-leaved 'Red Russian' kale, the crêpe-like Tuscan kale, along with cresses, purslanes, chicories and oriental greens. Lastly, I make full use of the many edible flowers and flowering herbs to infiltrate scent and pure colour into the garden: nasturtiums, pot marigolds, thymes, day lilies... it is an endless list. A favourite edging plant is the 'Gem' series of French marigolds (*Tagetes*) neat and bright all summer long and, to my mind, the flowers adding a real, fruity flavour to salads.

Not everyone wants a potager, but there is plenty of scope for slipping decorative salad plants into flower beds or growing them in containers on patios and balconies.

For over twenty-five years our garden has been run on organic lines, without using chemical fertilizers, weedkillers or pesticides other than the handful of non-persistent chemicals approved for organic gardening. Bar the endless war against slugs, we have encountered no major problems in growing organically and believe our plants are more robust, better-flavoured, and remain fresh for longer as a result.

When this book was first published in 1984, many of the plants it covered were virtually unknown outside a limited area. Now they can be found in supermarkets, street markets and restaurants, and, crucial for us gardeners, the seed is available mainly through mail-order seed catalogues, and increasingly in garden centres. Sadly, there are also commercial pressures to limit the number of old varieties in circulation. The legal restrictions imposed by the European Union and the vested interests of multi-national seed companies threaten some traditional vegetable varieties. I urge gardeners to support organizations such as Garden Organic, the working name of the Henry Doubleday Research Association in the UK, which runs a heritage seed library, and similar organizations elsewhere, to prevent the erosion of our genetic heritage.

Notwithstanding these pressures, there is still an enormous choice of varieties (or cultivars as they should be called) of the most popular salad plants. New varieties are constantly being introduced, sometimes to disappear a couple of seasons later. It is almost impossible to keep up to date. On the whole, I recommend only varieties I have grown or seen myself, and hope will remain available. But there are many other excellent varieties. Follow the gardening press to keep abreast of good new ones.

Approach salad growing in a spirit of adventure and enquiry. Every garden is unique, and there are few rights and wrongs in gardening. Be prepared to experiment; don't be bound by rules! Do, however, keep detailed records. Your own notes on sowing times, varieties grown, quantities sown, methods used and harvesting times will eventually become far and away the best guide to producing salads for your household.

An enormous range of plants can be used in salads, from familiar garden vegetables to wild plants and weeds. As space is limited, lesser known plants have

ABOVE A circular patch of sweet corn edged with colourful *Tagetes* 'Orange Gem'.

priority in *The Salad Garden*. For in-depth cultivation of mainstream vegetables, see Further reading p. 274.

The photographs for the original 1984 edition of this book were taken by Roger Phillips. Most of the plants illustrated were grown in my garden in Suffolk in one season. This is how, at the time, I described that season: '... an unusually odd season it was. We had more than twice the average rainfall in April, followed by an exceptionally cold May, and a very long drought in summer, which included the highest July temperature ever recorded here. So, as can happen in any garden, we had our failures, and a few specimens were not as good as we would have liked.' When shooting again with Roger for a new edition, eighteen years later, we then too experienced a year when weather records were being broken. Only now everyone is labelling it global warming. Who knows what lies ahead? But rest assured, whether it gets warmer, colder, drier, wetter or windier, there will always be something you can grow from the vast storehouse of salad plants.

Joy Larkcom, May 2001

leafy salad plants

—

Mild-flavoured leaves – lettuce above all – have always been the mainstay of the traditional salad. But oh how that salad can be enriched with the spiciness of salad rocket, the subtle flavours of the chicory tribe, the glorious colours of Swiss chard and red chicories… Then there's the sparkle of iceplant, the textures of summer and winter purslane, and the dainty beauty of curled endive. Some of the many possibilities are explored in this chapter.

Winter butterhead

Lettuce
Lactuca sativa

Lettuce is rightly one of the most widely grown salad plants. Not only is the quality and flavour of home-grown lettuce far superior to anything you can buy, but the colourful varieties now available are exceptionally decorative in the garden. Even in small gardens there is always space for a few lettuces. Pretty loose-leaf Salad Bowl types make excellent edges to vegetable and flower beds; small hearting types, such as 'Tom Thumb' and 'Little Gem', are ideal for intercropping; patches of seedling lettuce and 'leaf lettuce' require minimum space.

Lettuce is essentially a cool-climate crop, growing best at temperatures of 10–20°C/50–68°F. With the exception of the Asiatic stem lettuce, it does not do well in very hot climates. In most temperate climates you can grow it all year round, provided you sow appropriate varieties each season. Some protection is usually advisable for the winter crop, while in colder regions artificial heating is essential for a continuous winter supply. Where greenhouse space is limited in winter, it may be better to devote it to oriental greens grown as seedlings, salad rocket, Texsel, endives and chicories. Compared to lettuce, these are far more tolerant of the low light levels and damp weather typical of northern-latitude winters and probably far more nutritious than most winter lettuce varieties.

Types of lettuce

Lettuces can be divided roughly into hearting and non-hearting types, with a few intermediate, semi-hearting varieties. The principal hearting types are the tall cos or 'romaine' lettuce, and the flat 'cabbage' type, subdivided into 'butterhead' and 'crisphead' lettuce. Non-hearting types include the loose-leaf Salad Bowl varieties and stem lettuce. While lettuces are predominantly green, there are now red and bronze forms in virtually every type of lettuce. For varieties, see p. 25.

Cos These are large, upright lettuces with long, thick, crisp, distinctly flavoured leaves forming a somewhat loose heart. They are slower-maturing than other types, but stand hot and dry conditions well without running to seed, besides tolerating low temperatures. Several varieties are frost hardy and can be overwintered, and some are suitable for sowing thickly as leaf lettuce (see p. 24). Cos lettuces keep well after cutting. 'Semi-cos' lettuces are a smaller type, exemplified by 'Little Gem', a compact variety notable for its sweet, crisp leaves – and arguably the best flavoured of all lettuces.

Butterhead This is the softer type of cabbage lettuce, typified by a flat, round head of gently rounded leaves with a buttery texture and mild flavour. They tend to wilt quickly after picking. Butterheads generally grow faster than crispheads, but are more likely to bolt prematurely in hot weather. While mainly grown in the summer months, they are reasonably well adapted to the short days of late summer and autumn, and many winter varieties are in this group.

Crisphead This group of cabbage lettuce is characterized by crisp-textured, often frilled leaves. The term Iceberg has been adopted

Stem lettuce

for large crispheads sold with the outer leaves trimmed off, leaving just the crisp white heart. Crispheads generally take about ten days longer than butterheads to mature but stand well in hot weather without bolting – especially the American Iceberg varieties. Crispheads keep reasonably well after picking. Many are considered flavourless, but an exception is the group loosely known as 'Batavian'. Of European origin, they often have reddish-tinged leaves and tend to be relatively hardy.

Loose-leaf Lettuces in this group form only rudimentary hearts, but produce a loose head of leaves that can be picked individually as required. The heads normally resprout if cut about 2½cm/1in above ground. The group are also known as 'gathering' or 'cutting' lettuces, or Salad Bowl types, after the variety of that name. The leaves are often deeply indented (the 'oak-leaved' varieties closely resemble oak leaves) while others, notably the beautiful red and green Lollo varieties, which originated in Italy, are deeply curled. Loose-leaf lettuces are generally slower to bolt than hearting lettuce, which, coupled with their ability to regenerate, gives them a long season of usefulness. The

central leaves of reddish-tinged varieties tend to become darker-coloured with successive cuts. Loose-leaf types are suitable for cut-and-come-again seedling crops. Most are reasonably hardy, and seem less prone to mildew than other types. Leaves are generally soft, are easily damaged by hail and wilt soon after picking. They are amongst the prettiest lettuces for potager use; the red-leaved varieties make dainty pinnacles at least 45cm/18in high if left to run to seed.

Stem lettuce This Asiatic lettuce, also known as 'asparagus lettuce' or 'celtuce', is grown primarily for its stem, which can be 2½–7½cm/1–3in thick and at least 30cm/12in long. Its leaves are coarse and palatable only when young, unless cooked. Cultivate it like summer lettuce, spacing plants 30cm/12in apart each way. It is tolerant of both low and high temperatures, but needs fertile soil and plenty of moisture to develop well. The stem is sliced and used raw in salads, but can also be cooked. It has a distinct lettuce flavour. Mature, firm-stemmed plants can be uprooted in autumn and transplanted into cold frames, with the leaves trimmed back. This enables them to be kept in good condition for a month or more.

Red oak-leaved Salad Bowl type

Soil and site

Lettuces require an open situation, but in the height of summer and in hot climates can be grown in light shade. They can be intercropped between taller plants, provided they have adequate space and light. They do well in containers in fertile, moisture-retentive soil or compost.

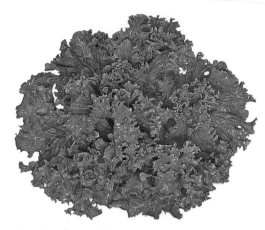

Green Lollo loose-leaf type

Cultivation

Lettuce can be sown *in situ*, 'indoors' in seed trays or modules for transplanting, or in an outdoor seedbed for transplanting (see Plant raising p. 191).

Sowing *in situ*

- for seedling cut-and-come-again crops and leaf lettuce (see p. 24);
- in very hot weather, when transplanted seedlings wilt badly after planting, unless raised in modules; for some overwintered sowings.

The disadvantage of sowing *in situ* is that germination and early growth are erratic if soil and weather conditions deteriorate, and, seedling and leaf lettuce crops apart, for good results thinning is essential.

Start thinning as early as possible – and use the thinnings in salads. Final spacing depends on the variety: small varieties like 'Little Gem' 12–15cm/5–6in apart; cabbage lettuces 23–30cm/9–12in apart; cos and 'Iceberg' types about 35cm/14in apart.

Sowing in modules (preferably) or seed trays for transplanting a reliable method of producing good-quality plants, which suffer minimal setback when planted out. It also allows for flexibility over planting.

Transplant young plants outside when conditions are suitable, or under the cover of cloches, frames, greenhouses or polytunnels. Lettuces are best transplanted at the four-to-five-leaf stage. Plant most types shallowly with the lowest leaves just above soil level, though cos lettuces can be planted a little deeper. I recommend planting at equidistant spacing, rather than in rows.

Sowing in an outdoor seedbed (Only advisable where there are no facilities for raising plants indoors, or no ground is available for direct sowing.)

Lettuce germinates at surprisingly low temperatures – it even germinates on ice – but some of the butterheads, and my favourite 'Little Gem', have 'high-temperature dormancy', which means that they germinate poorly at soil temperatures above 25°C/77°F. These temperatures frequently occur in late spring and summer. You can take various measures to overcome the problem, of which the main options are:

- Use crisphead varieties, which germinate at soil temperatures of up to 29°C/84°F.
- Sow between two and four in the afternoon. The most critical germination phase then

coincides with cooler night temperatures.

- Put seeds somewhere cold to germinate, such as in a cold room, in a cellar or in the shade. Or cover seed trays with moist newspaper to keep the temperature down until germination.
- If sowing outdoors, water the seedbed beforehand to cool the soil; or cover it with white reflective film after sowing and remove it as soon as the seeds germinate.

Watering

Common lettuce problems, such as bitterness, bolting and disease, are exacerbated by slow growth, often caused by water shortage. In the absence of rain, water summer crops at the rate of up to 18 litres per sq. m/4 gallons per sq. yd per week. If watering regularly is difficult, concentrate on one really heavy watering about seven to ten days before harvesting. Water autumn-planted lettuce well when planting, but subsequently water sparingly during the winter months as damp leaves invite disease. Lettuce responds well to being mulched with organic material or polythene film.

Sowing programme

For a continuous supply of lettuce, make several sowings during the year, using appropriate varieties for each season.

Summer supplies For the earliest outdoor summer lettuce, sow under cover in early spring, transplanting outside as soon as soil conditions are suitable. These early crops can be protected initially with some kind of cloche or low polythene tunnel. Continue sowing in spring and early summer by any of the

methods described above.

A problem in maintaining a steady summer supply of hearting lettuce is that growth rates vary during the season, from six and a half weeks to as much as thirteen weeks. Relevant factors include the variety, speed of germination, and soil and air temperature. In hot weather some varieties run to seed soon after maturing. In other words, regular sowing at ten- to fourteen-day intervals, as is often advocated, does not guarantee a steady supply.

Later sowings may overtake earlier sowings, leading to gluts and gaps. The best way to iron out fluctuations is to make the 'next' sowing when the seedlings from the last sowing have just emerged. The Salad Bowl types of lettuce stand well for several months. One or two sowings normally ensure a supply throughout the summer.

Autumn supplies Sow from mid- to late summer, using any of the methods on pp. 21–2. In areas where autumn is normally wet, grow mildew-resistant varieties. If the weather deteriorates in autumn, cover outdoor lettuces with cloches or low polytunnels to keep them in good condition. These sowings can also be transplanted into frames, polytunnels or greenhouses if space is available.

Winter supplies Sow winter-hearting varieties in seed trays or modules in late summer and early autumn, transplanting into frames, greenhouses or polytunnels in late autumn. Successful cropping depends to some extent on the weather: in poor winters plants may not mature until spring. They will, of course, crop earlier if grown in gently heated conditions with a minimum night temperature of 2°C/36°F and day temperature of 4½°C/40°F. Winter and early spring lettuce are very vulnerable to fungal diseases such as

'Winter Density' cos

'Little Gem' semi-cos

'Marvel of Four Seasons'
semi-hearting

Bronze-leaved butterhead

Crisphead type

grey mould and downy mildew (see p. 26). Avoid overcrowding and keep them well ventilated.

Spring supplies The earliest spring lettuce comes from crops grown in unheated greenhouses and polytunnels during winter. Use only varieties specifically bred for this period. Sow in autumn in seed trays or modules (each variety has a recommended sowing time), transplanting under cover. In slightly heated greenhouses, continue sowing in mid-winter/early spring for follow-on crops under cover.

The earliest outdoor spring lettuce comes from hardy varieties (capable of surviving several degrees of frost) that have been overwintered in the open. Sow *in situ* outdoors in late summer/early autumn, thinning initially to about 7½cm/3in apart, and to the final spacing the following spring. Plants will be of better quality, and more likely to survive in good condition, if protected from the elements under cloches or low polytunnels or in frames.

Alternatively, you can sow the same hardy varieties or plant them under cover in late summer/early autumn, and thin in the same way. You can also sow them in seed trays or modules in late autumn, overwinter them as seedlings under cover, and plant in spring in the open or under cover.

There is always an element of chance with overwintered lettuce because of the vagaries of winter weather. It is worth the gamble if you yearn for early lettuce.

Red Lollo loose-
leaf type

'Rouge d'Hiver'
cos type

heated frames in winter, providing out-of-season salading. The technique is still useful for early sowings under cover, as seedlings will be ready far sooner than hearting lettuce sown at the same time. You can make sowings throughout the growing season, a patch often providing two or occasionally three cuttings over several months. Seedling lettuce lends itself to intercropping and making decorative patterns. Besides the traditional 'cutting' lettuce varieties, it is worth experimenting with others, perhaps utilizing left-over seed. Only a few varieties prove bitter at the seedling stage. Lettuce is also a key ingredient in the many salad mixtures now widely available for sowing.

Leaf lettuce

This concept, based on the old seedling lettuce techniques, was developed in the 1970s at the vegetable reseach station which later became Horticulture Research International at Wellesbourne in the UK. The aim was to produce a crop of single leaves, to save caterers from having to tear apart the heart of a lettuce. The researchers discovered that if certain varieties of cos lettuce were sown closely, they grew upright

Seedling crops

Several varieties of lettuce are suitable for use at the seedling or baby leaf stage. In the past, seedling lettuce was commonly sown in without forming hearts, and regrew after the first cut, allowing a second crop within three to seven weeks. The method is easily adapted for use in the salad garden. A family of four could be kept in lettuce all summer by cultivating approximately 5 sq. m/6 sq. yd, and making ten sowings, each of about 80 sq. cm/1 sq. yd, cutting each crop twice.

The soil must be fertile and weed-free. Prepare the seedbed carefully to encourage good germination. Either broadcast the seed, thinning seedlings later to about 5cm/2in apart, or sow thinly in rows about 12cm/5in apart, thinning to about 3cm/1¼in apart. Plants must have plenty of moisture throughout growth.

Starting in spring, make the first seven sowings at weekly intervals. Make the first cuts in each case about seven weeks later, and a second cut a further six to seven weeks after that, during the summer. Make the last three sowings at weekly intervals in summer. These mature more rapidly, allowing the first cut after about three weeks (just overlapping with the tail end of the early sowings) and the second cut four weeks or so after the first. This gives continual cropping into autumn. Cut the leaves when 7½–12cm/3–5in high, about 2cm/¾in above ground level.

Varieties

A huge choice. These are old favourites and highly recommended newer varieties.

Cos lettuce 'Chatsworth', 'Cosmos', 'Density' syn. 'Winter Density' (hardy), 'Frisco', 'Lobjoits Green Cos', 'Musena', 'Parris Island', 'Pinokkio', 'Romany', 'Rouge d'Hiver' (hardy), 'Tan Tan' syn. 'Tin Tin'

Semi cos (Little Gem type) 'Atttico' (good mildew resistance), 'Little Gem', 'Little Gem Delight', 'Maureen'
Red varieties: see decorative below
Butterhead 'Arctic King' (hardy), 'Clarion', 'Tom Thumb', 'Marvel of Four Seasons', 'Valdor' (hardy)
Crisphead 'Challenge', 'Hollywood', 'Robinson', 'Valmaine' (hardy, good mildew resistance)
Loose-leaf 'Catalogna', 'Lettony', 'Lollo' (green and red), Salad Bowl/Oakleaf types, 'Veredes'
For seedling/babyleaf lettuce Salad Bowl varieties, smooth and curly-leaved cutting lettuce, most cos and semi-cos varieties, crisphead/'Minigreen'
For leaf lettuce 'Lobjoits Green Cos', 'Paris White Cos', 'Valmaine'
Shortlist for flavour all cos and semi-cos varieties, including 'Little Gem', 'Pinokkio', 'Sherwood'
Red Batavian: 'Red Batavian', 'Exbury', 'Relay', 'Rouge Grenobloise'
Green Batavian: 'Blonde de Paris', 'Regina Ghiacci'/'Queen of the Ice'
Red iceberg: 'Sioux'
Loose-leaf: 'Cocarde' (red), 'Catalogna' (also suitable baby leaves)
Shortlist for decorative quality
Red or red tinted os: 'Amaze', 'Cosmic', 'Nymans', 'Dunrobin', 'Little Leprechaun', 'Pandero', 'Rosemoor'
Loose-leaf: 'Cocarde' (green, red tinged), 'Freckles' (green, red splashed)
Red: 'Lollo Rosso', 'Mascara', 'Navara' (red, good mildew resistance), 'Revolution', 'Frillice', 'Red Parella' (hardy rosette)

Pests

These are the most common pests on lettuce. For protective measures and control, see p. 226.

Birds Seedlings and young plants are most vulnerable, though mature plants are attacked from time to time.

Slugs Slugs can cause serious damage at every stage, especially in wet weather and on heavy soils. Red-leaved varieties seem less prone to slug damage.

Soil pests Wireworm, cutworm and leatherjackets all destroy plants, and are most damaging in spring.

Root aphids Colonies of yellowish brown aphids attack the roots, secreting a waxy powder. Plants grow poorly, wilt and may die. There are no organic controls: practise rotation and check current catalogues for varieties with a measure of resistance.

Leaf aphids (Greenfly) Attacks are most likely outdoors in hot weather and under cover in spring.

Diseases

There are no organic remedies for diseases, so prevention is all-important. Watch in current seed catalogues for new varieties with disease resistance or some degree of tolerance. (As resistance eventually breaks down, resistant varieties tend to come and go.)

Damping-off diseases Seedlings either fail to emerge or keel over and die shortly afterwards. Avoid sowing in cold or wet conditions; sow thinly to avoid overcrowding; keep indoor crops well ventilated.

Downy mildew (*Bremia lactuca*) Probably the most serious lettuce disease, occurring in damp weather, mainly from autumn to early spring. Pale angular patches appear on older leaves and white spores on the underside. Leaves eventually turn brown and die. Avoid overcrowding; keep foliage dry by watering the soil rather than the plants; avoid watering in the evening; keep greenhouses well ventilated. Cut off infected leaves with a sharp knife. Burn them and debris from infected plants, which harbour disease spores. Use resistant varieties. Transplanted crops are less susceptible to mildew than direct-sown crops.

Grey mould (*Botrytis cinerea*) A rotting disease which commonly manifests itself at the base of the stem, causing plants to rot off. It is most serious in cold, damp conditions. Avoid overcrowding and deep planting; take preventive measures as above for downy mildew. Currently there are no varieties with effective resistance.

Mosaic virus A seed-borne disease causing stunted growth and yellowish mottling on the leaves, which become pale. Burn infected plants; try to control aphids, which spread the disease; use seed with guaranteed low levels of mosaic infection (less than 1 per cent); grow resistant varieties.

Green oak-leaved
Salad Bowl type

Chicory
Cichorium intybus

The chicories are a wonderfully diverse group of plants with a long history of cultivation for human, animal and medicinal use. The classical Roman writers often referred to the use of chicory as both a cooked and salad vegetable, and Italy is still the hub of the chicory world. The Italians grow an enormous range of chicories, some scarcely known further afield. 'Radicchio', a popular Italian name for chicory, has become widely identified with the red-hearted chicory. These red chicories have been embraced by the restaurant trade and have become a key ingredient in supermarket salad packs.

For the gardener, chicories have many merits. They are naturally robust, are mostly easily grown and have few pests, though the red chicories are prone to rotting diseases in autumn. Their main season is from late summer to spring, when salad material is scarcest, and they can often be sown or planted after summer crops are cleared, utilizing ground that would otherwise be idle in winter, both in the open and under cover.

Their acceptance in the English-speaking gardening world has been slow with the result that varieties available to home gardeners are more limited, even today, than they should be. If you become an aficionado, as I am, look to Italian, French and Belgian seed sources for a bigger choice.

Types of chicory

There are several distinct kinds of chicory. While the majority are grown for their leaves, some are cultivated for their roots and shoots.

The most striking of the leaf types are the red-leaved Italian chicories. Of the green-leaved chicories, the most widely grown is the Sugar Loaf type, used at the seedling stage, or when the crisp 'loaf-like' head has developed. Among other forms of leaf chicory are the rosette-shaped, extraordinarily hardy Grumolo chicory, and various wild, narrow-leaved chicories, not unlike dandelion. The Catalogna chicories, grown mainly for their spring shoots, are another distinct group.

Best known of the root chicories is Witloof (or Belgian) chicory. The roots are forced in the dark to produce white, bud-like 'chicons'. Other root chicories are used raw in salads, much like winter radishes, while a few varieties were traditionally dried and ground as a coffee substitute. The beautiful pale blue chicory flowers can be used in salads, fresh or pickled.

Chicories have a characteristic flavour, with a slightly bitter edge – addictive to those who acquire the taste, but less popular with the sweet-toothed. The bitterness can be modified by shredding the leaves, washing them gently in warm water, by mixing them with milder plants and, where appropriate, by blanching the growing plants. Chicories can also be cooked, typically by braising, acquiring an intriguing flavour in the process. Bitterness varies with the variety and the stage of growth. Seedling leaves are less bitter than mature leaves, the inner leaves of Sugar Loaf chicories less bitter than the outer, and the red chicories become sweeter in cold weather.

Traditional red-leaved
chicory showing root

Blanched red
'Treviso' chicory

Hearted red chicory
'Red Verona'

Traditional variegated red
chicory 'Sottomarina'

Typical improved hybrid chicory

Cultivation

Chicories are deep-rooting, unfussy plants. They adapt to a wide range of soils, from light sands to heavy clay, and even to wet, dry and exposed situations. They tolerate light shade. Although most are naturally perennial, for salad purposes it is best to treat them as annuals, resowing every year. Plants left to flower in spring will sometimes seed themselves but, because they cross-pollinate, resulting seedlings may not be true to type. In recent years plant breeders have improved the traditional varieties of red chicory beyond recognition. Unfortunately the high cost of this seed means that retail seedsmen supply only a limited choice. Mixtures of hardy chicories, sometimes sold as 'Miscuglio', make colourful seedling patches. Treat them initially as cut-and-come-again seedling patches, then allow a few plants to mature.

Red-leaved chicories

The outstanding feature of the so-called red chicories is their colour, which ranges from deep red and pinks to variegated leaves with flashes of red, yellow and cream on a green background. The old varieties were predominantly green in the early stages, but, chameleon-like, became redder and deeper-coloured with the onset of cold autumn nights. At the same time the leaves turned inwards, developing a nugget of sweeter, crisp, attractive leaves. The degree of hearting and colouring was always a lottery. Improved modern varieties develop earlier, more consistently, and are deeper-coloured. Varieties differ in their hardiness, from those that tolerate light frost, to 'Treviso', a unique loose-headed, non-hearting variety of upright leaves which, in our garden, has survived temperatures of -15°C/ 5°F.

In my experience the best hearting chicories are obtained by sowing in modules and transplanting. Red chicory can also be sown outdoors in rows, or in the traditional method of broadcasting, then thinning plants in stages to about 25cm/10in apart. In practice broadcast patches seem to 'thin themselves' by a kind of survival of the fittest. Varieties of the 'Treviso' type respond well to broadcasting.

Germination, particularly outdoors, can be erratic in hot weather, so take appropriate measures (see p. 197). Chicory is sometimes trimmed back on transplanting to 7½–10cm/ 3–4in above ground to stimulate growth, especially in hot weather. Space plants 25–35cm/10–14in apart, depending on variety.

For summer supplies Sow from mid- to late spring using suitable early varieties, or plants may bolt prematurely. Protect plants with perforated film or fleece in the early stages. (Be guided by information on the seed packet on suitability for early sowing.)
For autumn/early winter supplies Sow from early to mid-summer. The hardier varieties will survive mild winters outdoors.
For winter/early spring supplies Sow under cover from mid- to late summer. Transplant under cover, or cover the plants *in situ*, in late summer/early autumn. Do not overcrowd this useful crop.
For cut-and-come-again seedlings Sow patches from late spring to mid-summer, extending the season with slightly earlier and slightly later sowings under cover.
Harvesting With successive sowings you can have hearted chicories from late summer until the following spring. Either pick

individual leaves as required, or cut the heads about 2½cm/1in or so above ground level, leaving the lowest leaves intact. The stumps normally produce further flushes of leaf over many weeks.

With cut-and-come-again seedling patches, start cutting when leaves are 5–7½cm/2–3in high. Some will be tender at this stage; others may be bitter, depending on variety and the weather. You can later thin the seedlings, allowing a few to grow to maturity.

Winter protection The challenge with hearted chicories is to keep plants in good condition from late autumn into winter. In humid conditions they have a tendency to rot, usually starting with the outer leaves of the hearts. (Remove them carefully and you may find perfectly healthy hearts beneath.) Outdoor crops often keep well if protected with a light covering of straw, bracken or dry leaves – although there is a risk of attracting mice and even rats in severe winters. Glass cloches or low polytunnels can give additional protection, though polytunnels may encourage high humidity. We have harvested beautiful plants from under the snow: it can be a good insulator.

In unheated greenhouses and polytunnels, make sure there is good ventilation, and remove rotting leaves to limit the spread of infection. Keep plants reasonably well watered, or they may suffer from tipburn at the leaf edges. In spite of this, we have had some of our best hearted chicories from our polytunnel.

Forcing and blanching Certain varieties of red chicory, such as 'Red Verona' and 'Treviso', can be lifted and forced in the dark like Witloof chicory (see p. 35). They can also be blanched *in situ* by covering with an upturned pot with light excluded. Cut back hearted varieties such as 'Red Verona' to within 2½cm/1in of the stump, so that it is new growth that is blanched. You can force 'Treviso' this way, or alternatively blanch it more quickly by simply tying the leaves together before covering the plant. Blanched red chicories are exceptionally beautiful, the whitened leaves overlaid with pink hues. Blanching also makes them sweeter.

Varieties *Improved varieties:* 'Cesare' (suitable for early sowings), 'Indigo' F1 (unfortunately few other improved varieties are currently available to home gardeners)

Traditional varieties: 'Palla Rossa Bella', 'Rossa Verona' (Verona type), 'Castelfranco', 'Sottomarina' (variegated)

Treviso types: 'Treviso' syn. 'Rosso di Treviso'

Green-leaved chicories
Sugar Loaf chicory

A mature Sugar Loaf chicory forms a large, light green, tightly folded conical head, not unlike cos lettuce in appearance. The inner leaves are partially blanched by the outer leaves, and are pale, crisp, distinctly flavoured and sweeter than most chicories – though the 'sweetness' is only relative. They are naturally vigorous, responding well to cut-and-come-again treatment at every stage: seedlings, semi-mature and mature. Most varieties tolerate only light frost in the open, but if grown under cover in winter and kept trimmed back, are likely to survive winter well, giving regular pickings and resprouting vigorously in spring. They require fertile, moisture-retentive soil, but seem to have better drought resistance than comparable salad plants, such as lettuce, possibly because of their long roots.

Sugar loaf seedling

Mature
Sugar Loaf
chicory

Grumolo chicory

For a hearted crop Sow by any of the methods used for red-leaved chicory (p. 29). You can obtain good results by sowing in modules and transplanting, or by sowing *in situ*. Space or thin plants to 15–30cm/6–12in apart, the closer spacing for the older, less vigorous varieties.

For summer supplies Sow in spring/ early summer. (A few varieties are unsuited to early sowing: be guided by information on the seed packet.)

For autumn supplies Sow in early/mid-summer; transplant later sowings under cover for winter crops, or cover *in situ*. Again and again I have found this to be an invaluable crop, in some years providing robust, refreshing, salad well into winter.

For winter or early spring supplies Sow in late summer and transplant under cover. This crop is a gamble as tight heads may not form until the following spring. However, loose leaves can generally be cut during the winter. Like the red chicories, Sugar Loaf heads are prone to rot in damp winter weather. Keep plants well ventilated and remove rotting leaves, but leave the stumps: even 'hopeless cases' may regenerate in spring. Traditionally, Sugar Loaf plants were uprooted in early winter and stored for several weeks, in closely packed heaps covered with straw in cellars or frames.

Cut-and-come-again seedlings Some older varieties of Sugar Loaf chicory are primarily used for cut-and-come-again crops. Sow from late winter/early spring through to early autumn, making the earliest and latest sowings under cover. These protected sowings are exceptionally good value. The first sowing under cover can be made as soon as soil temperatures rise above 5°C/41°F in spring.

The late autumn seedling sowings under cover survive lower temperatures than mature plants, and start into renewed growth very early in the year.

Make the main sowings in succession throughout the summer for a continuous supply of fresh young leaves. They are best cut when 5–7½cm/2–3in high; older leaves may be coarse. Growth is rapid, sometimes allowing a second cut within fifteen days of the first. A patch can remain productive over many weeks, provided the soil is fertile and there is plenty of moisture. Supplementary feeding with a liquid fertilizer will help sustain growth towards the end of the season. Cut-and-come-again seedlings can eventually be thinned to about 15cm/6in apart and left to develop small heads.

Varieties *Traditional varieties, mainly recommended for cut-and-come-again seedlings:* 'Bianca di Milano', 'Bionda di Triestino', 'Imero – Dolce Greco'
Heading varieties: 'Jupiter' F1, 'Uranus' F1
As with the red-leaved chicories, the improved varieties are rarely available to home gardeners, probably on grounds of cost. If this changes, make use of them.

Grumolo chicory

This rugged little chicory from the Italian Piedmont survives the roughest winter weather to produce a ground-hugging rosette of smooth, rounded, jade-green leaves in spring. The leaves are upright during the summer months, but acquire a rosette form in mid-winter. They appear to die back in the depth of winter, but reappear remarkably early – green rosebuds at ground level! They tolerate poor soil, weedy conditions and low temperatures. They are naturally rather bitter, but you can blend them into mixed salads – they earn a place on the shape and colour of their leaves alone. The more mature leaves are coarser, but can be shredded or used cooked. Light and dark green forms are available.

Cultivation While Grumolo chicory can be sown from spring to autumn, the most useful sowings are in mid-summer, for autumn-to-spring supplies. Grumolo chicory lends itself to being broadcast thinly in patches but can be sown thinly in rows 15cm/6in apart. In hot climates mid-summer sowings can be made in light shade. During the summer cut the young leaves when 5–30cm/2–12in high, but in autumn leave them to form rosettes. Patches will not normally need thinning unless they have been sown too thickly, in which case thin to about 7½cm/3in apart.

In spring, or when the chicory is freshly sown, it may be necessary to protect from birds. Cloche protection in early spring will bring plants on earlier and make the leaves more tender. Cut the rosettes in spring, leaving the plants to resprout. The subsequent growth is never as prettily shaped and tends to become coarse, but may fill a gap in spring salad supplies.

Leave a few plants to run to seed – they form spectacular clumps 2m/7ft high, covered in pale blue flowers that tend to fade at noon. Pick these in the morning for use in salads. You can grow Grumolo chicory as a perennial by sowing a patch in an out-of-the-way place and letting it perpetuate itself.

Catalogna chicory

Also known as 'asparagus chicory', this tall chicory from south Italy has long, narrow leaves, which can be smooth-edged or serrated with green or cream stalks. The 'puntarelle' types are grown primarily for the chunky buds (puntarelle) and flowering stems that develop in spring; they are bitter raw, but delicious cooked and cold in salads. The young leaves can be used in salads. Other types (such as Catalogna frastagliata) are grown for the leaves, picked either small, or as a bunch when 20–40cm/8–16in tall. 'Red Rib' and 'Italico' are forms with attractive, dark red veins. They are naturally very bitter and for this reason are sometimes blanched.

The Catalogna chicories are reasonably heat tolerant but stand only light frost. They are undemanding about soil. Sow leaf types *in situ* in summer, as cut-and-come-again seedlings or thinning to 15cm/6in apart. Sow puntarelle types *in situ* or in modules and transplant, spacing plants about 20cm/8in apart. In temperate climates they can be planted under cover in late summer, and will form shoots the following spring. Catalogna chicories make beautiful flowering clumps in their second season.

Wild chicory

Capucin's beard or barbe de Capucin is the popular name for the jagged-leaved wild chicories. The young leaves can be eaten green (generally shredded), but blanching mature plants develops their unique flavour. Like many bitter and blanched plants, wild chicory is excellent *aux lardons* (see p. 267). Sow from late spring to early summer *in situ*, thinning plants to about 15cm/6in apart. Blanch *in situ* or transplant under cover (see pp. 245–7). The top of the root is edible and well flavoured.

Forced Witloof chicon

Wild chicory

Root chicory

Witloof chicory root
before forcing

Root chicories

Witloof chicory

Also known as Belgian chicory, this chicory was allegedly 'discovered' when a Belgian farmer threw some wild chicory roots into a warm dark stable. The whitened shoots which developed laid the foundations for the modern Witloof industry. Witloof chicory is easy to grow, tolerating a wide range of conditions. Avoid freshly manured ground, as it can result in lush plants and fanged roots. Improved modern varieties produce excellent, plump chicons.

Cultivation Sow in early summer, in drills 30cm/12in apart, or in modules for transplanting. Thin or space plants to about 23cm/9in apart. No further attention is required, other than keeping plants weed-free and watering in very dry weather.

Forcing Roots can be forced *in situ* or transplanted indoors. The latter is more convenient, but roots forced outside are said to be better flavoured. For forcing *in situ*, see p. 247. To force indoors, dig up the roots in late autumn/early winter, and leave them exposed to light frost or low temperatures for a week or so. In theory fanged or very thin roots should be rejected (they should be at least 4cm/1½in thick at the neck), but in practice even poor roots produce chicons of a sort. Cut back the foliage to 2½cm/1in above the neck, and trim the roots to about 20cm/8in. For a continuous supply, force a few at a time, storing surplus roots in layers in boxes of moist sand, kept in a frostproof shed or cellar.

The simplest way to force roots is to pot several roots close together in a 23–30cm/9–12in flower pot, filled with soil or old potting compost. (This is to support the roots, not supply nutrients, as nourishment comes from the roots themselves.) Water gently, and cover the pot with an inverted pot of the same size with the drainage hole blocked to exclude light. (See illustration on p. 247.) Alternatively put the pot in total darkness. Keep the pot at a temperature of 10°C/50°F or a little higher. Inspect it from time to time, water if the soil has dried out and remove any rotting leaves. The chicons will normally be ready in about three weeks. Chicory can, of course, be forced in any darkened container large enough to take the roots.

Witloof chicory can also be transplanted into frames and greenhouses, using various means to create darkness (see p. 247).

Once the chicons are ready, use them soon or they deteriorate. Cut them 2½cm/1in above the root, and keep them wrapped in aluminium foil or in a refrigerator, as they become green and bitter on exposure to light. The root can be left in the dark to resprout: it will normally produce more leaf, but not a dense chicon.

Varieties 'Apollo', 'Redoria' F1, 'Zoom' F1

Other root chicories

Some chicories have large, edible roots, white and surprisingly tender – a useful winter standby. They are used raw, chopped or grated in salad, or cooked and eaten cold. Sow in spring or early summer by broadcasting, or sowing in rows or modules for transplanting, spacing plants eventually about 10cm/4in apart. The roots are moderately hardy and can be lifted during winter as required.

Varieties Few now listed by name
Heritage varieties: 'Magdeburg', 'Geneva', 'Soncino'

Broad-leaved
'Cornet de Bordeaux'

Blanched head of
curly-leaved 'Minerva'

Curly-leaved
'Frisée de Ruffec'

Endive
Cichorium endivia

The endives are a versatile, attractive group of plants in the chicory family: indeed, in the non-English-speaking world they are known as 'chicory'. They are a cool-season crop, growing best at temperatures of 10–20°C/50–68°F and tend to become bitter at higher temperatures. Don't grow them in mid-summer where this is likely to be the case. All varieties survive light frost. Endives are more resistant to pests and disease than lettuce and, provided appropriate varieties are used, less likely to bolt in hot weather. They are also better adapted to the low light levels and dampness of autumn and winter. Their flavour is fresh and slightly piquant, but plants can be blanched before use, which makes the leaves milder, crisper and an attractive, creamy white colour. Many of the newer varieties are virtually self-blanching and naturally sweeter. Endive has become a popular ingredient in supermarket pre-packed salads.

Types of endive
Curly-leaved (frisée, staghorn, cut-leaved) These have a low-growing habit, and fairly narrow, curled, fringed or indented leaves, making a pretty head. They are more heat tolerant than broad-leaved endives, but more prone to rotting in damp and cold weather, making them the best varieties for summer use. They are among my potager favourites – neat and pretty: I often use them to outline vegetable patterns. They are also excellent as cut-and-come-again seedlings.

Broad-leaved (Batavian, escarole, scarole) These are larger plants, with broader, smoother, somewhat furled leaves, which can be upright or low-growing and compact. They can withstand temperatures as low as -9°C/15°F, so are generally the best value for winter-to-spring crops. Mature plants respond well to cut-and-come-again treatment, making them among the most productive salads in winter under cover. Modern plant breeding is producing intermediate varieties, with some of the characteristics of each type.

Cultivation
Endives like an open situation and fertile, moisture-retentive soil, with plenty of well-rotted organic matter worked in beforehand. Very acid soils should be limed.

Either sow *in situ* and subsequently thin out or transplant, or sow in modules for transplanting. Transplanted endive is said to grow faster and be less likely to become bitter. Seed germinates best at 20–22°C/68–72°F. Germination may be poor at higher soil temperatures, with slow-germinating plants being prone to premature bolting. (For sowing in hot conditions, see Lettuce p. 21.) Depending on variety, space plants 25–35cm/10–14in apart. On average endives take about thirteen weeks to mature. Use thinnings in salads or transplant to maintain continuity.

Sowing programme
Early summer supplies Sow under cover very early in spring, transplanting outdoors as soon as soil conditions allow. Protect with

37

cloches or crop covers. These early sowings may bolt prematurely if temperatures fall below 5°C/41°F for several days.

Main summer supplies Sow in mid- to late spring.

Autumn supplies outdoors Sow in early to mid-summer. Use hardier varieties for the late sowings; in mild areas they may stand well into winter. Protect with cloches or crop covers if necessary.

Autumn and winter supplies under cover Sow in mid-summer to early autumn, transplanting under cover in autumn. With cut-and-come-again treatment, of the broad-leaved types in particular, it may be possible to make several cuts during winter.

Late spring supplies Sow hardy broad-leaved varieties in modules under cover in late autumn, overwintering them as seedlings and planting early in the year, under cover or outside.

Cut-and-come-again seedling crops Sow from late winter to early autumn. Make the earliest and latest sowings under cover, provided the soil temperature is above 15°C/59°F. Curly endive makes particularly appealing salad seedlings, though all types can be used. They lend themselves to intercropping and being sown in decorative patches.

Blanching

Whether or not you blanch endives before harvesting is largely a matter of taste. I find most of them quite palatable 'as they are', although there is something irresistible about the crisp, white centre of a blanched curly-leaved endive. For blanching techniques see p. 245. In the main, endives are blanched *in situ*, using covering methods for compact, low-growing varieties and tying the heads of looser-leaved varieties. Curly-leaved endives benefit most from blanching in hot weather, when they tend to be more bitter. A simple, old-fashioned blanching method is to cover one endive with an uprooted one. Simply pull up one plant, then place it, with the head down and root in the air, on to the head of a growing plant. Mutual blanching results!

Varieties

Curled *For spring and summer supplies:*
Fine de Louviers
For autumn and winter supplies: 'Minerva' (Wallonne type), 'Naomi', 'Pancalière', 'Ruffec'

Broad-leaved *For supplies for any season:* 'Grosse Bouclée 2'
Hardiest: 'Cornet de Bordeaux', 'Géant (Giant) Maraîchère' racc 'Margot' and race 'Torino', 'Ronde Verte à Coeur Plein' ('Fullheart')

Spinach

Spinacia oleracea

My conventional English upbringing never led me to suspect that spinach could be a salad vegetable. It took a visit to the USA, where it has long been used in salads, for me to realize its merits and it has been a favourite ever since. To satisfy today's huge demand for 'baby leaf' spinach in prepacked salads, plant breeders are continually introducing improved hybrid varieties, whose good disease resistance and upright habit make for healthy plants.

Spinach has a unique flavour – 'spinachy' is the only word to describe it. The most popular varieties are round-leaved, though some older varieties and Asiatic spinach are pointed. Texture varies from thin, smooth-leaved types to those with thicker, puckered leaves, which are more robust, less easily bruised and bulkier, so predominate in the salad packs found in supermarkets.

Mature spinach can be used in salads, though leaves may need to be torn or shredded to make them a manageable size. On the whole it makes far more sense, in terms of space, time and an end product that's 'just right' for salads, to grow spinach as a cut-and-come-again, baby leaf crop.

Cultivation

Spinach is an annual, cool-season crop, with a natural tendency to run to seed in the lengthening days of late spring and early summer, and at high temperatures. It grows best in early spring and late summer. Mid-summer sowings of traditional varieties were often unproductive. The hardier varieties survive light to moderate frosts in the open, but will be of far better quality if grown under cover in winter. The secret of a year-round supply in temperate climates is to sow appropriate varieties for the season. See the sowing programme on p. 40 and be guided by seed packet and catalogue information.

Spinach needs fertile, well-drained, moisture-retentive soil that is rich in organic matter. Summer crops can be grown in light shade, provided there is adequate moisture. It is advisable to rotate spinach around the garden, as the resting spores of downy mildew, a scourge of spinach with no organic remedy, remain in the soil. However look out for newer varieties with reasonable mildew resistance.

On account of its tendency to run to seed rapidly, spinach is usually sown *in situ*, but it can be sown in modules and transplanted. For single plants sow in drills 27–30cm/11–12in apart, thinning to 15cm/6in apart. Depending on the season, these plants may respond well to cut-and-come-again treatment. For cut-and-come-again seedling crops, make successive sowings at roughly three-to-four-week intervals (but see the sowing programme on the next page). Bear in mind that very early sowings, or sowings in hot spells, run the risk of premature bolting. You can normally make the first cuts within thirty or forty days of sowing: two or three subsequent cuts are often possible. Seedlings can be thinned to 7½–10cm/3–4in apart and grown as small plants.

Sowing programme

For summer supplies Sow from late spring to early summer, using slow-growing, long-day varieties with good bolting resistance. The following are among many recommended for baby leaf crops: 'Emilia', 'Fiorano' F1, 'Medania' F1, 'Palco', 'Tetona' F1, 'Violin' F1

For autumn, winter and early spring supplies Sow from mid- to late summer outside, and early to mid-autumn under cover. The late sowings may stop growing in mid-winter, but will start again in early spring. You can also sow under cover in early spring if soil conditions are suitable. For all these sowings, use faster-growing, short-day varieties such as 'Giant Winter' 'Mikado' F1 (Oriento), 'Palco', 'Samish' F1, 'Triathlon' F1, 'Turaco' F1

Swiss chard and Perpetual spinach *Beta vulgaris* var. *cicla*

Swiss chard (also known as seakale beet, silver chard and silver beet) and perpetual spinach (or spinach beet) are both considered 'leaf beets' as they technically belong to the beetroot family. In appearance, however, they are far more like spinach. Their leaves are coarser than spinach and less distinctly flavoured, and were traditionally grown for use cooked. However, the development of 'baby leaves' has seen Swiss chard soar in popularity due to the colourful stems and reddish tints in some leaves, while perpetual spinach is a useful cut-and-come-again crop.

Swiss chard

These vigorous biennial plants have large, thick, glossy leaves and prominent leaf ribs and stalks, in some varieties yellow, orange, pink, purple or red. They can be almost luminescent, making them superb 'potager' plants. Mature chards require cooking, and it is advisable to cook the stems a little longer than the leaves. Stems and leaves, when coloured, retain some colour after cooking so merit being mixed into salads cold. However, the raw baby leaves are best suited to salads.

Chard is more heat, cold, drought and disease-tolerant than spinach and is probably one of the easiest vegetables to grow. Although slower-growing than spinach, it can be grown for much of the year, cropping over many months.

For both large plants and cut-and-come-again (baby leaf) seedlings, sow from spring to late summer outdoors, though very early outdoor sowings may bolt prematurely. For winter and spring supplies, sow in early autumn and early spring under cover. Seed catalogues list mixtures such as 'Bright Lights', as well as varieties with notable red, yellow, pink and silvery stems, and some with reddish leaves. 'Fordhook Giant' and 'Lucullus' are very productive, green-leaved, white-stemmed varieties.

Perpetual spinach (spinach beet)

More like spinach than Swiss chard, perpetual spinach is very versatile and far less likely to run to seed than spinach. So it remains productive over a much longer period. In practice it often perpetuates itself by self-seeding or simply surviving from one year to the next, if picked regularly. Cultivate as Swiss chard above. Where growing spinach proves difficult, perpetual spinach is an excellent alternative.

'Bright Lights'
Swiss chard

Salad rape

Leaf amaranth

Red orache

Texsel greens

Mild-flavoured leaves

These are easily grown, undemanding salad plants, with relatively mild flavours. Look on them as supplying the 'gentle notes' in a salad, softening the 'discords' of sharp flavours. They are listed here alphabetically according to their Latin names.

Leaf amaranth (calaloo, Chinese spinach) *Amaranthus* spp.

These highly nutritious, spinach-like plants are normally cooked, but the young leaves are surprisingly tasty in salads. Amaranths need a temperature of 20–25°C/68–77°F to flourish outdoors, and will not stand any frost. For salads, sow *in situ* from spring to summer, under cover or outside, provided the soil is above 20°C/68°F and there is no danger of frost. Grow it either as cut-and-come-again baby leaf, or space plants 10–15cm/4–6in apart and harvest the young leaves. The deep red and blotched red- and green-leaved varieties are very productive and the most colourful in salads, but the pale, so-called 'white-leaved' varieties have a tender, buttery flavour. Deep red varieties such as 'Red Army' and 'Garnet Red' are popular subjects for microgreens.

Orache (mountain spinach) *Atriplex hortensis*

Orache is a handsome annual plant, growing up to 2m/7ft high. Green- and red-leaved forms are the most widely grown, sometimes available as mixtures. So-called 'red' strains range from muddy brown to pure scarlet, so if you have a nicely coloured one, save your own seed! Use only young orache leaves in salads; they have a faint spinach flavour and almost downy texture. Either pick leaves from young plants, or grow cut-and-come-again seedlings.

For larger plants, sow *in situ* in spring and early summer, thinning to 20cm/8in apart. Plants grow rapidly, so keep them bushy and tender by regularly picking the topmost tuft of leaves. Even so, they eventually 'get away' from you! Leave a few of the best to self-seed. Bountiful seedlings appear early the following year. Alternatively, to grow as cut-and-come-again seedlings, make continuous sowings from late spring under cover, followed by outdoor sowings until late summer, with a final sowing under cover in early autumn. Summer sowings may bolt prematurely, but late sowings under cover may remain in usable condition for much of the winter.

Texsel (texel) greens *Brassica carinata*

This brassica was developed in the late twentieth century from an Ethiopian mustard. Its small glossy leaves have a distinct, clean flavour with a delightful hint of spinach in them. It is very nutritious and rich in vitamin C. It is reasonably hardy (plants have survived -7°C/20°F in my garden) and very fast-growing. For this reason it is often grown where clubroot disease is a problem: it can be harvested before becoming seriously infected. It is useful for intercropping. Texsel is appreciated as cooked greens in the Indian community, the plants being harvested when

25–30cm/10–12in high. At this stage the smaller leaves and young stems can be eaten raw in salads. Palatable leaves can even be picked from the flower stems. However, small seedling leaves are, in my view, the best-flavoured. This last spring it was my star performer. I had sown a tiny patch in my greenhouse in late winter, and was able to make frequent pickings of perky tasty leaves over two months, before it ran to seed. And now I'm saving the seed for another year.

In the USA Texsel is being sold under the name 'amara'. To quote Jamie Chevalier, who writes the Bountiful Gardens seed catalogue, 'I love the bitter almond and garlic overtones in its flavour, so much more complex than most brassicas.' Incidentally a totally different use for Texsel is as game cover, sometimes grown up to 1½m/5ft high!

Texsel may bolt prematurely in hot and dry conditions, and it grows best, and is best value, in the cooler, autumn-to-spring period. It is usually sown *in situ*. Make early cut-and-come-again seedling sowings under cover in late winter/early spring; continue sowing outdoors in late spring and early summer; avoid mid-summer sowings, but start sowing again outdoors in late summer/early autumn, with final sowings under cover in mid-autumn. You can sometimes make the first cut of seedling leaves within two to three weeks of sowing, with a second cut a few weeks later; occasionally these leaves are bitter.

Research has shown that small plants produce the highest yields when sown in rows 30cm/12in apart, thinned to 2½cm/1in apart, or in rows 15cm/6in, thinned to 5cm/2in apart. In clubroot-infested soils, you can make successive sowings if you pull up plants by the roots when harvesting, leaving a three-week gap before the next sowing. Texsel is generally a healthy crop, but flea beetle (see p. 229) may attack in the early stages. Growing under fine-mesh horticultural nets is a solution.

Salad rape *Brassica napus*

Salad rape is often used as a mustard substitute in 'mustard and cress' packs; it has a milder flavour than mustard with a hint of cabbage in it. It is a very useful garden cut-and-come-again seedling crop, being much slower to run to seed than mustard or cress. I have had spring-sown patches that remained productive for four months. Moreover it does not become unpleasantly hot when mature. It germinates at low temperatures and in my experience survives -10°C/14°F. Seed can be sprouted and grown in shallow containers.

In temperate climates, sow as cut-and-come-again seedlings outdoors throughout the growing season. For exceptionally useful winter-to-spring supplies, sow under cover in late autumn and early winter, and again in late winter and early spring. Cut-and-come-again seedlings may give three, even four successive cuts. If left uncut, salad rape grows to about 60cm/24in high. At this stage the small leaves on the stems are still tender enough to use in salads. It grows very fast, so if you want it with cress, sow it three days later. Salad rape has one failing: it is very attractive to slugs (for control, see p. 229). I have even considered sowing strips as slug decoys!

Tree spinach *Chenopodium giganateum* 'Magentaspreen'

This handsome relative of fat hen or lamb's quarters (*Chenopodium album*) grows rapidly

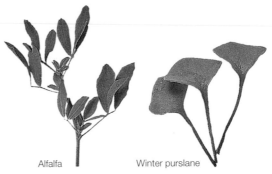

Alfalfa | Winter purslane

to at least 1¾m/6ft high. The tips of many leaves and the leaf undersides are a beautiful magenta pink, as are the flowering spikes. The leaves have a floury texture and a flavour reminiscent of raw peas. Only use young leaves in salads. Either grow it as cut-and-come-again seedlings, sowing throughout the growing season; or sow it in spring and early summer, *in situ* or in modules, spacing plants about 25cm/10in apart – in which case pick the young leaves for salads. It self-seeds prolifically, with abundant seedlings appearing early the following spring – ready for use in salads. It can become invasive, but it is a genial, easily uprooted invader, deserving a place (at the back) of any potager border.

Alfalfa (lucerne, purple medick)
Medicago sativa

Alfalfa is a hardy semi-evergreen perennial in the clover family, with attractive blue and violet flowers. Mature plants can grow up to 90cm/36in high, becoming quite bushy. It is deep-rooting, so withstands dry conditions well. As both foliage and flowers are decorative, it is sometimes grown as a low hedge, dividing the garden into sections. The clover-like young leaves, which have a distinct, pleasant flavour, are used in salads. The seeds can be sprouted, and it is also grown as a green manure.

Grow it either as a perennial or as cut-and-come-again seedlings (you can use seed sold for sprouting). For perennial plants, sow *in situ* in spring or late summer to autumn, thinning to 25cm/10in apart, or alternatively sow in modules and transplant. Pick the young shoots for salads. Cut the plants back hard after flowering to renew their vigour. After

three or four years, it is best to replace them or they become very straggly. For cut-and-come-again seedlings, sow in spring and early summer, and again in late summer and early autumn. For an extra tender crop, make the earliest and latest sowings under cover. You can make pickings throughout the growing season, but the leaf texture becomes tougher as the plants mature.

Winter purslane (claytonia)
Montia perfoliata (syn. *Claytonia perfoliata*)

A native of North America, where it is known as miner's lettuce and spring beauty, this dainty hardy annual is an invaluable spring salad plant. Its early leaves are heart-shaped, but the mature leaves, borne on longer stalks, are rounded and wrapped around the flower stem as if pierced by it. Leaves, young stems and the pretty white flowers are all edible. They are refreshingly succulent, if slightly bland, which may be why children seem to like them. Avoid the pink-flowered 'pink purslane' (*Montia sibirica*): its leaves have an acrid aftertaste.

Winter purslane flourishes in light, sandy soils but, provided drainage is good, adapts to most conditions, including quite poor, dry soils. It is reasonably hardy outdoors in well-drained soil, but its winter quality is vastly

45

improved with protection. Grow it as a cut-and-come-again, baby leaf crop or – probably the most productive method – as single plants.

It can be grown for much of the year, but it is best value, and grows best, in late autumn and early spring. Crops under cover stop growing in mid-winter, but burst into renewed growth early in the year. The seeds are tiny, so sow shallowly, *in situ* or in modules for transplanting, spacing plants about 15cm/6in apart. For summer supplies, sow in early to late spring. For autumn and early-winter-to-spring supplies, sow in summer, planting the later sowings under cover, unless you are sowing *in situ*. Pick leaves from mature plants as required, or cut the whole head 2½cm/1in above ground: it will resprout vigorously before eventually running to seed in late spring. Cut-and-come-again crops give at least two cuts.

Once established, winter purslane self-seeds prolifically, carpeting the ground with seedlings in autumn and spring. They are shallow-rooted, but can be carefully transplanted, perhaps under cover in autumn. If it becomes invasive, dig it in as a green manure in spring.

Iceplant *Mesembryanthemum crystallinum*

Iceplant is an attractive, sprawling plant with thick, fleshy leaves and stems covered with tiny bladders that sparkle in the sun like crystals. It grows wild on South African and Mediterranean shores. In hot climates it is perennial, and is cultivated as a substitute for spinach in summer. I feel it is far better raw in salads – if only for its unusual appearance. Leaves and sliced stems have a crunchy

succulence (not to everyone's taste!) and an intriguing, albeit variable, salty flavour. It grows best in fertile soil, but tolerates poorer, but well-drained, soil.

Although it is a sun-lover, in mid-summer it can be grown undercropping sweet corn. It makes an attractive ground-cover plant in a potager, and, with its trailing habit, looks effective in pots or hanging baskets.

Iceplant is not frost hardy, so make the first sowings in modules or seed trays under cover and plant out, initially with protection if necessary, when all danger of frost is past. Space plants 30cm/12in apart, and protect against slugs in the early stages (see p. 229). In warm climates, sow *in situ* outdoors in late spring or early summer. You can take stem cuttings in early summer (they root quite quickly) to provide a follow-on crop, which you can plant under cover in late summer.

You can normally pick individual leaves or small 'branches' of leaves and stems a month or so after planting. Keep picking regularly, to prevent plants from running to seed and getting coarse, and to encourage further shoots. Surprisingly, mature plants tolerate

Iceplant

light frost and, if given protection, continue growing well into autumn, though the quality is slightly impaired.

_____

February orchid (Chinese violet cress) 'shokassai' (Japanese) *Orychophragmus violaceus*

Essentially an Asiatic weed, February orchid can be grown as an annual or biennial. It has light green leaves, which vary in shape from roundish to deeply serrated, and can be up to 7½cm/3in in width. It is naturally vigorous, young plants in their leafy stage being 10–15cm/4–6in high but then shooting up to 45cm/18in or more when running to seed. This results in masses of beautiful, lilac flowers, not unlike the flowers of honesty (*Lunaria annua*). Their fresh brightness boosts my spirits every spring, their natural time for flowering, hence one of its (several) Chinese names, February orchid. The flowers are edible and decorative in salads. Evidently in the past *Orychophragmus violaceus* was cultivated as an ornamental in European flower borders and cool greenhouses.

The raw leaves have an interesting, mild flavour – my personal opinion, not everyone agrees. They can also be cooked like spinach or used in stir-fries. The great merit of this plant is its tolerance of low winter light levels. It flourishes when so many of our salad plants are in the doldrums, its mildness a good foil to the bitterness of endives and chicory.

The main problem is that there are few sources of seed. (See seed suppliers p. 275 or 'Google' for new suppliers.) Once you have grown it however, you have it for life. It self-seeds readily, though is easily pulled up if showing signs of becoming invasive. It is very easy to save your own seed, the best way being to leave a few plants in spring, in a cold greenhouse or polytunnel, collecting the seed in early summer. It will also self-seed outdoors in areas with relatively mild winters.

February orchid is not fussy about soil provided drainage is good, and is reasonably hardy, overwintering outside if temperatures don't fall below about -5°C/23°F. While the most useful sowings are in late summer to early autumn, for an autumn and spring crop to be grown under cover, it can be sown from early spring to early summer for an outdoor crop. Sow *in situ* or in modules for transplanting. It can be grown as a cut-and-come-again baby leaf crop, or thinned to 15cm/6in apart for larger plants. Leaves can be picked as they reach a reasonable size, even from the stems of seeding plants. If you want flowers, simply leave a few plants to run to seed.

_____

Summer purslane *Portulaca oleracea*

Forms of purslane (not to be confused with winter purslane, which is a different plant) grow wild throughout the temperate world and have been cultivated for centuries. It is a low-growing, half-hardy plant with succulent, rounded leaves and slender but juicy stems. There are green and yellow forms. The green are more vigorous, thinner-leaved and, some say, better-flavoured; the yellow or 'golden' form has thicker, shinier leaves, and is more sprawling, but is very decorative in salads. The leaves and stems are edible raw and have a refreshing, crunchy texture but a rather bland flavour. In the past all parts were pickled for winter use. It is a pretty plant and a favourite in the summer potager; 47

I love to make striped patterns with alternating rows of the two colours. They are productive for many weeks in summer, looking good throughout.

Purslane does best on light, sandy soil but succeeds on heavier soils if they are well drained. It grows profusely in warm climates, but in cooler conditions choose a sheltered, sunny site or grow it under cover.

It can be grown as single plants or, probably the more productive method, as cut-and-come-again baby leaves. As the seed is tiny, and the fragile young seedlings are prone to damping-off diseases (see p. 226), you gain nothing by sowing before the soil has warmed up. For an early start, sow in a heated propagator in late spring, planting out after all danger of frost is past – under protection if necessary. Sow *in situ* outdoors from late spring (in warm areas) to mid-summer. Space plants 15cm/6in apart. For very useful early summer and late autumn cut-and-come-again seedling crops, sow under cover in mid-spring and late summer.

Cut-and-come-again baby leaves are normally ready within four or five weeks of sowing, and may give two or three further cuts. You can make the first pickings from single plants about two months after sowing. Pick individual leaves or stemmy shoots, always leaving two leaves at the base of the stem, where new shoots will develop. It is essential to pick regularly or plants run to seed, becoming coarse.

Remove any seed heads that develop: they are knobbly and unpleasant to eat. Keep plants well watered in summer. The gold-leaved forms are said to remain brighter if watered in full sun. Plants naturally decline in autumn, but may get a new lease of life if you cover them with cloches or fleece.

Yellow purslane

Green purslane

Corn salad (lamb's lettuce, mâche)
Valerianella locusta

This small-leaved hardy annual and closely related species are found wild in much of the northern hemisphere. Rarely more than 10cm/4in high, its fragile appearance belies its robust nature. Its gentle flavour and soft texture make it invaluable in winter salads, although it can be grown most of the year. The flowers are inconspicuous but edible. It is undemanding, tolerates light shade in summer and is ideally suited to intercropping. A traditional European practice was to broadcast corn salad seed on the onion bed prior to lifting the onions. The larger-seeded type has pale green, relatively large, floppy leaves, while the smaller-seeded types, known as verte or 'green', are darker, compact plants with smaller, crisper, upright leaves. They are reputedly hardier, and mainly used for late sowings.

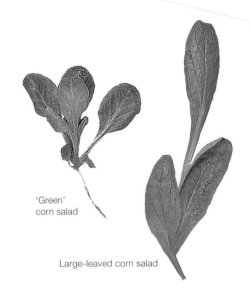

'Green' corn salad

Large-leaved corn salad

While the traditional varieties still give reasonable results, improved selections and varieties are becoming available, which are more productive and versatile. Some are listed below.

Corn salad can be grown as cut-and-come-again seedlings or as individual plants, the latter probably being more productive. As plants are so small corn salad is normally sown *in situ*, although you can sow it in modules or seed trays and transplant, spacing plants 10cm/4in apart. It must be sown on firm soil, and may germinate poorly in hot, dry conditions. If so, take appropriate measures (see p. 197).

For early and mid-summer supplies, start sowing under cover in late winter/ early spring (the first cuttings will help fill the 'vegetable gap'), continuing outdoors in mid- and late spring. For the main autumn/ early winter supplies, sow from mid-summer to early autumn outdoors, making a final sowing in early winter under cover for top-quality winter plants. Although corn salad

is very hardy, surviving at least -10°C/14°F, outdoor plants are always more productive if protected with, say, cloches or fleece.

Corn salad grows slowly, taking about three months to develop to maturity. Baby leaf seedlings are ready several weeks sooner. Pick individual leaves from the plants, or cut across the head to allow resprouting, or pull them up by the roots, as is done commercially – otherwise leaves wilt rapidly. Cut seedlings as soon as they are a useful size. They will resprout at least once. A patch can more or less perpetuate itself if you leave a few plants to self-seed.

Varieties *Large-leaved varieties:* 'Dutch', 'English', 'Pulsar'
'Green' varieties: 'Baron', 'Favor', 'Verte de Louviers', 'Verte de Cambrai', 'Verte de Cambrai' race 'Cavallo', 'Verte de Louviers', 'Vit'

Young leaf of
broad-leaved
sorrel

Young leaf of
red-leaved
sorrel

Watercress

French sorrel

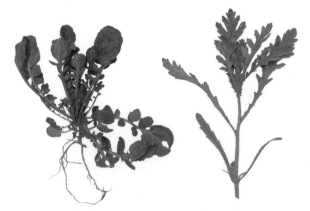

Land cress

Chrysanthemum greens

Strong-flavoured leaves

Not all the strong-flavoured plants in this group are to everybody's liking. But mixed into salads in small quantities, especially blended with mild-flavoured leaves, they can be the catalyst for wonderfully individual salads. The herb coriander (p. 150) could be included here. They are listed here in alphabetical order by their Latin names.

Land cress (American, belle isle, upland or winter cress)
Barbarea verna

A very hardy, low-growing biennial, land cress has dark green, shiny, deeply cut leaves that remain green all winter. Its strong flavour is almost indistinguishable from watercress, and it is used in the same way, cooked or raw in salads. It grows best in moist, humus-rich soils; in hot, dry soils it may run to seed prematurely unless kept well watered. You can grow it in light shade in summer, and intercrop it between taller vegetables.

It is at its best in the winter months, making a neat edging for winter beds. Although it is hardy to at least -10°C/14°F, the leaves will be far more tender to eat if you protect plants with, say, cloches. You can grow it as single plants, spaced 15cm/6in apart, or as cut-and-come-again seedlings. For sowing times and cultivation, see Corn salad, p. 48. The first leaves are normally ready for use within about eight weeks of sowing and cut-and-come-again seedlings several weeks sooner. Young plants are susceptible to flea beetle attack; for control, see p. 229. Land cress runs to seed in its second season. You can leave patches in out-of-the-way corners to perpetuate themselves. This sometimes seems the simplest way to grow it!

There is also a pretty variegated form of land cress, the green leaves dappled with white or pale yellow blotches. It seems to be less hardy, and slightly milder flavoured than standard land cress.

Chrysanthemum greens (shungiku, garland chrysanthemum, chop suey greens) *Chrysanthemum coronarium*)

This annual chrysanthemum, grown as an ornamental, has indented or rounded leaves, depending on variety, and pretty, creamy yellow flowers. The nutritious leaves are used widely in oriental cookery, but with their strong, aromatic flavour should be used only sparingly in salads when raw. The Japanese plunge them into boiling water for a few seconds, then into cold water, before mixing them into salads.

The flower petals are edible, but discard the centre, which is bitter. Mature plants can grow over 60cm/24in high; for salads it is best grown as small plants or cut-and-come-again seedlings.

It thrives in moist, cool conditions, and you can grow it in light shade in summer. Being tolerant of low winter light and moderately hardy, it is best value in the leaner months, from autumn to spring.

The leaves stand well in winter, especially under cover.

For cut-and-come-again baby leaves (it makes a pretty intercrop), start sowing under cover in early spring. Continue sowing outdoors as soon as the soil is workable. For an autumn to early spring supply, sow in late summer outdoors and in early autumn under cover, protecting outdoor sowings if necessary. You can usually cut seedlings four or five weeks after sowing; further cuts may be possible, but uproot plants once the leaves become tough. You can also sow chrysanthemum greens in seed trays or modules, spacing plants 15cm/6in apart. These will be ready eight to ten weeks after sowing. Pick frequently to encourage further, tender growth, and remove flowering shoots. Bushy plants usually regenerate if cut back hard. Give them a liquid feed to stimulate growth. Plants left to flower may self-seed. Use improved named varieties where available.

Rocket (arugula) *Eruca vesicaria* subsp. *sativa* and wild rocket (sylvetta) *Diplotaxis tenuifolia*

There has been an explosion of interest in rocket in the last decade, driven by chefs looking for interesting, spicy leaves to add to salads. Of Mediterranean origin, in the past the annual rocket was far and away the most widely grown type. It has gently indented or straight leaves, creamy white (edible) flowers and a moderately spicy flavour. The perennial wild rocket has far more deeply indented, darker leaves, yellow flowers and a fiery flavour. Plant breeders have now developed improved varieties of both types

– wild rocket now including varieties of wild rocket with ferocious heat, and others with striking, red-veined leaves. Some of the old distinctions of leaf form have been eroded in the process, so there are annual rocket varieties with deeply indented leaves and wild rocket varieties with broader leaves. It's a changed scene, but for everyday use in salads, I still prefer the classic 'old fashioned' type to the more exotic wild rockets. Use these very sparingly when you're looking for an extra kick!

Rocket is a small but fast-growing plant. It can stand several degrees of frost, and undoubtedly grows best in cool weather. Plants run to seed very rapidly in hot, dry conditions, or if stressed in any way – by lack of water, poor soil or overcrowding for example – in which case the leaves become coarser and more pungent. It is inadvisable to buy pots of seedlings from garden centres for this reason: they are very liklely to bolt when planted out. The younger the leaves, the more appealing their flavour, hence their widespread use as microgreens, seed sprouts and cut-and-come- again baby leaves. It responds well to cut-and-come-again treatment at every stage. Its fast growth makes it very useful for intercropping.

In temperate climates, it is possible to have a year-round supply, sowing outdoors from early spring (as soon as the ground is workable) until autumn, followed with sowings under cover. I sow in my polytunnel in mid- to late winter for very early crops and early to mid-autumn for late crops. It is one of the first and last crops I sow every year.

Rocket is normally sown *in situ*; it doesn't transplant well. Either grow it as cut-and-come-again seedlings or as single plants,

Straight-leaved rocket

Rocket with indented leaves

Red-veined rocket

Garden cress

biological control for gardeners in the future. Rocket is a powerful plant.

Varieties A selection of reliable varieties from a wide and expanding choice:
Annual rocket: 'Apollo', 'Esmee', 'Green Brigade', 'Serrata', 'Sorrento', 'Victoria'
Wild rocket: 'Napoli'; 'Tirizia'; 'Dragon's Tongue', 'Fireworks' (both red veined); 'Wasabi' (exceptionally pungent)

Turkish rocket *Bunias orientalis*

True Turkish rocket is a very hardy perennial with dandelion-like leaves, and edible flower buds. It is native in southern and eastern Europe where it is used as greens and in salads. It was traditionally forced and blanched like seakale. Belgian nurseryman Peter Bauwens recommends growing a few plants for use in spring, which he blanches (see p. 245). Germination can be slow, but Turkish rocket is trouble free, and self-seeding. Strains of salad rocket are sometimes misleadingly sold as 'Turkish rocket'.

Garden cress (pepper cress) *Lepidium sativum*

For centuries hot-flavoured cress seedlings have been used in salads, partnered with mustard and, recently, salad rape. Cultivate it in shallow containers indoors or as cut-and-come-again seedlings in the garden. It does best on light soil with plenty of moisture during growth. A fast grower, it is invaluable for intercropping, making dense green patches in ornamental schemes. For sowing, see salad rape p. 44. It has a shorter season of usefulness than rape, running to seed in

spaced 15cm/6in apart. Make summer sowings in light shade, and keep them well watered. You can cut seedlings within three or four weeks of sowing, and make as many as four further cuts. It is easy to save seed, especially from plants seeding in early summer. The main problem is flea beetle, to which summer sowings are particularly susceptible (see p. 229).

Wild rocket, being perennial, can be cut down at the end of the season and left to regenerate the following year. Generally speaking wild rocket is slower to germinate, and growth is slower than annual rocket. With both types, it is easy to save your own seed. In addition, plants left in the ground will often self-seed.

Salad rocket is noted for its levels of vitamins, minerals and glucosinolates. This last has led to current research into its potential as a crop grown to control soil nematodes, notably in potatoes. Who knows, this might become a practical means of hot weather unless grown in light shade.

Garden cress survives only light frost, but you can grow it under cover from mid-autumn to late winter, if you maintain temperatures of 10°C/50°F. At lower temperatures it will become dormant, but it will burst into growth again in spring. Spring sowings can be highly productive: a patch sown in my unheated greenhouse in spring yielded five cuts, boosted by one seaweed extract feed. Cut seedlings at any height from 4 to 15cm/1½ to 6in. They are usually ready within three to four weeks of sowing. It is easy to save seed, especially from plants running to seed in spring.

The traditional, fine-leaved types (probably fastest growing) and stronger flavoured, broad-leaved types have been joined by more exciting looking varieties with distinct flavour. These include 'Bubbles' and 'Wrinkled Crinkled' (ruffled and blistered, decorative leaves), 'Greek Olympus' (frilled spicy leaves), 'Sprint' (fast growing).

Watercress *Nasturtium officinale*

This hardy aquatic perennial has shiny pungent leaves, which are rich in vitamins and minerals. It is a cool-season crop, growing best in spring and autumn in temperate climates. It is a native of fresh running streams in limestone areas and its ideal requirements are clean, flowing, alkaline water, a constant temperature of about 10°C/50°F and dappled shade: that is, bright light but not full sun – conditions not easily met in most gardens. If you have a stream, plant young, rooted pieces of watercress in the soil along the edges in spring, 15cm/6in apart. (Sprigs of watercress root quickly in a jar of water.) Pick lightly in the first season, pinching out tips and flowering shoots to encourage branching. You can usually cut established plants two or three times a season.

Small quantities of watercress can be grown in, say, 20cm/8in wide flower pots. Line the bottom of each pot with gravel or moss to prevent soil from being washed out, then fill it with rich garden or potting soil, to which some ground limestone has been added. Plant several young, rooted pieces in the pot, taken from established plants, or rooted as above. Stand the pot in a dish of cool, clean water, changing the water daily in hot weather, less frequently in cool weather. Put it somewhere sheltered in good light. Apply occasional liquid feeds and harvest as above.

Sorrel *Rumex* spp.

Sorrel is a hardy perennial, found naturalized in the wild all over the world. The leaves have a delicious, sharp, lemon flavour: in salads, it is superb partnered with rocket. It also makes excellent sauces and soups. Two species are grown for the kitchen. The most productive is *Rumex acetosa*, popularly known as common, garden or broad-leaved sorrel (and wrongly as French sorrel). This has fairly large, arrow-shaped leaves, up to about 25cm/10in long, and grows into clumps 30cm/12in wide. The best known variety is 'Large de Belleville' The true French or buckler-leaved sorrel (*R. scutatus*) has small shield-shaped leaves roughly 2½cm/1in wide.

A sprawling plant about 30cm/12in high, it makes excellent ground cover and is pretty

Salsola

as a container plant. It has good drought tolerance. But beware: its spreading roots and self-seeding habit can make it invasive. The tiny leaves have an exceptionally strong flavour, and remain green much longer in winter than common sorrel. It has an attractive, silver-leaved form. There is also a beautiful, red-leaved form of sorrel, *R. acetosa* subsp. *vineatus*, which I have only seen growing in France. The seed is apparently sterile, so the plant can only be propagated by division. It is worth cultivating if found.

Sorrel does best in fertile, moist, slightly acid soil but tolerates a range of conditions, including light shade. It is a good plant for shaded urban gardens. It is normally grown as a perennial. You can renew plants every two or three years by division in the autumn, or leave a plant to run to seed and transplant the seedlings. You can raise plants by sowing in spring, by any method, finally spacing them 30cm/12in apart. Pick leaves as required, and cut off any seed heads which develop. Sorrel naturally dies back in mid-winter, but you can extend the leafy phase by covering with cloches or low tunnels in autumn; similarly covering in spring will encourage earlier growth. For mid-winter pickings, plant young plants under cover in late summer.

Closely related to garden sorrel is herb patience, *R. x patienta* (lemon spinach) with leaves of a distinct lemon flavour. They are tasty and tender in salads, provided they are used young: they become fibrous later. They respond well to cut-and-come-again treatment. Yet another traditional salad plant, red-veined sorrel or red-veined dock *R. sanguineus* var. *sanguineus* (see p. 166) has striking red veins, which have won it a place in contemporary baby leaf mixes and for microgreens. Because of their astringency, they are best used at a very young stage – with only two to four true leaves – primarily for their decorative qualities.

Salsola (saltwort, agretti, roscano) *Salsola* spp.

Members of the Salsola group are by nature salt marsh plants, traditionally collected wild and cultivated both in Asia, especially Japan, and in Italy. They are closely related to the European *Salicornia europaea*, glasswort, also known as marsh or sea samphire (see Wild plants and Weeds, p. 162). The Japanese form of *Salsola komarovii*, okanijiki (meaning 'land seaweed') is probably the most productive, and has become the most widely grown species in the west. This is the form discussed below.

Young leaves and leaf tips of larger plants are used raw in salads, but otherwise it is lightly cooked, sauteed, boiled for a couple of minutes, braised, or dipped briefly into soups before serving. It is often served with seafood. The sparse, frond-like leaves have an appealing, crunchy texture when eaten raw, and a somewhat salty, slightly sour flavour. If left to mature, plants grow into a tuft up to 20–30 cm/8–12in high and 30–45cm/12–18in in diameter.

Salsola can be grown on fairly poor soil, doing best on alkaline soil. It is normally sown *in situ*, thinning plants to about 6cm/2½in, if growing for salad use. If larger plants are wanted, thin to 20–30cm/8–12in apart. The first cuts can be made at a very young stage, when seedlings are no more than 2½cm/1in high, a stage sometimes reached within a month of germination. The fresh salsola I saw in little salad packs in Japan were at a matchstick stage, about 6cm/2½in long. They looked and tasted delicious.

First sowings can be made under cover in spring, followed by outdoor sowings in late spring and early summer. Left in the ground to mature, salsola will sometimes seed itself. It is relatively free of pest and disease problems: some people grow it simply because it is not attacked by flea beetle.

But there is a snag. Salsola seed is notoriously unreliable, losing its viability very rapidly so that sowings often end in failure. Moreover germination can be erratic and slow, and the process is strange. Here's a description from nurseryman Peter Bauwens: 'There's actually a kind of little spiral inside the seed that opens and pushes the young root into the ground. Very unusual.' To increase the chance of success always use fresh seed, keep it at a low temperature before sowing, say in a domestic fridge, and sow as soon as possible. Lovers of salsola are convinced the effort is worthwhile!

White mustard seedlings

White mustard *Sinapsis alba*

White mustard has long been partnered with cress in seedling packs; the hotter-flavoured black mustard (*Brassica nigra*) can also be used. Seeds of both types are used in making mustard. It has a peppery flavour and pretty leaves. Grow as salad rape (see p. 44), but avoid mid-summer sowings, as it runs to seed fast in hot weather, becoming unpleasantly hot. Its useful life is shorter than rape, as once it is past the seedling stage, 5–7½cm/2–3in high, the leaves can become tough and bristly. If you want it with cress, sow it three days later than cress. In areas of high rainfall, growth can be rampant. Varieties 'Tilney' and 'Albatros' are improved varieties.

Dandelion *Taraxacum officinale*

Wild and improved forms of the hardy perennial weed dandelion (see illustration on p. 163) have been grown for culinary use for centuries. All parts – flowers, leaves and roots – are edible. Use young leaves raw in salads, but older leaves are fairly tart unless blanched. The root tops have an excellent flavour and can be sliced raw into salads. Dandelion is most valuable in winter and spring; in temperate climates the leaves often remain green all winter.

It tolerates most conditions, except waterlogged soil. Sow in spring and early summer, in seed trays or modules for transplanting, or *in situ*, spacing plants 35cm/14in apart. You can also thin out

Blanched dandelion
leaves

quite spicy; the smallest seedlings are faintly curry-flavoured; while larger seedlings, notably the leaf tips, have a pea flavour.

Fenugreek tolerates a wide range of conditions, and survives temperatures as low as -16°C/3°F, which makes it a valuable winter salad under cover in cool climates. It requires plenty of moisture throughout growth. Grow it as a cut-and-come-again seedling crop, sowing every three weeks or so, as seedlings quickly become thick-stemmed and coarse. Sow in mid autumn/early winter under cover for winter pickings, setting mouse traps if necessary: mice love fenugreek seeds! Cut seedlings when they reach 5–7½cm/2–3in high – normally four or five weeks after sowing.

seedlings to 5cm/2in apart, so that a group can be blanched under one pot.

From late summer onwards, blanch a few plants at a time. The simplest method is to cover them *in situ*. Allegedly plants covered with leaves or soil have the finest flavour. Where winters are severe, lift plants from mid-autumn onwards and blanch in frames or cellars. They can also be cut back and forced like Witloof chicory (see p. 35).

Varieties Where available, use the more prolific improved named varieties, such as 'Amelioré Géant à Forcer'.

Fenugreek (methi) *Trigonella foenum-graecum*

Fenugreek is a hardy, pretty, aromatic legume, grown for its spicy seeds and leaves (and more recently as microgreens), as well as for green manuring and as a fodder crop. Several stages are used in salads, each, I think, with subtly differing flavours. Sprouted seeds, eaten 1cm/½in long, are

Fenugreek

59

brassica tribe

—

The Brassica tribe, also known as Crucifers, are the backbone of our vegetable gardens, mainly grown for use when cooked. However, they also fulfil an invaluable role in salads, and earn their place by being easily grown, nutritious and in many cases colourful. The key is to choose appropriate varieties and growing methods.

Typical round-headed early
summer cabbage

Typical pointed spring cabbage

Typical green savoy

Cross section of a
summer cabbage

Cabbage
Brassica oleracea Capitata Group

Cabbage is among the most widely grown of cool-climate crops, and for aficionados there is a cabbage for every season. In spring there are loose-headed 'spring greens' and perky, mainly pointed hearted cabbages; in summer and autumn there are large green and red cabbages; while in winter there are hardy savoys and red-tinged 'January King' types, and the option of stored Dutch Winter White cabbage. Any cabbage can be used as a raw salad or coleslaw, especially if finely shredded, but in my view the light green, sweeter spring and summer cabbages, the thin-leaved Dutch Winter Whites, the tasty savoys and the colourful red cabbages are the best for salads, simply because they are the most palatable raw. (For ornamental cabbages and kales see p. 68.)

Soil and site

Cabbages require fertile, well-drained, slightly acid soil, though if clubroot is endemic, it should be limed to bring the pH to marginally alkaline. Cabbages have high nitrogen requirements, and are a good crop to follow a nitrogen-fixing green manure. They are among the many brassicas (in the Cruciferae family) that should be rotated, ideally over a three-or-four-year cycle, to avoid the build-up of clubroot and brassica cyst eelworm.

Cultivation

The most reliable way of raising cabbages is to sow in modules for transplanting, though traditionally they were sown in seedbeds and transplanted. Plant in their permanent positions when quite small, at the three-or-four-leaf stage, planting firmly with the lower leaves just above the soil. Always plant into firm ground, never into freshly manured soil. It is often sufficient just to clear or rake the ground prior to planting, without digging. Otherwise fork the soil several weeks in advance, leaving it to settle before planting.

In very light soil or windy, exposed gardens, plant in shallow furrows about 10cm/4in deep, filling in the soil as the plants grow. Secondary roots develop on the buried stem, increasing the plant's stability. Large plants may need staking during the winter months.

Space cabbages from 30–45cm/12–18in apart, depending on the type and the size of head required. As a general rule, the wider the spacing, the larger the head will be. As cabbages are slow-growing and relatively widely spaced, they lend themselves to intercropping.

Cabbages need plenty of moisture throughout their growth. In the absence of rain, water weekly at the rate of 9–14 litres per sq. m/2–3 gallons per sq. yd. Failing this, aim to give them at least one very heavy watering two or three weeks before harvesting. If growth seems slow mid-season, apply a liquid feed.

Cabbages will often resprout after the main head is cut, producing a very useful crop of smaller secondary heads later in the season (see p. 239). This works best with spring cabbages.

Sowing programme

For spring and early summer supplies
In areas where winter temperatures rarely fall below about -6°C/21°F, sow in late summer, by any method, transplanting seedlings into their permanent positions in early autumn. Space plants 30cm/12in apart for headed cabbages.

For summer and autumn supplies
Make the first sowings in gentle heat, at about 13°C/55°F in late winter/early spring, planting out after hardening off as soon as soil conditions allow. (In my previous East Anglian garden, with its low rainfall, I found late winter sowings far better than spring sowings for the main summer red cabbage crop. Seedlings were overwintered in a cold frame and planted out as early as soil conditions allowed in spring.)

Continue sowing in late spring, initially under cover then in the open. Space summer cabbage 35–45cm/14–18in apart, depending on the size of head required. Older varieties of summer cabbages tended to bolt rapidly when mature but improved varieties, such as F1 hybrid 'Stonehead', stand in good condition for up to three months. Plant autumn cabbage by mid-summer; space them 50cm/20in apart.

'Mini' cabbage These are tiny cabbages with no wasted outer leaves, produced by growing plants very close together. They are exceptionally tender in salads. Only certain varieties are suitable. Sow from early to late spring, *in situ* or in modules, thinning or planting to 12cm/5in apart. Harvest heads about twenty weeks after sowing.

For winter storage supplies These are mainly Dutch Winter White cabbages, though you can also store late varieties of red cabbage. Sow in mid-spring, planting in early summer 50cm/20in apart. Use heads fresh in early winter, but lift them before heavy frost, pulling them up by the roots or cutting with 5–7½cm/2–3in of stalk attached to use as a handle. Store them hung in a frost-free shed or cellar, or in cold frames, raised off the ground on wooden slats and covered with straw. Ventilate the frames on warm days. Cabbages can also be stored in heaps on a cellar floor, on a bed of straw with straw between the heads. Inspect stored heads regularly, and gently roll off any rotting outer leaves. They will often keep for three or more months.

For fresh winter supplies These are the hardiest cabbages, surviving outdoors where temperatures normally remain above about -10°C/14°F. The well-flavoured, crêpe-leaved savoys are the backbone of the hardy cabbages; more recently introduced cabbages are crossed with Winter White types. Sow in late spring, planting by mid-summer 50cm/20in apart each way. Some will stand until the following spring, helping to fill the 'vegetable gap'.

Varieties

Recent developments in the cabbage world include the introduction of varieties with clubroot resistance, and two groups of exceptionally sweet varieties, the pointed 'Sweetheart' types, (indicated with a 'p' below which can be grown all summer) and the flat headed, thin-leaved Japanese varieties. I have chosen the varieties listed here primarily for their suitability for salads.

Spring supplies 'Advantage' F1, 'Duncan' F1, 'Spring Hero'

Early summer supplies As above plus:
'Cabbice' F1 (flat Japanese), 'Candisa' F1,
'Caramba' F1, 'Elisa' F1, 'Tinto' F1 (red, p)
Summer supplies 'Alcosa' (F1) (summer
savoy), 'Caraflex' F1 (p), 'Dutchman' F1 (p),
'Elisa' F1, 'Regency' F1 (p), 'Primero' F1 (red),
'Stonehead' F1
Autumn supplies 'Charmant' F1, 'Kalibos'
F1 (red), 'Primero' F1 (red), 'Ruby Ball' F1
(red), 'Stonehead' F1
Mini cabbage 'Alcosa' F1 (savoy), 'Candisa'
F1, 'Elisa' F1, 'Primero' F1 (red), 'Puma' F1
Winter storage 'Bison' F1, 'Brigadier'
F1, 'Dutch Winter White Kilaton' (clubroot
resistant), 'Lodero' F1 (red, clubroot resistant)
Winter hardy 'January King Hardy Late
Stock 3', 'Deadon' F1
Savoy x *Dutch White hybrids:* 'Renton' F1,
'Tundra' F1
Savoys: 'Cappriccio' F1, 'Rigoletto' F1

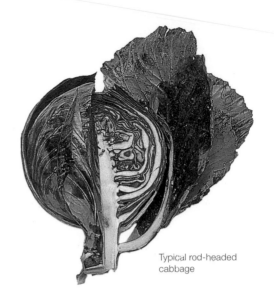

Typical rod-headed
cabbage

undersides of leaves in late summer and can
be very destructive. Colonies of whitefly, which
flutter up from plants in summer, are normally
less serious. As aphids overwinter in brassica
stumps, and emerge in late spring, old plants
should be pulled out and burnt after cropping.

Pests

Unless otherwise stated, for protective measures
and control, see p. 226.
Birds Attack seedlings and mature plants,
especially in winter.
Slugs and snails Potentially serious at any
stage, but most damaging on seedlings and
young plants in wet weather.
Cabbage root fly Often a serious pest. Small
white maggots attack the roots, causing plants to
wilt and die. When planting, take measures to
prevent the adult flies from laying eggs near by.
Flea beetle Tiny, blue-black beetles nibble
holes in seedling leaves of all brassicas; *in situ*
sowings are the most vulnerable.
Caterpillars Attacks are most damaging in
late summer.
Aphids Grey mealy aphids appear on the

Diseases

Clubroot This serious soil-borne disease
manifests itself as solid swollen galls on roots
of the brassica family. Plants eventually wilt
and die. Practical measures to reduce clubroot
are improving drainage and liming acid soils
to a neutral or slightly alkaline level, and
rotation. Remember that swedes, turnips and
radishes are also brassicas. In badly infected
soils grow only fast-growing brassicas such as
Texsel greens and oriental cut-and-come-again
seedlings. Or give plants a head start on the
disease by sowing in modules and potting into
10cm/4in pots before planting out. Watch out
for new remedies and resistant varieties.
Damping-off diseases Seedlings are
vulnerable when sown in adverse conditions.

65

'Red Russian' kale

Cavolo nero

Thin-leaved 'Hungry Gap' kale

Thin-leaved 'Pentland Brig'

Curly kale 'Redbor' F1

Typical curly kale

Kale

(borecole) *Brassica oleracea* Acephala Group

I used to think kales were too harsh for anything but the most sparing use in salads. I've changed my mind, for several reasons. First, I realized how tender some of the thinner-leaved kales can be, such as 'Hungry Gap', 'Pentland Brig' and 'Red Russian'. (The latter has very pretty, blue-green leaves brushed with purple.) Then I discovered two exceptionally beautiful crisp-leaved kales: the old Italian Tuscan kale, also known as cavolo nero, black kale, palm cabbage and dinosaur kale, with its flavoursome, narrow, crêped blue leaves, and the newer 'Redbor' variety, probably bred from an old heirloom kale, which is as hardy as the old forms but with striking, deeply curled, bronze-red leaves. And I realized how productive and appealing these, and the traditional curly kales, are when grown as cut-and-come-again seedlings. Indeed, baby-leaved 'Redbor' and 'Red Russian' are popular ingredients in prepacked salads.

Seedling kales can be sown throughout the growing season, but come into their own in the colder months when salading is most scarce. Two or three cuts of small leaves can generally be made from one sowing. Mix them with other salad leaves, or use them on their own, accentuating their flavours with a strong dressing such as the Ginger and Sesame dressing on p. 263.

Cultivation

These rugged kales often succeed where other brassicas fail. They need well-drained, reasonably fertile soil, but are otherwise undemanding. They have some tolerance to clubroot. For mature plants, cultivate as for summer cabbage, sowing in late spring and early summer (see p. 64). Varieties mentioned below are as hardy as savoy cabbages. Mature leaves and the shoots that develop in spring are used as cooked vegetables from autumn to spring, but small leaves could be picked for salads.

For cut-and-come-again seedling crops, start sowing under cover in late winter; continue sowing outdoors from mid-spring to late summer (or later in mild areas). Make the last sowings under cover in early autumn. Kales are relatively slow-growing, but, depending on the variety and time of year, the first cutting of small leaves can be made any time from about six weeks after sowing.

Varieties

These varieties can be grown as mature plants, but are also recommended for cut-and-come-again seedlings.

Black kale: 'Black Magic', 'Cavolo Nero'
Green curly kale (med. sized): 'Darkibor' F1, 'Kapitan' F1, 'Reflex' F1, 'Starbor' F1 (compact)
Red curly kale: 'Redbor' F1
Thin-leaved kales: 'Bolshoi' F1, 'Hungry Gap', 'Pentland Brig', 'Red Russian' and 'Ragged Jack' ('Ragged Jack' is similar to 'Red Russian' in appearance and texture, but may be less hardy), 'Siber-Frill' (very curled and indented)

Ornamental cabbages and kales

These loose-headed cabbages and kales are notable for their wonderful colouring: the blue-green leaves are tinged with varying combinations of red, white, cream, purple and yellow. The leaves are also decorative shapes – deeply serrated, frilled or waved – sometimes packed into rosette heads in rings of contrasting colours. Some varieties have been bred with exceptionally long stems for flower arranging. They are all ideal plants for the decorative potager.

They are at their best late in the year, as the colours deepen when night temperatures fall to about 10°C/50°F. There are dwarf, intermediate and tall forms, ranging from 30 to 60cm/12 to 24in tall. Seed catalogues rarely distinguish between cabbages and kales, but those with flat heads and relatively smooth leaves are generally cabbages, while the deeply serrated, coarser-leaved types are kales. The significance is that the kales are hardiest, surviving temperatures of about -10°C/14°F, which would destroy the cabbages. Mainly used in salads as a decorative garnish, small leaves can be eaten whole and larger leaves shredded.

Soil and site

Soil must be well-drained and moisture-retentive, but these ornamental forms tolerate poorer soil than most brassicas. In rich soil they may become lush and fail to colour well. They like an open situation, but can be protected, or grown under cover, in winter in cold climates. Dwarf types can be grown as winter houseplants in cool conservatories.

For top-quality plants, sow in modules or seed trays, eventually potting into 8–10cm/3¼–4in pots before planting out. Make the main sowings in late spring or early summer; modern varieties take only three months to mature. Space plants 30–40cm/12–16in apart, depending on variety, planting firmly at the five-to-seven-leaf stage, with the lower leaves just above soil level. For a late crop under cover, pot on into 15cm/6in pots and plant in early autumn. For winter container plants, pot dwarf varieties into 15cm/6in pots; or plant two or three closely into a 35cm/14in pot in good potting compost. For pests, see Cabbages, p. 65. Caterpillars tend to be the worst pest (for control, see p. 229).

Harvesting

Unless using a whole head for decoration, pick individual leaves just before use, as they wilt rapidly. Plants resprout over many months, sometimes lasting two seasons, with small secondary leaves developing on the stems. To perpetuate good varieties, cuttings can be made from young shoots.

Varieties

Ornamental cabbages and kales are often listed in the flower section of seed catalogues. In each distinct type 'series' have been bred, each variety with a different dominant colour, usually red, white, or pink. All are F1 hybrids.

Round leaved Pigeon series, Osaka series, Songbird series

Fringed leaved Chidori series, Kanome series, Nagoya series, Northern Lights series, Buttonhole kale Stargazer

Serrated leaved Coral series, Feather series, Peacock series

Red 'Osaka' ornamental kale

oriental greens

—

A whole range of exciting oriental greens have gradually become available to gardeners in the West. Their subtle flavours when raw, crisp texture, lively colours and nutritional qualities make them valuable additions to the salad garden. Many are in their prime in autumn and early winter and, being fast growing, lend themselves to cut-and-come-again techniques. More recently, the popularity of 'baby leaf' salads has led to new varieties being developed – beautiful, pink-leaved forms in some cases, and delightfully frilly leaf forms in others.

The oriental greens are in the main cool-season crops, ideally suited to summer and early winter cultivation in temperate climates, though there are varieties for warmer and tropical climates. They generally make excellent winter crops under cover. Some of the mustards are very hardy.

Oriental brassicas must be grown in fertile soil, rich in organic matter, with plenty of moisture throughout growth. It is just not worth growing them in poor, dry soils. Ideally soil should be neutral or slightly alkaline, as clubroot can be a problem (see p. 65). Soil fertility apart, a key factor in growing oriental brassicas is overcoming a tendency to bolt prematurely. This is caused by various interlocking factors, such as day length and low temperatures in the early stages of growth, and can be exacerbated by transplanting. For this reason be wary of buying oriental vegetable plants from garden centres early in the year: they are likely to bolt.

The problem scarcely arises with cut-and-come-again seedlings, as they are harvested young. However, when growing plants to maturity, the safest bet is to delay sowing until early summer – that is, after the longest day – and to protect plants if a sharp temperature drop is expected. Some varieties are more bolt-resistant than others. Late sowing means that oriental greens, which are fast-growing, can follow early harvests of potatoes, peas, beans or salads, making full use of garden space.

On the whole, oriental brassicas do not transplant well, so sow them either *in situ* or in modules. They tend to have shallow roots, so, unlike other brassicas, need to be watered frequently, but moderately, especially when nearing maturity. Mulching, with organic materials or plastic films, seems to be beneficial for these greens. Unless the soil is exceptionally fertile, growth can be boosted with liquid feeds during the growing season. Oriental brassicas are subject to the same pests and diseases as Western brassicas (see p. 65). Caterpillars and slugs cause the most trouble (for control measures see p. 229). Growing under fine nets is highly recommended.

While they are all superb cooked vegetables, the most suitable for salads are the mild flavoured greens, typified by Chinese cabbage and pak choi, and some of the mustards and flowering brassicas. All are excellent with Ginger and Sesame dressing (see p. 263).

A major barrier to adopting oriental vegetables is their confusing names. Not only are plants known by several names, but the same names are used for different plants. Then, to overcome the difficulties in pronouncing the original names, misleading Westernized names have been coined. 'Pak choi', for example, is often called 'celery mustard' – yet it is neither celery nor mustard. I try to use the most sensible, or currently acceptable, name for each plant.

Chinese cabbage
Brassica rapa Pekinensis Group

Popularly known as Chinese leaves, the hearted types of Chinese cabbage (known as Napa cabbage in the USA) form a barrel-shaped, rounded or tall cylindrical head of closely folded leaves, usually creamy to light green in colour, with a crinkled texture, prominent white veining and white midribs broadening out at the base. The tall cylindrical types are generally later and slower-maturing.

'Loose- or semi-headed' types are a distinct group that do not form hearts, used mainly as cut-and-come-again crops at the seedling and semi-mature stages. Varieties dubbed 'fluffy tops' have beautiful, butter-coloured centres of crêpe-like leaves, ideal for salad use. All Chinese cabbages are crisp-textured with a delicate flavour. They grow best at temperatures of 13–20°C/55–68°F. They tolerate light frost in the open, but with cut-and-come-again treatment plants remain productive under cover in the winter months. They have survived -10°C/14°F in my polytunnel. They are amongst the fastest growing of all leafy vegetables. In good conditions mature heads can be cut ten weeks after sowing, loose-headed types two to three weeks sooner, and seedlings four to five weeks after sowing.

Chinese cabbage is a very thirsty crop: a single plant may need as much as 22 litres/ 5 gallons of water during its growing period. Harvested Chinese cabbage heads will keep for several weeks in a fridge, frost-free cellar or shed.

For the main late summer and autumn supplies

Sow early to late summer. Space plants about 30cm/12in apart.

For an earlier summer crop

Try sowing in late spring in a propagator, using bolt-resistant varieties; maintain a minimum temperature of 18°C/64°F for the first three weeks after germination. Protect plants with cloches or crop covers after planting.

For an autumn/early winter crop

Sow in late summer, transplanting under cover in early autumn. The plants may not have time to develop full heads. Plant either at standard spacing or about 12cm/5in apart – in which case cut the immature leaves when 7½–10cm/3–4in high. Do not overcrowd autumn plants, as the leaves tend to rot in damp weather. Cut hearted plants 2½cm/1in above the base and allow them to resprout during the winter. In spring let remaining plants run to seed: the colourful flowering shoots make a tender salad and are colourful too.

For cut-and-come-again seedlings

Use only loose-headed varieties, as hearting types often have rough, hairy leaves at seedling stage – though new, smoother-leaved varieties may be developed. Make the first sowings under cover in spring. Follow with outdoor sowings as soon as the soil is workable, giving protection if necessary. Continue outdoor sowings until late

Typical loose-headed
Chinese cabbage

Typical tall-headed
Chinese cabbage

Typical barrel-shaped
Chinese cabbage

summer, and make final sowings under cover in early autumn. Cut seedlings as soon as they reach a useable size, leaving stems to resprout unless they have started to bolt.

Varieties

With modern breeding programmes the choice of varieties is constantly changing, and in practice, gardeners have to be guided by information in current seed catalogues.

F1 varieties tend to be of better quality and more reliable than older varieties. For headed Chinese cabbage, varieties described as compact, 'mini' or short are easier to grow than large varieties. All are excellent for salad use. For cut-and-come-again seedlings use loose headed types, sometimes listed as 'bunching' varieties; these include 'Santo' selections and 'Tokyo Bekana'.

Pak choi
(bok choy/celery mustard) *Brassica rapa* Chinensis Group

The typical pak choi has smooth, shiny, somewhat rounded leaves, traditionally pale or dark green in colour but now with the addition of beautiful, reddish leaved varieties. The pronounced midribs merge into stems that swell out at the base into a characteristic, almost bulb-like butt. They are normally white-stemmed, but some varieties are a beautiful light green. The many types range from small, stocky

varieties 7½–10cm/3–4in high, to medium 15cm/6in-high varieties, to tall forms up to 45cm/18in high. (See also Rosette pak choi opposite.) Varieties differ in their tolerance to heat and cold, but most only stand light frost. Like Chinese cabbage, they are excellent winter crops under cover. All parts, from seedling leaves to the flowering stems, are edible raw or cooked. Pak choi has a delightful fresh flavour, succulent

74

texture, and to me, an irresistible, bonny appearance.

Pak choi is closely related to Chinese cabbage and grown in the same way (see p. 73). For the headed crop, use slow-bolting varieties for the earliest sowings. Space small and squat varieties 12–15cm/5–6in apart, medium-sized varieties 18–23cm/7–9in apart and large types up to 45cm/18in apart. Allow up to ten weeks from sowing to harvest, though small heads are sometimes ready within six weeks of sowing. Leaves can be picked individually or the whole head cut, leaving the stump to resprout.

Cut-and-come-again seedling crops can be very productive. Depending on the season, the first cut of small leaves may be made within three weeks of sowing; it is sometimes possible to make two or three successive cuts.

Typical green-stemmed pak choi

Varieties As with Chinese cabbage, varieties are constantly changing and most give good results. The following are reliable, compact varieties, with good bolting resistance. 'Baraku' F1, 'Choko' F1, 'Mei Qing Choi' F1, 'Shuko' F1, 'Summer Breeze' F1, 'Red Choi' F1 (among many new, reddish-leaved varieties)

Rosette pak choi
(ta tsoi/tah tsai and similarly spelt names)
Brassica rapa var. rosularis

This unique form has crinkled, rounded, blue-green leaves, which, although upright initially, in cool weather develop into a flat, extraordinarily symmetrical rosette head. It is hardier than other pak chois, and in well-drained soil may survive -10°C/14°F. This makes it a favourite in my winter potager. Its pronounced flavour is highly rated by the Chinese; the leaves are very decorative in salads.

Grow it as single plants or cut-and-come-again seedlings. It is slower-growing and somewhat less vigorous than other pak chois and prone to bolting from early

sowings, so it is best to sow it from mid- to late summer. Like Chinese cabbage and pak choi, it can be transplanted under cover for an excellent-quality winter crop. Adjust spacing according to the size of the plant required: 15cm/6in apart for small, unrosetted heads; 30–40cm/12–16in apart, depending on variety, for large plants. Pick individual leaves as required, or cut across the head, encouraging it to resprout. As a baby leaves crop, it stands well over many weeks.

Varieties Mainly sold as 'Tatsoi' or 'Tahtsai'; improved varieties include 'Rozette' F1

Komatsuna
(mustard spinach) Brassica rapa Perviridis Group

This extraodinarily diverse group of robust greens originated by crossing various brassicas. Most have large, glossy leaves, which radiate an aura of healthiness, especially in the winter months. They tolerate a wide range of climates, some being very hardy. They are less prone to bolting, pests and diseases than many oriental brassicas and, being vigorous, respond well to cut-and-come-again treatment at any stage. Essentially a vegetable for cooking, large mature leaves can be shredded for use in salads, but leaves from small plants and baby, cut-and-come-again seedling leaves are more suitable. The young flowering shoots are also very sweet and palateable in salads. Depending on variety, the flavour has hints of cabbage, spinach and mustard. They are said to be very nutritious.

For general cultivation, see Chinese cabbage, p. 73. Sow outdoors from early to late summer, spacing plants 10cm/4in apart for harvesting young, or 30–35cm/12–14in apart, depending on variety, for large plants. For cut-and-come-again seedlings, start sowing in mid- to late winter under cover for a very early crop; sow outdoors from early spring to late summer, making a final sowing under cover in early autumn for a high-quality winter crop.

Plant breeders are developing varieties especially suited to baby leaf crops, including varieties with ruby red leaves.

The 'Senposai' hybrids are a group with a marked cabbage flavour, bred in Japan and widely used for seed sprouting. I found them a useful cut-and-come-again seedling crop for late summer in the open and winter under cover.

Varieties *Older varieties:* 'Green Boy' F1, 'Komatsuna', 'Tendergreen'
Red leaved: 'Comred' F1. Watch out for new F1 hybrid varieties in seed catalogues.

Mizuna
(kyona, potherb mustard) *Brassica rapa* var. *nipposinica*

This beautiful Japanese brassica has glossy, serrated, dark green leaves, often 25cm/10in long. Mature plants can form bushy clumps well over 30cm/12in wide. It is an excellent plant for edging or infilling decorative potagers, and for various forms of intercropping. Mizuna tolerates high and low temperatures: if kept cropped it will survive about -10°C/14°F in the open. With its natural vigour and healthiness it responds well to cut-and-come-again techniques at every stage, and can remain productive over many months. The leaves have a mild mustard flavour. Mature and seedling leaves can be used in salads, the latter being daintier and more decorative. Young flowering shoots are also sweet and colourful in salads. Cultivate as komatsuna above. Sowings in hot weather are susceptible to flea beetle attacks.

Besides the more traditional, serrated leaved varieties, there are now broader-leaved varieties such as 'Waido', some very finely cut, feathery-leaved varieties, and red and reddish tinged leaved forms. See seed catalogues for what is currently available.

Rosette pak choi

Seedling leaves of komatsuna

Broad-leaved
mizuna greens

Finely serrated
mizuna greens

Red mizuna
greens

Mibuna greens
Brassica rapa var. nipposinica

Mizuna's twin, mibuna, has narrow, strap-like leaves 30–45cm/12–18in long, which are less glossy and probably milder-flavoured than mizuna but add an interesting dimension to salads. Mature plants form handsome architectural clumps. It is less productive than mizuna and less hardy – surviving temperatures of about -6°C/21°F in the open. It is a cool-season crop and best value in the late summer/early winter period, in the open or under cover. For cultivation, see Mizuna p. 76. Currently 'Green Spray' F1 is the only named variety. The flowering shoots of both mibuna and mizuna can be used in salads.

Mustards
Brassica juncea

This vast and rugged group of hardy vegetables has rather rough leaves with varying degrees of fiery flavour. They not only add a spicy zing to a salad, but also often a colourful and decorative element. Use them sparingly. Mature leaves can be shredded to moderate the flavour, which tends to intensify as plants age and run to seed. The flowering stems are edible too – again, approach them cautiously. Some time back I discovered, through serendipitous nibbling, that both the ordinary and flowering stems of the pickling or stem mustards have a delectable, almost sweet flavour – superb in salads. It may be necessary to peel the outer skin before use.

The main salad use of the oriental mustards is as 'baby leaves', and they feature prominently in the popular mixes now sold for stir-fries and salads. Look out for 'spicy' in the mixture names; 'Bright and Spicy', 'Nice and Spicy' etc. Because so many are hardy, they are particularly useful in winter months.

The mustards are slower growing than most oriental brassicas. They are mainly sown in mid-summer, *in situ* or in modules. For mature plants space them 25–40cm/10–16in apart, depending on variety and the size required. They can be planted under cover in late summer or early autumn for a more tender crop.

When grown as cut-and-come-again seedlings for baby leaf, early sowings are very liable to bolt, so sowings from mid-summer to late summer are recommended. Regrowth is less vigorous than in many seedling crops, but they will stand in reasonable condition for many weeks.

The varieties being used alone, or in mixtures for salads, come mainly from the mustard groups below.

Giant-leaved mustards

This group includes the handsome, purple- and red-tinged mustards, typical traditional varieties being 'Red Giant' and the slightly finer 'Osaka Purple'. They are reasonably hardy, often acquiring deeper colours as temperatures lower. I saw them grown as seedling crops in summer in the Napa Valley in California, with the leaves cut for salads about 2½cm/1in diameter. There are also green varieties, such as 'Miike Giant'.

Possibly originating from the giant mustards and these smaller-leaved types, are exciting new varieties bred for baby leaf use. Some have beautifully coloured red leaves: 'Red Dragon' and 'Red Lace' are two currently available. Another decorative group are the 'Frills' varieties, with beautiful, serrated feathery leaves. There are red, green, and very light coloured forms. 'Red Frills', 'Green Frills,' 'Golden Streak', 'Ruby Streak', are some of these new varieties currently available, but the choice is constantly changing. Look out for them in current seed catalogues and in the seed mixtures. All are best eaten young in salads, though they can be stir-fried when larger.

Common or Indian mustards

There are many somewhat smaller-leaved, rugged and spicy mustards, sometimes labelled Common or Indian mustards. One of the best known is the serrated-leaved 'Green in the Snow' (Serifong, Xue li hong and assorted spellings). The Chinese name means 'Red in the Snow', indicating how hardy it is – though the leaves are, in fact, green! It can develop into a large plant, but for salads can be grown either as cut-and-come-again seedlings, or spaced 15–20cm/6–8in apart for small plants cut young before the leaves become too hot.

Another useful, though less hardy variety, is 'Amsoi', used in China as a pickling mustard. Pick young leaves and stems for use in salads; they have an interesting flavour.

The flowering brassicas
Brassica juncea

The flowering shoots of almost all oriental brassicas can be used raw in salads. Most are pleasantly sweet-flavoured, though mustards have a characteristic hot flavour. Pick shoots from mature plants when in bud, before the flowers open. The plants generally produce a succession of shoots.

The following are types traditionally cultivated primarily for their flowering stems. Plant breeders have been developing improved varieties with more substantial, and more succulent edible shoots, though few are listed by name in home gardeners' catalogues. Where available, they can often be found under the general names below and are well worth growing.

Choy sum *Brassica rapa* var. *parachinensis* (often listed as flowering pak choi)

The standard green-stemmed type has yellow flowers, and is moderately hardy. Sow from early to late summer, *in situ* or in modules for transplanting, spacing plants 12–20cm/5–8in apart. Cut the shoots when 10cm/4in long.

The well-known purple form 'Hon Tsai Tai' (the Chinese name means red shoots), has purple flower and leaf stalks, with leaves varying from dark green to purple. It is quite hardy, surviving -5°C/23°F outdoors. Grow as above or space them up to 38cm/15in apart for large plants.

'Green in the
Snow' mustard

Purple-leaved
mustards

Edible oil seed
rape leaves

Mibuna
greens

Edible oil seed rape *Brassica rapa* var. *oleifera* and *B. r.* var. *utilis* (sometimes listed as flowering Chinese cabbage)

Not to be confused with the ordinary oil seed rapes – but developed from them – are hybrid varieties with chunky, succulent stems, yellow flower buds, and pretty, crêpe-textured leaves. Some varieties are even used as cut flowers in Japan. Grow them like Choy sum (see p. 79). They generally tolerate light frost and do well under cover in winter. 'Shuka' F1 is one of the newer varieties.

Chinese broccoli (Chinese kale, Gai laan) *Brassica oleracea* var. *algoglabra*

This distinct, thick-stemmed, white-flowered brassica is appreciated for its exceptional flavour. While normally cooked, it can be used raw in salads, though the stems may need to be peeled before use. It tolerates several degrees of frost and does best from mid- to late summer sowings. Space plants 10–15cm/4–6in apart for harvesting whole when flowering shoots appear, or 25–38cm/10–15in for large plants, where individual shoots are picked over a longer period. 'Green Lance' F1 is one of the older varieties, 'Kaibroc' F1 a newer variety.

Oriental saladini

Oriental saladini was originally a mixture I created in 1991 with the seed company Suffolk Herbs to introduce Westerners to the wonderful diversity of oriental greens. The mixture included loose-headed Chinese cabbage, pak choi, komatsuna, mibuna, mizuna and purple mustard. The various 'spicy green' mixtures on the market can be used in the same way. Its main use is for cut-and-come-again seedlings for salads or stir-fries, though you can prick out or transplant individual plants and grow them on to maturity. Sow as for Chinese cabbage cut-and-come-again seedling crops, p. 73. Spring and early summer sowings may allow only one cut before the plants start to bolt: the most productive sowings are from mid-summer onwards. Make the last sowings under cover in early to mid-autumn for use in winter and early spring. Patches often seem to 'thin themselves out' after several cuttings, leaving just a few large plants. Oriental saladini can be sown in containers or spent compost bags.

Many of the oriental greens and salad mixtures listed today are variations on the 'oriental saladini' theme. They are excellent value for salad greens, often productive over several months.

stems
and
stalks

—

Interesting flavours and exceptional textures lurk in plants grown for their edible stalks and stems. Kohl rabi and fennel earn their place here, as their bulb-like swellings are, botanically speaking, swollen stems.

Standard leaf celery   Leaf celery 'Parcel'

Celery
Apium graveolens

The celeries are biennial, marsh plants in origin, grown mainly for the distinct flavour and crisp texture of their stems. The stems of some types, mainly the classic 'trench celery' are blanched to make them paler, crisper and sweeter. The strong-flavoured leaves are used for seasoning and garnishing, both fresh and dried. The seeds are also used in flavouring. There are several closely related kinds, of varying hardiness.

General cultivation

The celeries are all cool-season crops, requiring fertile, moisture-retentive soil that is rich in organic matter, and preferably neutral or slightly alkaline. Very acid soils are unsuitable. All types need generous watering and mulching to conserve moisture, and generally benefit from supplementary feeding.

Celery seed germinates at 10–15°C/50–59°F. The seed is small, so it is normally sown in seed trays or modules, in a heated propagator if necessary. It requires light to germinate, so sow on the surface or just covered lightly with sand or fine vermiculite. Keep the surface damp until germination. Prick out seedlings as soon as they are large enough to handle. Plant them at the five-to-six-leaf stage after hardening them off well. Seedlings may bolt prematurely if, after germinating, they are subjected to temperatures below 10°F/50°C for more than about twelve hours, so try and keep them at an even temperature. If cold threatens while they are hardening off, give them extra protection.

Pests and diseases

Slugs Can be very damaging to young plants and mature stems. For protective measures and control see p. 229.

Celery fly/leaf miner Tiny maggots tunnel into leaves, causing brown, dried patches. Discard any blistered seedlings, remove mined leaves on mature plants by hand and burn infested foliage. Growing under fine nets helps prevent attacks.

Celery leaf spot Pinprick brown spots appear on leaves and stems. There are no organic remedies, but rotation, growing plants healthily and removing old plant debris all help prevent the disease.

Leaf celery (cutting celery, soup celery) *Apium graveolens*

This is the hardiest and least demanding type of celery, closely related to wild celery. It can survive -12°C/10°F, so can be a source of glossy green leaves all year round. It is a branching, bushy plant, 30–45cm/12–18in high, but in northern Europe it is also grown as fine-stemmed cut-and-come-again seedlings for use in salads and soup. It is naturally vigorous and responds to cut-and-come-again treatment at every stage. Varieties such as 'Fine Dutch' were developed for this purpose, but are no longer easily obtained. 'Parcel' is a distinct variety introduced to the West from Eastern Germany. It has crisp, shiny, deeply curled leaves with a strong celery flavour – a most decorative edging plant for a winter potager. 'Red Soup' is a variety with reddish stems.

Cultivation For single plants, sow as described above throughout the growing season, indoors, or, when soil conditions are suitable, *in situ* outdoors. Space plants 23–30cm/9–12in apart. You can space them closer initially, then remove alternate plants and leave the remainder to grow larger. Make the first cuts within about four weeks of planting. Pot up a few plants in late summer and bring them under cover for winter. Leaf celery often perpetuates itself if one or two plants are left to seed in spring: seedlings pop up everywhere!

For cut-and-come-again seedlings, make successive sowings outdoors. You can make earlier and later sowings under cover. Cut seedlings as required when 10–12cm/4–5in high. You can obtain nice fine-stemmed clumps by multi-sowing up to eight seeds per module and planting the clumps 20cm/8in apart.

Self-blanching celery *Apium graveolens* var. *dulce*

These long-stemmed plants, about 45cm/18in high, are the most widely grown type of celery today. The standard type, once called 'Gold', have cream to yellow stems; planting them close will enhance their paleness and make them whiter, crisper and possibly sweeter. The 'American' and 'Green' varieties have green stems, are considered naturally better flavoured and do not need supplementary blanching.

Now these are joined by a new, and increasingly popular group, the 'Apple Green' varieties. They are midway between the traditional green trench celery and the original self blanching types, and are considered better flavoured.

There are also beautiful varieties with a pink flush to the stem. Purists consider self-blanching celery less flavoured than traditional 'trench' celery but it is far easier to grow. It is not frost hardy, so is used mainly as a summer crop.

Cultivation Sow as described on p. 85 in spring in gentle heat in a propagator. Plant at even spacing in a block formation, to get the blanching effect. Do not plant too deeply. Space plants 15–27cm/6–11in apart: the wider apart they are, the heavier the plants and the thicker the stems will be. If you plant them close, you can cut intermediate plants when they are small, allowing the remainder to grow larger. For a late crop under cover, sow in late spring and plant under cover in late summer. This will crop until frost affects it.

Take precautions against slugs in the early stages (see p. 229). Keep plants well watered to prevent premature bolting and 'stringiness'. Feed weekly with a liquid feed from early summer onwards. If you are growing standard varieties, tuck straw between the plants in mid-summer to increase the blanching effect.

Start cutting before the outer stems become pithy. You can dig up plants by the roots before the first frost and store them for several weeks in cellars or cool sheds. Traditionally plants were transplanted into frames and covered with dried leaves or straw.

Varieties *Standard:* 'Celebrity', 'Lathom Self-Blanching', 'Galaxy', 'Loretta'
'Apple green' type: 'Octavius' F1, 'Tango' F1, 'Victoria' F1
Dark green: 'Monterey', 'Green Sleeves'
Pink: 'Pink Blush'

Green self-blanching celery

Golden self-blanching celery

Self-blanching
celery 'Pink Blush'

Trench celery *Apium graveolens* var. *dulce*

This is the classic English celery. The long white or pink stems are crisp, superbly flavoured and handsome, but have to be blanched to attain their full flavour and texture – a labour-intensive procedure. Trench celery is mainly grown today for exhibition purposes.

Cultivation In essence, raise plants as described on p. 85 and plant in a single row, spaced 30–45cm/12–18in apart. You can use various blanching methods, depending on whether planted on the flat or in trenches.

On heavy soils, plant at ground level. Blanch in stages by wrapping purpose-made collars, heavy lightproof paper, or black fillm around the stems. Wrap them fairly loosely to allow for expansion, leaving one-third of the stem exposed each time.

In light soils, plant in trenches at least 38cm/15in wide and 30cm/12in deep. Tie plants loosely to keep them upright, and blanch in stages by filling in the trench initially, then spading soil up around the stems, each time up to the level of the lowest leaves, until only the tops are exposed.

Cut from early winter onwards. Trench celery will not stand much frost unless protected with straw or bracken. The red and pink varieties are slightly hardier and can be used later.

Varieties *White:* 'Giant White'
Pink: 'Mammoth Pink'/'Giant Pink', 'Red Martine', 'Starburst' F1 (pink tinge)

Celeriac

(turnip-rooted celery) *Apium graveolens* var. *rapaceum*

Celeriac is a bushy plant, grown for the knobbly 'bulb' that develops at ground level. It has a delicious, mild celery flavour, is an excellent winter vegetable, cooked or as soup, and is good in salads grated raw or cooked and cold. Its strongly flavoured leaves can be used sparingly in salads or for flavouring cooked dishes. It is less prone to disease and much hardier than stem celery.

Cultivation

Celeriac tolerates light shade, provided the soil is moist and fertile. The secret to growing large bulbs (essential, as much is lost in peeling) is a long, steady growing season. Raise plants as described on p. 85, sowing in gentle heat in mid-spring. Germination is often erratic: be patient! Celeriac needs to be hardened off before planting out, but don't start moving seedlings outside until the weather is warm. Celeriac is notoriously prone to premature bolting later in its life cycle if subjected to sudden drops in temperature as young plants. If there's a risk of this happening, it is better to harden them off indoors, using the 'stroke' method (see p. 207).

Plant in late spring or early summer 30–38cm/12–15in apart, with the base of the stem at soil level – no deeper. Celeriac normally benefits from feeding, every two weeks or so, with a liquid feed.

Plants stand at least -10°C/14°F, but tuck a thick layer of straw or bracken around them in late autumn for extra protection and to make lifting easier in frost. They can be lifted and stored, but their flavour and texture are better if they remain in the ground though there is risk of slug damage. A few leaves may stay green all winter, which are useful for flavouring and garnish.

Celeriac

Varieties

'Kojak', 'Monarch', 'Prinz', 'Rowena' F1 – among many good varieties

Sea kale
Crambe maritima

This handsome hardy perennial, with its glaucous, blue grey leaves, is a native of the seashore. It has long been cultivated for its deliciously flavoured young leaf stalks. These are usually eaten raw after blanching, though some people find the natural young stems very palatable as they are.

Cultivation

Establish a sea kale bed in good, light, well-drained soil in a sunny position: lime acid soil to about pH7. They make excellent ground cover plants, if undisturbed often lasting at least seven years. Raise them by sowing fresh seed (seed loses its viability rapidly) in spring, *in situ*, in a seedbed or in modules for transplanting. Alternatively, buy young plants or rooted cuttings ('thongs') for planting in spring or autumn. Space plants 30–45cm/12–18in apart. They die right back in winter.

In its third season plants are strong enough to force into early growth. In late winter/early spring, cover the bare crowns with 7½cm/3in of dry leaves and a traditional clay blanching pot, or any light-excluding pot or bucket at least 30cm/12in high (see p. 245). The shoots may take three months to develop. Cut them when they are about 20cm/8in long, then leave the plants uncovered to grow normally. Give them an annual dressing of manure or seaweed feed. You can also lift plants and force indoors at 16–21°C/60–70°F. They will be ready within weeks, but the plants will be weakened and must be discarded afterwards.

Kohl rabi
Brassica oleracea Gongylodes Group

Kohl rabi is a beautiful but strange-looking vegetable, growing about 30cm/12in high. The edible part is the graceful bulb, 5–7½cm/2–3in diameter, which develops in the stem, virtually suspended just clear of the ground. There are purple and green ('white') forms, the purple possibly sweeter but more inclined to be fibrous. Kohl rabi has a delicate turnip flavour. Normally cooked, it is also grated or sliced raw into salads; young leaves are also edible. It is fast-growing, withstands drought and heat well, and is less prone to pests and disease, clubroot included, than most brassicas. It is rich in protein, calcium and vitamin C. The old 'Vienna' varieties quickly became fibrous on maturity, but much-improved modern varieties stand well.

Kohl rabi grows best in light, sandy soil, with plenty of moisture, but tolerates heavier soil. It stands low temperatures, but grows fastest, and so is most tender, at 18–25°C/64–77°F, the optimum being 22°C/72°F. For salads, it should be grown fast, or grown as 'mini kohl rabi'. Rotate it within the brassica group.

Purple kohl rabi

Green kohl rabi

Cultivation

For the main crop, sow from spring to late summer *in situ* outdoors. Soil temperature should be at least 10°C/50°F, or early sowings may bolt prematurely. Thin in stages to 25–30cm/10–12in apart. Alternatively sow in modules and transplant. You can multi-sow with three or four seedlings per module, and plant as one.

For an earlier summer crop, sow in mid-winter/early spring in gentle heat; for an early winter crop under cover, sow indoors in late summer/early autumn. For mini kohl rabi, sow *in situ* from late spring to late summer in drills 15cm/6in apart and thin to 2½cm/1in apart. Use recommended varieties. Harvest at ping-pong-ball size, normally within eight weeks of sowing. Take precautions against flea beetle in the early stages (see p. 229).

Varieties

Purple 'Azur Star' F1, 'Kolibri' F1
Green 'Korist' F1, 'Lanro', 'Quickstar' F1, 'Rapidstar' F1
For mini kohl rabi 'Korist' F1, 'Kolibri'

Florence fennel

Florence fennel
(sweet fennel, finocchio) *Foeniculum vulgare* var. *dulce*

Florence fennel is a beautiful annual with feathery, shimmering green foliage, growing about 45cm/18in high. It is cultivated for its swollen leaf bases, which overlap to form a crisp-textured, aniseed-flavoured 'bulb' just above ground level.

Fennel does best in fertile, light, sandy soil, well drained and rich in organic matter, but will grow in heavier soil. A Mediterranean marsh plant, it needs plenty of moisture throughout growth and a warm climate. Sudden drops in temperature or dry spells can trigger premature bolting without it forming a decent bulb. This tendency is exacerbated by transplanting and early sowing. Some new varieties have improved bolting resistance, but are not infallible.

Cultivation

Fennel should be grown fast. To minimize the risk of bolting, preferably sow in modules and delay sowing until mid-summer, unless you are using bolt-resistant varieties. Otherwise sow in seed trays, prick out the seedlings when they are very small, and transplant them at the four-to-five-leaf stage. Space plants 30–35cm/12–14in apart. For an early summer outdoor crop, sow in mid- to late spring using bolt-resistant varieties, at a soil temperature of at least 10°C/50°F. For a main summer crop, sow in early summer. For an autumn crop that can also be planted under cover, sow in late summer or even early autumn.

Watch for slugs in the early stages (for control, see p. 229); keep plants watered and mulched. Occasional feeding with a seaweed-based fertilizer is beneficial.

In good growing conditions, fennel is ready eight to twelve weeks after sowing. When it reaches a usable size, cut bulbs just above ground level. Useful secondary shoots develop which are tasty and decorative in salads. Mature plants tolerate light frost, but plants that have previously been cut back survive lower temperatures. Late plantings under cover may not develop large succulent bulbs, but the leaf bases can be sliced finely into salad, and the tender 'fern' often lasts well into winter.

Annual fennel is also being used to grow fine stemmed seedling leaves for garnish or what chefs are calling 'pencil fennel', a fairly accurate description of their size. These are used in salads. CN seeds told me that by sowing on the surface in small modules (2–2½cm/¾–1in), seeds are sown evenly and there is no need to thin out which disrupts the delicate roots. The module trays are then put on the soil, so the roots grow out into the soil, making it easier to water them without a check, which may cause bolting. They reach the pencil size in five to six weeks.

Varieties
Standard 'Perfection', 'Sirio'
Bolt resistant 'Zefa Fino'
For baby leaf 'Di Firenze'/ 'Sweet Florence'
For herb fennel *Foeniculum vulgare*, see p. 151

fruiting vegetables

—

No group of vegetables repays the gardener more handsomely for their efforts than those with edible fruits. People who have never tasted a home-grown tomato, cucumber or pepper can hardly believe the richness of flavour in freshly picked produce, grown from carefully selected varieties. The pods of peas and beans, technically their fruits, as well as some of the leafy parts of peas, are sources of unsuspected delights for salad-lovers.

Italian plum type

Tomato

Lycopersicon esculentum

The tomato is a tender South American plant, which was introduced into Europe in the sixteenth century as an ornamental greenhouse climber. It has deservedly become one of the most universally grown vegetables. Tomatoes are beautiful, rich in vitamins and versatile in use, both cooked and raw.

Types of tomato

Tomato fruits are wonderfully diverse in colour, shape and size. They can be red, pink, orange, yellow, red- and orange-striped, black, purple, green and even white. Size ranges from huge beefsteaks to the aptly named 'currant' tomatoes. They can be roughly classified on the basis of fruit shape and size, red and yellow forms being found in most types.

Standard Smooth, round, medium-sized fruits of variable flavour.

Beefsteak Very large, smooth, fleshy, multilocular fruits (that is, several 'compartments' evident when sliced horizontally); mostly well flavoured.

Marmande Large, flattish, irregular, often ribbed shape, multilocular, fleshy, usually well flavoured, but some so-called 'improved' varieties though more evenly shaped are not necessarily as well flavoured as the old.

Oxheart Medium-sized to large, conical, fleshy; some are exceptionally well flavoured.

Plum-shaped Generally small to medium sized, though 'San Marzano' can be very large. More or less rectangular in shape, firm, generally late maturing; variable flavour, mostly used cooked. (On account of their shape and firmness the 'Roma' varieties in this group were originally selected for the Italian canning industry.) Cherry plum tomatoes are a small, firm, distinctly flavoured form of plum tomato for eating raw, typified by 'Santa'.

Pear-shaped Smooth, small to medium-sized, 'waisted', mostly unremarkable flavour and texture.

Cherry Small, round fruits under $2\frac{1}{2}$cm/1in diameter, mostly sweet or distinctly flavoured. Some have a tendency to split on ripening, so must be picked as soon as ready.

Currant Tiny fruits about 1cm/$\frac{1}{2}$in diameter; exceptionally rambling plants; hitherto not notably flavoured.

Growth habit

The growth habit of tomatoes affects how they are cultivated.

Tall or 'indeterminate' types The main shoot naturally grows up to 4m/13ft long in warm climates, with sideshoots developing into branches. These are grown as vertical 'cordons', which are trained up strings or tied to supports. Growth is kept within bounds by nipping out or 'stopping' the growing point and removing sideshoots. It is also possible to allow sideshoots to develop and train plants into U-shaped double cordons, or even triple cordons, which at the same time reduces the vigour of the main stem. I have done this recently to keep tall-growing cherry tomatoes within reach. Appropriate varieties, for example tiny currant tomatoes, can even be trained as 'fans'.

'Green Zebra'

'Pink Pear'
pear-shaped type

'Supermarmande'
F1 'Marmande' type

'Yellow Perfection'
yellow-skinned

Typical round
standard tomato

'Jubilee'
orange-skinned

Typical beefsteak tomato

'Golden Boy' F1 beefsteak type

In a 'semi-determinate' sub-group, the main shoot naturally stops growing when about 1m/3ft high. Most Marmande types are in this latter group.

Bush or 'determinate' types In these types the sideshoots develop instead of the main shoot, forming a naturally self-stopping bushy plant of 60–125cm/2–4ft diameter that sprawls on the ground. They do not require stopping, sideshooting or supports. They are often early maturing, quite decorative when growing, and can be grown under cloches and films (see p. 218). Some varieties are suitable for containers, but usually need some kind of support to keep them within bounds. Where blight is a limitation on growing tomatoes outdoors, early bush varieties are the best option, as they should fruit before being seriously affected.

Dwarf types These are exceptionally small and compact, often no more than 20cm/8in high. They require no pruning, and are ideal for containers and edgings.

Flavour

The quest for excellent flavour, which is rarely found in bought tomatoes, is a major incentive for growing your own. Nothing can compare with thick slices of a freshly picked 'Golden Boy' beefsteak on home-made bread, sprinkled with basil and black pepper. Flavour, essentially a balance between acidity and sweetness, is in practice determined by a number of factors, of which the hours and intensity of sunshine are probably paramount. Sunshine apart, flavour can vary from plant to plant, and fruit to fruit, depending on the season, maturity and even the time of day. My personal view is that overwatering and overfeeding commonly destroy flavour. Start with a potentially well-flavoured variety, and err on the side of 'starving' and 'underwatering'. You may not have the highest yields, but they will be the best tasting. Currently heirloom varieties are being reintroduced on the basis of their flavour. Some, undoubtedly, are exceptionally flavoured, but not all. In comparison with modern varieties, they tend to suffer from poor disease resistance and late maturity. Incidentally, green tomatoes are among the most highly rated for flavour. Most must be picked while still green, though 'Green Grape' should be picked when the skin is 'green chartreuse'. The whole question of flavour is extraodinarily subjective: two people, tasting the same variety at the same time, can have totally opposing views. Experiment… and grow what you like!

General cultivation

The optimum temperature for tomatoes is 21–24°C/70–75°F. They grow poorly at temperatures below 10°C/50°F and above 32°C/90°F. They need high light intensity and most varieties require at least eight frost-free weeks from planting to maturity. Beefsteaks require somewhat higher temperatures in the early stages, pear-shaped tomatoes may not develop a true pear shape at low temperatures, and the slow-maturing 'Roma' varieties need a fairly long season. The method of cultivation depends on climate. If you are new to tomato growing, be guided by current practice in the locality. The main options, graduated from warm to cool climates, are:

- Outdoors, directly in the ground or in containers.
- Outdoors, initially protected by cloches or in frames which are removed when outgrown, using tall or bush types.
- Outdoors, under cloches or in frames, using bush types. Bush types can also be planted under perforated film or fleece which is removed later (see pp. 224–5).
- Indoors, in unheated greenhouses or polytunnels. They can be grown in the ground unless soil sickness has developed in which case they must be grown in containers or growing bags, or by systems such as ring culture (see p. 220), or using plants grafted on disease-resistant rootstocks. Polytunnels are invaluable for tomato growing, as they can be moved every three or four years, so avoiding the development of soil sickness.
- Indoors, in heated greenhouses. For culture in heated greenhouses see Further reading.

Some tomato varieties are bred solely for cultivation in greenhouses, but in practice, in my experience, most 'indoor' varieties can be grown outside and vice versa. It really depends on your locality.

Soil and site

In temperate climates, tomatoes can be grown outdoors, but the main problem is infection from potato blight, which has become increasingly serious in recent years and can lead to failure. A key factor in success, which may help offset blight, is planting in a warm sheltered position, for example against a wall (ideally south-facing) which will reflect warmth on to the plants. (See also Cultivation of outdoor crops, p. 100).

Tomatoes are in the potato family and vulnerable to the same soil pests and diseases so should be rotated accordingly. Grow them as far away from potatoes as possible. Growing in polytunnels and unheated greenhouses is a practical option, and gives considerable protection against infection from the airborne blight spores. In polytunnels and greenhouses it is inadvisable to grow tomatoes in the same soil for more than three or four consecutive years.

Tomatoes need fertile, well-drained soil, at a pH of 5.5–7. Ideally prepare the ground beforehand by making a trench 30cm/12in deep and 45cm/18in wide, working in generous quantities of well-rotted manure, compost and/or wilted comfrey leaves (whose high potash content benefits tomatoes).

Plant raising

Sow in early to mid-spring, six to eight weeks before the last frost is expected. For a follow-on crop of container-grown bush tomatoes for patios or under cover, a second sowing can be made in late spring. Seed germinates fastest at 20°C/68°F, though outdoor bush varieties germinate at slightly lower temperatures. Sow in a propagator, either in seed trays, pricking out into 5–7½cm/2–3in pots at the three-leaf stage, or in modules. These can later be potted on into small pots. Seedlings can withstand lower temperatures, of about 16°C/60°F once germinated, but must be kept above 10°C/50°F. Keep them well ventilated, well spaced out and in good light. They are normally ready for planting in the ground or into containers six to eight weeks after sowing, when 15–20cm/6–8in high, with the first flower truss visible. When buying plants, choose sturdy plants in individual pots, with healthy, dark green foliage.

Cultivation of outdoor crops

For outdoor growing it is advisable to choose varieties with a degree of resistance to blight. Modern plant breeding is continually improving the options, though the quality of flavour is variable. None is totally resistant. On the whole cherry tomatoes are less prone to blight than larger-fruited varieties, and early bush tomatoes will often mature before the onset of blight.

Raise seeds as above, and harden off well before planting outside. If the soil temperature is below 10°C/50°F or there is any risk of frost, delay planting. Plant firmly with the lowest leaves just above soil level. Planting through white reflective mulch keeps plants clean and reflects heat up on the fruit – an asset in cool climates. Unless planted through polythene film, keeping plants mulched with straw is beneficial, and prevents blight spores being washed up on to the plants.

Tall types (grown as cordons) Plant 38–45cm/15–18in apart, in single rows or staggered in double rows. For supports, use strong individual canes, elegant metal spiral supports or posts at least 1½m/5ft high; or erect 1½/5ft posts at either end of the rows, running two or three parallel wires between them. Tie plants to the supports as they grow. In cool climates, protect plants in the early stages, for example with polythene film side panels. These can be left in place, where feasible, and will give some protection against blight infection. Remove sideshoots as they develop, and in mid- to late summer remove the growing point, so that remaining fruits mature. Depending on the locality, this will be after three to five trusses have set fruit.

Except in very dry conditions, plants do not normally require watering until they are flowering and setting fruit. At this stage apply about 11 litres per sq. m/2 gallons per sq. yd weekly. If growth seems poor when the second truss is setting, feed weekly with a seaweed-based or specially formulated organic tomato feed, or liquid comfrey. In cool climates, towards the end of the season cut plants with unripened fruit free of the canes (without uprooting them), lie them horizontally on straw and cover with cloches to encourage further ripening. You can also uproot plants and hang them indoors for several weeks to continue ripening. Individual fruits ripen slowly wrapped in paper and kept in the dark indoors.

Bush and dwarf varieties Plant bush types 45–60cm/18–24in apart and dwarf types 25–30cm/10–12in apart. Closer spacing produces earlier crops, but wider spacing produces heavier yields and is advisable where there is a risk of blight. Water and feed as tall varieties above. Protect bush and dwarf varieties with cloches or grow in frames. (Low polytunnels are unsuitable, unless the film is perforated, as humidity and temperatures rise too high.) Keeping plants reasonably dry is a key factor in preventing and limiting blight.

As a measure against blight, if there has been wet weather for about three days when the plants are starting to fruit, Belgian nurseryman Peter Bauwens covers outdoor plants with polythene film anchored over hoops. The hoops (1m/3ft high) cover two rows of bush tomatoes.

For an earlier crop, plant under perforated polythene film or fleece, anchored in the soil and laid directly on the plants or over low hoops (see pp. 224–5). Once the flowers press against the covering, make intermittent slits (about 60cm/2 ft long) down the centre, to allow insect pollination and to start 'weaning' the tomatoes, ie acclimatizing them to colder conditions. About a week later cut the remaining gaps so that the film falls aside. Leave it there as a low windbreak. Water and feed as for tall outdoor plants. These will normally be ready two weeks before other outdoor tomatoes.

Cultivation of indoor crops

To grow crops in unheated greenhouses and polytunnels, prepare the ground and raise plants as above. Tall varieties make optimum use of this valuable space. Plant in single rows 45cm/18in apart, or at the same spacing in

'Gardener's Delight' cherry type

double rows with 90cm/36in between each pair of rows. I interplant with French marigolds (*Tagetes* spp.) as a deterrent against whitefly. To conserve moisture, tomatoes can be planted through polythene film, ideally opaque white film which reflects light up on to the crop, or double-sided black and white film. (For growing in containers see overleaf.)

Plants need to be supported, with strong individual canes or stakes, or some other system. One of the simplest is to suspend heavy-duty strings (man-made fibres tend to be stronger than natural fibres) from a horizontal overhead wire or horizontal bars beneath the greenhouse roof, looping the lower end around the lowest leaves of the tomato plant, or for greater stability, around the root ball before planting. Twist the plant carefully around the string as it grows, or tie it to the cane or stake, preferably with a figure-of-eight tie, so the stem doesn't rub directly on the support.

Whatever system is used, make sure it is robust enough to support the weight of a mature plant with a heavy crop of fruit. It is hard to envisage this when planting out a relatively small plant, and sometimes plants do snap off. If a leader snaps, it is often possible to encourage a lateral shoot into replacing it. First aid is another option. I have several times repaired what looked like severe breaks by 'bandaging' them with non-porous, transparent

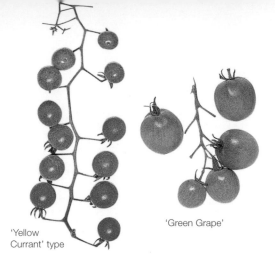

'Green Grape'

'Yellow
Currant' type

waterproof surgical tape. Provided the damaged stem is adequately supported, the wound will heal and it will continue growing normally. Tomato plants have great resilience.

Unless planted through polythene film, keep plants well mulched with up to 12cm/5in of organic material. (Wilted comfrey can be used.) Water well after planting, then lightly until the fruits start to set, when heavier watering is necessary. Plants need at least 9 litres/2 gallons per plant per week. One school of thought maintains that flavour is best if they are watered, at most, once a week, allowing the soil almost to dry out between waterings. To limit the risk of fungal disease, water carefully without splashing the leaves, and water either in the morning or early afternoon, rather than in the evening, to keep greenhouse humidity low at night.

If fruit is slow to set in late spring/early summer, tap the canes or wires around midday to spread the pollen and encourage setting. Keep plants well ventilated, removing some of the lower leaves, especially any that are yellowing, to improve air circulation around plants. In hot weather, 'damp down' at midday – that is, sprinkle the greenhouse and plants with water. Humidity during the day helps fruit to set and deters pests.

Remove sideshoots as for outdoor tomatoes and stop plants, ie remove the growing point, in late summer, either when they reach the roof or when it seems that further fruit is unlikely to mature during the season. Vigorous plants may produce seven or eight trusses, continuing to ripen into early winter. Continue removing withered and yellowing leaves and dig up and burn any seriously diseased plants. For high yields, indoor tomatoes normally need weekly feeding, once the first truss has set, with a high potash tomato feed.

Growing tomatoes in containers

(For container growing in general see p. 240.) Tomatoes are one of the most popular vegetables for growing in containers. They are widely used in greenhouses and polytunnels, especially where the soil is unsuitable for tomato growing or has developed 'soil sickness', and also on patios, courtyards, balconies and in similar situations. Containers used range from plastic growing bags filled with potting compost, to hanging baskets. The size of the container has to be suited to the type of tomato being grown and the variety.

Types best suited to container growing, especially outdoors on patios, are the very compact dwarf varieties, bush varieties, with their natural branching habit, and self-stopping determinate varieties. There are some varieties with a cascading habit, which can look stunning in hanging baskets or containers raised off the ground. For suitable varieties see below; consult seed catalogues for detailed information on their growth habit. Probably few of these have the flavour of the tall-growing, determinate varieties, but new varieties are continually being introduced.

Where tall-growing, determinate varieties are grown in containers it is crucial to ensure a high level of fertility and an adequate support system.

The general container rule – the larger the container the better – holds for tomatoes. The minimum size would be about 25–30cm/ 10–12in width and depth. Sarah Wain, supervisor of the famous Dean Gardens in Sussex, grows cherry tomatoes in 35–40cm/14– 16in diameter pots, getting six to eight trusses in a season. Three plants can be fitted into a standard growing bag, but two plants per bag is preferable. To minimize evaporation, cut small square holes in the bag for planting, rather than removing the top plastic completely.

Very compact and cascading varieties don't need supports, but larger varieties generally need supports such as canes, strong wire mesh, or a purpose-made plastic frame.

Use good quality potting compost – working in well-rotted garden compost is always beneficial – water very carefully so they are never too wet nor too dry, and start feeding weekly as soon as the fruits start to set, as for indoor tomatoes.

Pests and diseases

With outdoor tomatoes the main problems are poor weather and potato blight, which manifests as brown patches on leaves and fruits. There is no organic remedy. (See Soil and site p. 99).

Indoor tomatoes, which are being forced in unnatural conditions, are prone to various pests, diseases and disorders. You can avoid many of these by growing disease-resistant varieties, by growing plants well with good ventilation and avoiding overcrowding. Use biological control against whitefly (see p. 228). Interplanting with French marigolds may help deter whitefly.

Varieties

The choice today is vast and constantly changing. The following are my personal favourites and a few highly recommended, chosen for flavour, texture or some specific use or quality.

Standard round *Tall:* 'Alicante', 'Cristal' F1, 'Ferline' F1, 'Green Zebra', 'Nimbus' F1, 'Orkado' F1 (good outdoors)
Bush: 'Maskotka', 'Red Alert', 'Sleaford Abundance'
Beefsteak and marmande 'Costoluto Fiorentino', 'Brandywine', 'Golden Boy' F1 (gold), 'Marglobe', 'Supermarmande' F1, 'Marmande'
Plum-shaped 'Britain's Breakfast', 'San Marzano' (both excellent for freezing)
Cherry and small plum 'Apero' F1, 'Cherry Belle' F1, 'Gardener's Delight' (large cherry), 'Golden Crown', 'Rosella' (dark skinned), 'Sakura' F1 (large cherry), 'Sun Belle' (yellow)
Misc. heirloom 'Black Cherry', 'Green Grape', 'Green Zebra' (striped), 'Nepal', all 'Oxheart' varieties
Bush and dwarf vars for containers/ hanging baskets 'Balconi Red', 'Balconi Yellow', 'Cherry Falls', 'Garden Pearl'/'Garten Perle', 'Lemon Sherbert' (yellow), 'Losetto' F1, 'Maskotka', 'Red Alert', 'Terenzo' F1, 'Tumbler' F1, 'Tumbling Tiger', 'Totem', 'Tumbling Tom Red', 'Tumbling Tom Yellow', 'Vilma'
Varieties currently available with varying degrees of blight resistance
Bush a semi-determinate: 'Losetto' F1, 'Lizzano' F1
Cordon: 'Clou' (yellow) 'Crimson Crush', 'Dorado' (yellow) F1, 'Ferlline' F1, 'Mountain Magic' F1, 'Resi', 'Primabella', 'Primavera' (orange fruit)

Mini
cucumber

Greenhouse
cucumber

Burpless cucumber

White cucumber

'Sunsweet' F1
'lemon' cucumber

'Crystal Apple'
cucumber

Gherkin

Cucamelon

Cucumber

Cucumis sativus

With their crisp texture and refreshing flavours, cucumbers are quintessential salad vegetables. In origin climbing and trailing tropical plants, for practical purposes they can be divided into several main groups: the European greenhouse type, the outdoor ridge type, and heirloom cucumbers.

Types of cucumber

European greenhouse

These have smooth, dark green skin and fine-quality flesh, and are often over 30cm/12in long. The more recently developed 'mini cucumbers', however, are mature when 10–15cm/4–6in long. The traditional greenhouse cucumbers are vigorous plants, requiring high temperatures (roughly 18–30°C/64–86°F), and are normally grown in heated or unheated greenhouses. The fruit was mainly borne on side shoots/laterals, which had to be trained in. In older varieties (now mainly grown for showing), male flowers had to be removed as pollination made the fruits misshapen and bitter.

Modern 'all female' varieties Most modern varieties are 'all female' F1 hybrids. They are 'parthenocarpic', so set fruit without insect pollination. This virtually eliminates the problem of bitterness and the need to remove male flowers, though occasional male flowers appear, especially if the plants are stressed: these should be removed. (The female flowers are distinguished by the visible bump of the embryonic fruit which develops behind the petals.) Fruit develops on the main stem, so plants are easily trained up a single string or tied to a support. Many of these varieties have good disease resistance. The downside is they are less robust than the ridge varieties, require higher temperatures for growth and germination, and the seed tends to be expensive. In practice it is often as economic for gardeners to buy young plants. Many of the 'mini cucs' are all female varieties.

Outdoor ridge

The original ridge types – so called as they were grown in Europe on ridges to improve drainage – were short and stubby, with rough, prickly skin, normally dark or light green, but occasionally white, yellow or cream. There are some compact bush forms which are suitable for growing in containers. The plants have male and female flowers and need pollination. They are notably hardier and healthier than greenhouse cucumbers, tolerate much lower temperatures but are considered 'rough' in comparison with the greenhouse types, though often are well flavoured. All ridge cucumbers can be grown outside or under cover.

Japanese and 'burpless' hybrids Asian in origin, plant breeding has given us a range of excellent improved varieties, often approaching greenhouse cucumbers in length, smoothness and flavour. They tend to be healthy plants with good disease resistance. They climb up to about 1¾m/6ft, with fruits up to 30cm/12in long. They are suited to cultivation outdoors (except in cold or exposed sites) or in unheated greenhouses or polytunnels. They produce male flowers but there is no bitterness if pollinated, and fruit primarily on the main stems.

Gherkins are a distinct group of ridge cucumber with thin or stubby fruits, notably prickly skinned, averaging 5cm/2in in length. They tend to be sprawling plants. Although grown for pickling, they can be used fresh in salads.

Heirloom types

In this group are several more or less round-fruited varieties which are juicy, moderately well flavoured and decorative. They include the pale-skinned 'Crystal Apple', yellow-skinned, lemon-shaped 'lemon' cucumbers and the Italian 'melon cucumber' or 'carosello', which is credited with exceptional drought resistance.

When it comes to deciding what type to grow, I would suggest you play safe with Japanese hybrids and Burpless varieties or, if you are prepared to do a bit of 'coddling' in creating a warm environment, go for all female hybrids and try the mini cucs.

Ridge and all-female types should not be grown in proximity, or cross-pollination will occur. Only grow one type within the confines of a polytunnel or unheated greenhouse.

Soil and site

Cucumbers will not tolerate any frost. Outdoor plants require a warm site sheltered from wind, sunny but not liable to be baked dry. They tolerate light shade in mid-summer. Cucumbers do best where the roots can romp freely through reasonably fertile, humus-rich, moisture-retentive soil. Good drainage is essential. Very acid soils should be limed. Prepare the ground by making individual holes (or a trench) about 30cm/12in deep and 45cm/18in wide, working in well-rotted manure or garden compost. Cover with about 15cm/6in of soil, made into a small mound to improve drainage.

Plant raising

In the north European climate cucumbers require 100–140 frost-free days from sowing to maturity, so do not plant outside until all risk of frost is past. Where summers are cool or short, start them indoors in mid- to late spring, about four weeks before planting out. (A second sowing can be made about four weekls later for a follow on crop.) For germination, they need a minimum temperature of 18°C/64°F to at least 21°C/70°F for the all female varieties. As cucumbers transplant badly, sow in modules or in 5–7½cm/2–3in pots. Sow seeds singly or two to three per module or pot, removing all but the strongest one after germination. (Old gardening books advocated sowing seed on its side, but the Michaud organic growers demonstrated this is unnecessary: seed germinates equally well when sown flat.) Try to avoid further watering until after germination, to prevent damping-off diseases. Maintain a temperature of at least 16°C/60°F – preferably higher, for all female hybrids, with minimum night temperatures of 16–24°C/60–75°F.

Seedlings grow fast. If you are growing cucumbers outdoors, plant them out at the three-to-four-leaf stage in early summer after hardening them off carefully. Take care not to bury the stem when planting, which invites neck rot. Protect plants if necessary in the early stages. Once the soil feels warm to the touch, seeds can be sown *in situ* outdoors, under jars or cloches if necessary. Space climbing plants 45cm/18in apart, and bush plants 90cm/36in apart.

Supports

Climbing cucumbers can be trained against any reasonably strong support suitable for climbing beans, against trellises, metal or cane tepees, pig or sheep wire net, or nylon netting of about 23cm/9in mesh. Few varieties grow much over 1³⁄₄m/6ft high. They are largely self-clinging, but may need tying in the early stages. Less vigorous varieties can sprawl on the ground – gherkins are usually grown this way – but plants are healthier, and less prone to slug damage, if trained off the ground even on low supports.

Nip out the growing point when plants reach the top of the supports. Modern hybrids bear fruit on the main stem, whereas older varieties tend to bear on lateral sideshoots. (In this case nip out the growing point above the first six or seven leaves, to encourage fruit-bearing sideshoots. Tie these sideshoots in if necessary. To control growth, nip them off later, two leaves beyond a fruit.)

Once the plants are established, give them an organic mulch. Keep them well watered, but not waterlogged. If growth is not reasonably vigorous, apply an organic feed weekly from mid-summer onwards. Pick regularly to encourage further growth, picking the fruits young before the skins harden. If the cucumbers are too long for household use, cut the lower half and leave the top attached. The exposed end will callus over and can be cut later.

Growing in greenhouses

To grow ridge cucumbers in a greenhouse or polytunnel, cultivate as above. They generally grow taller than outdoors, so may need higher supports. You can train them up strings (see Tomatoes p. 97), but a strong structure such as rigid pig or sheep net or reinforced concrete mesh is more satisfactory. To build up really strong plants, rub off the early flowers that form on the first five or six leaves. If plants produce masses of laterals at a later stage, trim them back – a few at as time rather than all at once – to a few leaves, to allow good air circulation.

The warmer, protected conditions in unheated greenhouses and polytunnels increase the risk of pests and disease, so you need to strike a fine balance between creating humidity and ventilation. In hot weather, shading may be necessary. We sometimes simply peg light shading net over the plants during the day. Damp down plants and soil regularly (see p. 219) to prevent the build-up of pests such as red spider mite. Mulch the whole floor area, paths included, with straw; this helps maintain humidity and keeps the roots cool. Water regularly, and once fruits are developing, combine watering with a liquid feed. If roots develop above ground, cover them with garden compost as an extra source of nutrients.

Growing in containers

Cucumbers are not 'naturals' for containers, as containers restrict their roots and the soil temperature tends to rise too high. With care they can be grown in growing bags or in pots of at least 30cm/12in diameter. Choose compact varieties: bush ridge varieties are among the most suitable. Put them in a sheltered position. (See p. 240 for container growing in general.)

Pests and diseases

Cucumbers flourish in suitable climates, but are prone to various disorders and diseases in less favourable conditions. Good husbandry is the key to success. Never, for example, take a chance on planting in cold soil. Destroy diseased foliage, and uproot and burn diseased plants.

The most common problems are:

Slugs Young and trailing plants are the most vulnerable.

Aphids Colonies on the underside of leaves cause stunted and puckered growth.

Red spider mite Cucumbers grown under cover are very susceptible. Use biological control as soon as any signs of attack are noticed.

Cucumber mosaic virus This aphid-borne disease causes mottled, yellowed and distorted leaves; plants may become stunted and die. Remove and destroy infected plants and where possible control aphids. Varieties with a degree of resistance are becoming available.

Powdery mildew White powdery patches occur on leaves in hot weather, often spreading rapidly, weakening and killing the plant. Good ventilation helps prevention. Currently some varieties have impressive resistance.

Varieties

Just a selection from the wide choice available.

Greenhouse, all-female with mildew resistance 'Carmen' F1, 'Euphya' F1, 'Tiffany' F1

Mini *All female:* 'Cucino' F1, 'Hana' F1, 'La Diva' F1 (indoors and outdoors), 'Passandra' F1, 'Primatop' F1, 'Socrates' F1; *Male & female flowers:* 'Greenfingers' F1 (compact)

Japanese and 'Burpless' ridge type 'Burpless Tasty Green' F1, 'Jogger' F1, 'Tokyo Slicer' F1

Ridge types for outdoor cropping 'Bush Champion' F1 (compact), 'Marketmore' (good mildew resistance) 'White Wonder' (long white)

Gherkins 'Agnes' F1, 'Alhambra' F1, 'Partner' F1, 'Patio Snacker' F1 (compact), Vert Petit de Paris

Cucamelon *Melothria scabra*

This plant has burst upon the scene in recent years, grown for its tiny, grape-sized fruits, variously described as having a cucumber or watermelon flavour with a hint of lime. It is a rampant, climbing or trailing plant, capable of growing up to $2\frac{1}{2}$m/8ft high. It will grow outdoors in a sheltered spot or in a cool greenhouse. It is self-pollinating, very resistant to pests and has good drought tolerance. Fruits are used raw in salads or pickled.

Not having grown it myself, I've been sounding out gardening friends for their views. I have to say 'other people like it' was a common comment. Some thought it pretty; others not. Some found the skins tough and hard, and fruits bitter and full of seed. Some said children love it, others got tired of picking! Virtues include being very easily grown, prolific and fruiting all summer long! It should probably be classed as an edible novelty.

If you want to make up your mind, sow as for cucumbers, plant out about 45cm/18in apart against some kind of trellis support. For maximum production stop the main stems at $2\frac{1}{2}$m/8ft, and trim back sideshoots to 45cm/18in. The first season they may fruit from July to September, but in a sheltered situation will overwinter and start fruiting earlier in their second season.

Sweet pepper
(capsicum) *Capsicum annuum* Grossum Group

Sweet peppers, also known as capsicums, are tender tropical annuals that produce very varied, beautiful fruits. Most of these are green when immature, becoming red, yellow, orange or even a deep purple-black when fully ripe. Fruit shape is also very variable. They can be square, box-shaped (almost rectangular), bell-shaped, squat (for example, the 'bonnet-' or 'tomato-shaped' pepper) and long. The long-fruited types can be broad-shouldered or narrow, some tapered varieties having twisted ends like goat (or bull) horns. Fruits can be thin- or thick-walled, upright or pendulous. The plants are bushy in habit, with popular cultivars usually 30–45cm/12–18in high, though some are taller. (For chili peppers, see p. 111.)

Sweet peppers are superb salad vegetables, contributing colour, flavour and crisp texture when raw. As they mature, their flavour undergoes subtle changes. Coloured ripe peppers are sweeter and richer-flavoured – and richer in vitamins. Flavours can also modulate to wonderful effect when peppers are cooked or blanched then cooled to use as salads.

Cultivation

Broadly speaking, sweet peppers require much the same conditions as tomatoes (see p. 99), though they prefer marginally higher temperatures. They grow best at temperatures of 18–21°C/64–70°F. Depending on variety, most peppers reach a usable size slightly faster than tomatoes, but you should allow anything from three to six weeks for them to turn from the immature green stage to fully ripe. Like tomatoes, they need high light intensity to flourish. For the cultivation options in temperate climates, see Tomatoes p. 99. Being dwarfer in habit than tomatoes, sweet peppers can be easier accommodated under cloches and in frames or, in the early stages, under fleece.

Peppers are in the potato and tomato family and susceptible to the same soil pests and diseases, so should be rotated accordingly. Fortunately, they seem to be less susceptible to potato blight and generally healthier than tomatoes. They also have lower fertility requirements. Digging in plenty of well-rotted manure before planting is normally sufficient: indeed, too much nitrogen can encourage leafiness at the expense of fruit production.

Bonnet-shaped types   'Gypsy' pepper   Red bell pepper   Yellow bell pepper

Peppers perform well in containers such as growing bags, pots and even hanging baskets, but choose suitable, compact varieties. Three medium-sized peppers can be fitted into a standard growing bag; single peppers can be grown in pots of about 25cm/10in (equivalent to a 7–7½ litre pot) diameter.

Plant raising

For plant raising, see Tomatoes p. 100. It is advisable to sow fresh seed, as viability drops off after a year or two. The aim with peppers is to produce sturdy, short-jointed plants. You can achieve this by potting on several times before planting out, initially into 7½cm/3in pots, and subsequently into 10cm/4in pots. Seedlings are normally ready for planting about eight weeks after sowing, when they are about 10cm/4in high with the first flower truss showing. Harden them off well before planting outside, protecting them if necessary. Space standard varieties 38–45cm/15–18in apart and dwarf types 30cm/12in apart. You can interplant indoor plants with dwarf French marigolds to deter whitefly.

Peppers need to develop a strong branching framework. If growth seems weak, nip out the growing point when the plant is about 25–30cm/10–12in high to encourage sideshoots to develop. A small 'king' fruit may develop early, low on the main stem, inhibiting further development. Remove it at either the flower bud or young fruit stage. Once plants are setting fruits, nip back sideshoot tips to 20cm/8in or so to concentrate the plant's energy.

Branches can be brittle, and plants may need support if they are becoming top heavy. Tie them to upright bamboo canes, or support individual branches with small split canes. Earth up around the base of the stem for further support. Water sufficiently to keep the soil from drying out, but do not overwater. Heavier watering is required once fruits start to set. Mulching is beneficial. Keep plants under cover well ventilated, and maintain humidity by damping down regularly in hot weather (see p. 219). This also helps fruit to set. If fruits are developing well, supplementary feed is unnecessary. If not, apply a liquid feed as fruits start to set. At this point plants in containers should be fed every ten days or so with a seaweed-based fertilizer or high-potash tomato feed.

Start picking fruits young to encourage further cropping. Pick green fruits when the matt surface has become smooth and glossy. Where the season is long enough, you can leave fruits from mid-summer onwards to develop their full colour. Plants will not stand any frost. Towards the end of the season, uproot remaining plants and hang them in a sunny porch or greenhouse. They continue to colour up and may remain in reasonable condition for many weeks.

Pests and diseases

Poor weather is the main enemy of outdoor peppers. Under cover, red spider mite, whitefly and aphids are the most likely pests. For control measures, see p. 229.

Varieties

In warm climates, the choice is infinite. The following are reliable croppers in cooler climates: 'Ariane' F1, 'Bell Boy' F1, 'Bendigo' F1, 'Californian Wonder', F1, 'Corno di Toro/di Toro Rosso'/'Bull's Horn', 'Diablo'

F1, 'Gourmet' F1, 'Gypsy' F1, 'Long Red Marconi', 'Tequila' F1

Compact varieties suitable for containers, patios

* = suitable for hanging baskets
'Hamik' (yellow), 'Mira', 'Mohawk' F1*, 'Oda' (purple fruit), 'Paragon' F1, 'Redskin' F1, 'Roberta' F1, 'Snackbite' F1 series, 'Sweet Sunshine' F1, 'Marconi Rossa'

Chili peppers *Capsicum annuum, C. frutescens* and other spp.

Chili peppers are universally grown for their fiery flavours. Some are annuals, being the same species as sweet peppers, others are perennials from several species such as *C. frutescens.*

They are a very diverse group, both in the form of their fruits and in the degree of 'heat'. Many are beautiful plants and compact enough to be grown in patio containers and even hanging baskets.

Because of their hot flavours, very few are suitable for use raw in salads, the exceptions being the milder, fleshier 'Hungarian Hot Wax' type. The chili experts at Sea Spring Seeds suggest that others, such as some of the 'Anaheim' and 'Jalapeno' chilies, are better grilled, peeled, then used cold. They have wonderful, subtle flavours. Just make sure to remove the placenta, to which the seeds are attached, and every seed: both can be overwhelmingly pungent. There is a huge choice available today.

Cultivate as sweet peppers. Rather surprisingly, they seem to be more robust and easier to grow than sweet peppers.

Milder, fleshy varieties

Hungarian Wax type: 'Hungarian Hot Wax', 'Inferno' F1

Jalapeno type chili

'Corno di Toro' (Bull's horn chili)

Hungarian Wax type, semi-mature chili

Hungarian Wax type chili

Anaheim group: 'Anaheim', 'Antler Joe E. Parker', 'Beaver Dam', 'Hot Mexico'
Jalapeno type: 'Early Jalapeno', 'Jalapaeno M', 'Telica'

Compact decorative varieties for containers 'Apache' F1, 'Basket of Fire', F1, 'Cheyenne' F1, 'Firecracker', 'Gusto' F1, 'Hot Thai', 'Loco' F1, 'Nu Mex', 'Twilight', 'Pikito' F1, 'Prairie Fire', 'Stumpy', 'Super Chili' F1

Sugar Snap type of
sugar pea

Flat-podded
sugar pea

Peas
(Garden peas) *Pisum sativum*

Peas are deservedly among the most popular vegetables for gardeners, not least because fresh peas are so rarely on sale. (The money lies in the vast frozen pea market.) While any pea can be used raw in salads, there is no doubt in my mind that the most tempting raw are the 'mangetout' or sugar peas, grown for their edible, parchment-free pods. The classic mangetout peas are flat-podded and sickle-shaped, eaten when the peas are miniscule. They tended to be large, some well over 10cm/4 in long, but there are also varieties with very much smaller pods. There are a few purple- and yellow-podded varieties which are very attractive in salads. Very distinct is the Sugar Snap type. Uniquely, these are round in cross-section, with the round young peas virtually 'welded' to the outer skin. Peas and pods are eaten as one, and for flavour and texture they are hard to beat raw, though they can of course be cooked. All the mangetout peas are sweet and refreshingly crisp, and can, if left to maturity, be shelled and used as normal peas. Plants vary in size from the very tall 'Carouby de Maussane' to compact dwarf varieties. Peas have tendrils which enable them to cling to supports. Compact varieties can be grown in large containers.

Of the 'shelling peas', the best flavoured, and sweetest for use raw, are wrinkled-seeded varieties. These are preferable to the rather starchy, round-seeded hardy peas used for early sowings.

Apart from the pods, tender young pea leaves and tendrils are also edible, in salads or cooked. Pea tendrils and 'pea shoots' – the top pairs of leaves at the tip of the stem – are a delicacy in many parts of the world, notably China. They are traditionally grown by sowing peas closely together and harvesting the shoots as they develop. For Westerners, a more economical, and very acceptable, alternative are the tendrils of 'semi-leafless' peas, ordinary varieties with leaves modified into wire-like tendrils. A bonus for gardeners is that these enable neighbouring plants to twine together, so virtually becoming self-supporting. Clumps look beautiful in a potager. Nip off the tendrils while they are still soft and pliable, and enjoy the most delicate pea flavour. The plants will still produce a crop of normal peas.

Peas can also be sprouted, for young shoots harvested about 5cm/2in high. (See Seed sprouting p. 248.)

Some currently available varieties
Mangetout type *Large podded:* 'Carouby de Maussane', 'Oregon Sugar Pod'
Small podded: 'Delicata', 'Norli', 'Sweet Horizon', 'Shiraz' (purple podded), 'Golden Sweet' (yellow podded)
Snap peas 'Delikett', 'Jessy', 'Sugar Snap', 'Sugar Snap Zucolla', 'Sugar Ann'
Semi-leafless 'Ambassador', 'Charlie', 'Quartz' (snap pea), 'Style'

Beans

Gardeners use the term 'beans' to embrace several distinct crops: runner beans (*Phaseolus coccineus*), French beans (*Phaseolus vulgaris*), and broad beans (*Vicia faba*). What they all have in common, and is not always appreciated, is that they must be cooked before eating, to destroy the toxins in raw beans. So their primary salad use is as cooked, cold ingredients, whether using immature pods or the bean seeds inside the pods.

Runner bean pods

Broad bean pods

Runner beans *Phaseolus coccineus*

Originally introduced to Europe from America as climbing ornamentals, these robustly flavoured beans made the British Isles their home. The flattish pods can be well over 23cm/9in long, but are most tender picked at roughly half that length. They are excellent cooked and eaten cold, but the beans inside are normally too coarse for salads, unless used very small. The beautiful flowers can be red, white, pink or bicoloured. In some varieties, particularly the older varieties, the edges of the pods were tough and needed to be removed or 'stringed' before use. This has been eliminated in some newer varieties. Most runner beans grow over 3m/10ft tall, but there are some very decorative dwarf varieties, less productive than climbers, but pretty enough to grow in flower beds. They can also be grown in large containers.

French beans (Kidney beans) *Phaseolus vulgaris*

French beans are used at several stages: the immature pods as 'green beans' (though they can be other colours); the semi-mature bean seeds as 'flageolets'; and the mature, ripened beans dried as 'haricot' beans, usually stored for winter. All can be used in salads after being cooked, though some varieties are more suited to one use than another. Be guided by catalogue descriptions. Varieties grown for pods are green, purple, yellow or red and cream flecked; in my view the yellow 'waxpods' (the pods are waxy) and the purple-podded varieties have the best flavour. Pod shape varies from flat (in some climbing varieties) to the very fine, 'filet' or Kenya beans, which have a melting quality. When dried, French beans display a huge range of colour and patterning, which can be used to great effect in salads. Among my favourites are 'Borlotto Fire Tongue'/'Lingua di Fuoca', a red-flecked white bean (available in both climbing and bush forms), and the bicoloured 'pea bean' so called because of its rounded, pea-like shape. As with runner beans, there are climbing and bushy dwarf forms of French beans. The latter can be grown in large containers.

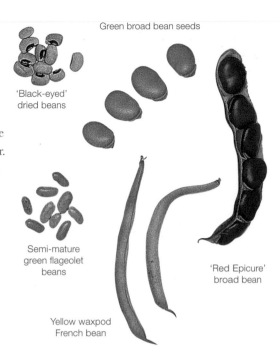

Green broad bean seeds

'Black-eyed' dried beans

Semi-mature green flageolet beans

Yellow waxpod French bean

'Red Epicure' broad bean

Broad beans *Vicia faba*

The seeds of these large, very hardy beans have a unique flavour which seems to be enhanced when used cooked and cold. For salads, either pick ordinary varieties young, before the seeds develop their own tough skin, or use the smaller-seeded, more delicate varieties grown primarily for freezing, such as 'Stereo'. The shorter-podded green- or white-seeded 'Windsor' broad beans, sown in spring, are more refined and generally better-flavoured than the hardier, autumn-sown, mainly 'longpod' types. There are a few pink-seeded varieties, which add a colourful dimension to salads. It is advisable to steam, rather than boil them, to retain their colour. Most broad bean varieties tend to be too top

heavy for containers, but the compact, early, cropping variety, 'The Sutton', can be grown in large containers. It can be sown in autumn or spring,

Another treat lies in the leafy tips of broad bean plants. Picked young and tender, once the pods are developing they can be steamed as greens or used raw in salads, though sparingly, as they are strongly flavoured. The tops of fodder bean plants, which I grow for green manure, are equally tender.

Broad bean flowers are ornamental and flavoursome in salads; particularly beautiful are those of the heirloom 'Crimson Flowered' bean.

Pink seeded varieties 'Grando Violetto', 'Karmazyn', 'Red Epicure'

the onion family

—

It's impossible to imagine a good salad that doesn't make use of a member of the onion (Allium) family. There is such a choice: from the varying pungency of sliced bulb onions to the freshness of salad and green onions, to a sprinkling of chives or their colourful flowers, to the uniqueness of garlic, whether worked into a dressing or simply rubbed into a wooden salad bowl.

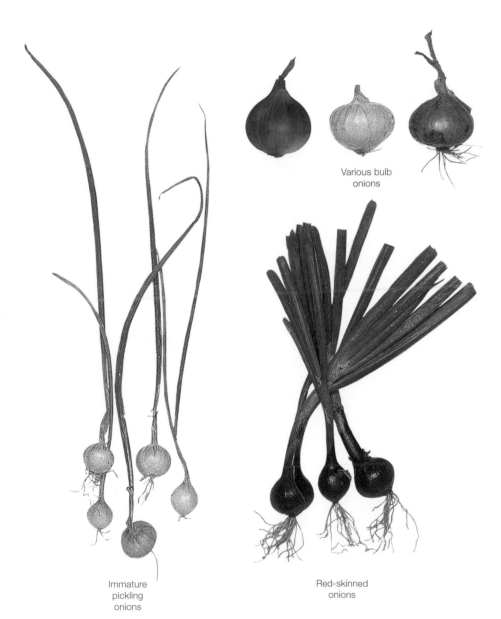

Various bulb
onions

Immature
pickling
onions

Red-skinned
onions

Bulb onions
Allium cepa

The onions are a large family of biennials and perennials, with a characteristic flavour. Using appropriate types, it is feasible to have a year-round supply: all can be used in salads. They divide into bulb and 'green' types. Bulb onions (*Allium cepa*) are adapted to temperate climates, and are used fresh or stored, sliced, chopped or grated raw into salads. Most are creamy or white-fleshed, but some are pink-skinned, and a few brown-skinned varieties have pretty, pink-hued flesh. Flavour varies from mild to piquant depending on variety, climate and growing conditions. Very small bulb onions are grown for pickling.

Soil and site

Bulb onions need an open site and fertile, thoroughly dug soil. Prepare it several months before sowing or planting, as growth will be too lush in freshly manured ground. Good drainage is essential. Lime acid soils to a pH of at least 6.5. In spite of the 'onion patch' tradition, try to rotate on a four- or at least three-year cycle to prevent the build-up of eelworm and soil-borne diseases.

Cultivation

Bulbs are the compact, swollen bases of the leaves. Bulb onions are very responsive to day length, and once a certain point is reached (about mid-June in the British Isles) no further leaves are initiated. In effect the bulb has reached its maximum potential: there is no 'catching up' if they were sown late. Success hinges on contriving the longest-possible growing season. It is essential to grow varieties suited to your climatic zone. 'Foreign' onions rarely succeed.

Sets or seed? Onions are grown from 'sets' – tiny, specially produced bulbs – or from seed. Each has its merits. Sets, being a more advanced stage of development, mature earlier, are easy to plant, can be planted in soil conditions unsuitable for sowing and escape onion fly attacks. Drawbacks are that planting dates are more critical, they are more prone to premature bolting and they are only available for certain varieties. Seeds are cheaper, available for all varieties, are more flexible over sowing times, and premature bolting is less likely. They require more attention, and are more liable to onion fly attack. Where good-quality sets are available (as in the British Isles) their use simplifies onion growing!

Sowing programme To ensure a continuous supply in temperate climates, make two sowings or plantings. Sow in late winter/early spring, for (a) main summer supplies of fresh onions, ready from mid-summer onwards and (b) storage onions, ready to lift in late summer/early autumn. These normally keep until mid- to late spring the following year. Make a second sowing in late summer/early autumn, for the first fresh onions, which will mature in early to mid-summer the following year. Only hardy varieties capable of overwintering outdoors are suitable: most of these are in the category known as 'Japanese onions'. An increasing range is becoming available, both as seeds and sets for autumn planting. Most only keep for a few months after lifting. The sowing date is critical and depends on your area. The onions need to be about 15–20cm/6–8in high by mid-autumn to survive winter conditions, but if too large, they are more likely to bolt prematurely or be affected by adverse weather. Be guided by catalogue information and local practice. It is a gamble worth taking for an early crop.

Growing from sets Use appropriate sets for the planting season (for varieties see opposite). Plant firm, small to medium-sized sets, as large sets are more likely to bolt prematurely. Some varieties are 'heat treated' to destroy the flower embryo and prevent premature bolting: these must be planted later. Follow the supplier's instructions.

For the main summer and storage crops, plant standard sets *in situ* from late winter to mid-spring as soon as the soil is workable. Plant heat-treated sets later. If soil conditions are poor, start sets singly in 5cm/2in modules and plant out when conditions improve. Plant overwintering sets in early to mid-autumn.

Plant sets by pushing them gently into the soil, until only the tip is visible. For the highest yield of medium-sized onions, space them 15cm/6in apart; closer spacing gives smaller onions, wider spacing larger ones. If birds tweak the sets aside, uproot and replant carefully: pushing them back in damages developing roots.

Growing from seed For that invaluable early start, sow indoors from late winter to early spring in seed trays or modules, at 10–16°C/50–61°F. If sowing in seed trays, prick out seedlings at the 'crook neck' stage, when they are still bent over, spacing them 5cm/2in apart. Onions can be multi-sown with up to six seeds per module. Once the seeds have germinated, maintain a temperature no higher than about 13°C/55°F before planting out, after hardening off. For maximum yields of medium-sized onions, space them 15cm/6in apart, or 4cm/1½in apart in rows 30cm/12in apart. As with sets, wider spacing produces larger onions and vice versa. Space groups of multi-sown onions 25–30cm/10–12in apart each way.

Follow with *in situ* sowing outdoors as soon as the soil is warm. Prepare the ground ten days before sowing, effectively making a 'stale seedbed'. This allows the soil to settle, deterring onion fly, which is attracted by freshly disturbed soil. Onion seed is small, so rake the seedbed to a fine tilth. Sow thinly in rows 20–30cm/8–12in apart, thinning to the spacings above. Use thinnings as green salad onions. Sow hardy overwintering varieties in late summer to early autumn, according to the date recommended for the variety. (See Sowing programme p. 119).

Weeding and watering

Keep onions weed-free, especially in the early stages, as the narrow, upright leaves never form a weed-suppressing 'canopy'. An onion hoe is the ideal weeding tool. In dry weather, water carefully until plants are well established. Further watering is normally unnecessary.

Harvesting and storage

For long-term storage, allow the foliage to die back and bend over naturally. Never forcefully bend it, as the resulting wounds lead to storage rots. Ease bulbs gently out of the ground. Dry them for about ten days, either outside off the ground on upturned boxes or racks, or, in wet weather, under cover, until the outer skins are papery. Store them hung in bunches or plaits, or loose in shallow boxes, in cool, well-ventilated, frost-free conditions.

For fresh and short-term storage, lift onions as required, once they are large enough to use. After the foliage has died back in late summer, the remaining onions must be lifted, or they deteriorate. Treat them as storage onions, using them up first.

Pests and diseases

Onion fly Groups of seedlings will turn yellow and die as a result of attacks from tiny maggots. Onion fly is most prolific in hot, dry conditions. Sow into a stale seedbed as described on the opposite page, or grow under fine nets. Remove and burn damaged plants.

Mildews and rots There are no organic remedies for the diseases which attack in poor seasons, but look out for varieties with mildew resistance, which are becoming available. Handle storage onions gently, as rots start with cuts and bruises.

Recommended varieties

Spring-planted bulb onions from sets
Brown: 'Autumn Gold', 'Centurion', 'Jaro', 'Rumba', 'Santero' (mildew resistant), 'Setton', 'Sturon'
Red: 'Garnet', 'Red Baron', 'Red Ray', 'Redspark', 'Marshalls Fen Red' (all of these need heat treatment).
Spring-sown bulb onions from seed
Brown: 'Arthur', 'Golden Bear', 'Hybound', 'Hytech', 'Marco', 'Santero' (mildew resistant),

'Supersweet'/'Dulcinea'
Red: 'Kamal', 'Red Baron', 'Red Ray', 'Redspark'
Autumn-planted bulb onions from sets (Japanese onions) 'Radar', 'Senshyu Semi-Globe Yellow', 'Shakespeare'
Autumn-sown bulb onions from seed (Japanese onions) 'Element', 'Hikeeper', 'Imai Early Yellow', 'Senshyu Semi-Globe Yellow', 'Toughball'
Misc. 'Long Red Florence' (long, mild, red, sweet salad onion)

Pickling onions *Alliium cepa*

Varieties suitable for pickling never develop a papery outer skin, and are lifted when they are small and immature. There are white- and purple-skinned varieties. They grow best in fertile soil, but tolerate poorer conditions than bulb onions.

Sow in spring in a sunny situation in wide drills or bands, spacing seeds about 1cm/½in apart, or in rows 30cm/12in apart, spacing seeds 8mm/½in apart. The high density keeps the bulbs small; thinning is normally unnecessary. Seeds are usually sown about 1cm/½in deep, but in Holland they are sometimes sown 4–5cm/1½–2in deep, to make the bulbs whiter. Allow the foliage to die down, then harvest as bulb onions. If left in the ground longer they will resprout. They can be stored a while before pickling, and can at any stage be used fresh in salads.

Popular varieties
White: 'Barletta', 'Paris Silver Skin', 'Pompeii'
Red: 'Purplette'

Tree onion
bulbils

Egyptian or
tree onion

Egyptian onion (Tree onion) *Allium cepa* Proliferum Group

These curious onions produce clusters of tiny aerial bulbils, not unlike hazelnuts, which in turn sprout and develop further clusters, so the plant becomes two- or sometimes three-tiered. In due course the stems bend to the ground, where the bulbils root, the plant thus perpetuating itself. Egyptian onions are low yielding but extremely hardy: 'mid-air' bulbils can be picked in mid-winter.

Egyptian onions grow in most soils in a sunny spot, but prefer fertile, well-drained soil. Plant single bulbils or a cluster about 25cm/10in apart, in spring or autumn. The plants will keep going for several years, but may need thinning periodically.

Shallots *Allium cepa* Aggregatum Group

Typical shallots are globe to flask-shaped bulbs, multiplying into a cluster at ground level. There are three main groups.

Yellow Round to flask shaped, with the outer skin a straw or bronze colour, and white flesh. They tend to be large.

Red Round to flask shaped, bronzy outer skins, but pink-tinged flesh; generally smaller than the yellow type. Some are very strongly flavoured.

French Jersey type Elongated shape; often pinkish flesh. Beloved of chefs, as they are easily sliced and are considered to have an excellent flavour. Some are only suitable for short-term storage.

Shallots have a distinct, clean onion flavour, with varying degrees of pungency. With the

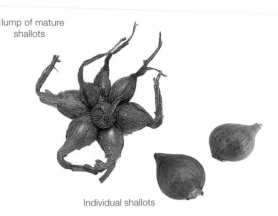

lump of mature
shallots

Individual shallots

exception of the French Jersey types, a major
asset is their ability to keep sound, often for
nine months, ie until early or mid-summer
the year after harvesting. This bridges the
gap in late spring/early summer between
stored and fresh onions. European varieties
are moderately hardy and withstand higher
temperatures much better than bulb onions..
Besides being grown for their bulbs, shallots
can be planted close for use as 'green onions'
or scallions.

Cultivation
For soil and site, see Bulb onions, p. 119.
Shallots are easily grown, traditionally from
individual sets or small bulbs, but more
recently also from seed.

Growing from sets is very simple (each will
develop into a cluster of eight to ten bulbs),
but there is a tendency to bolt prematurely,
and stocks can become virused and low
yielding. Always buy certified stock from a
reputable supplier: beware of cheap offers!
Some sets are suitable for autumn planting;
others only for spring planting. Be guided by
supplier or catalogue information.

Plant single sets in late autumn in
mild areas, otherwise in late winter/early

spring, depending also on the variety.
The optimum size for planting is about
1cm/½in circumference; larger sets may bolt
prematurely. Remove the loose, dry outer skin
and plant as onion sets (see p. 120), spaced
18cm/7in apart each way for the highest
yield. Harvest and store as for bulb onions.
There is no need to break up the clusters until
required for use.

Raising from seed is more labour intensive, and
requires a longer season. However there is less
risk of bolting, and plants are more disease
resistant. Each seed normally produces one
bulb – occasionally split into two or three.
Sow indoors in early spring as bulb onions,
planting 5cm/2in apart each way. Cultivate,
harvest and store shallots as bulb onions
(pp. 120–121).

Provided the shallots look healthy, keep
some for replanting the following season.
They eventually become infected with virus,
so buy fresh, clean stock every few years.

Recommended varieties
Globe shaped from sets: Brown/yellow: 'Bistro',
'Golden Gourmet', 'Yellow Moon'
Red/pink: 'Sante'
Jersey Long type from sets: Brown/yellow:
'Griselle', 'Jermor', 'Longor', 'Pesandor'
Red/pink: 'Mikor', 'Picasso', 'Zébrune'
Globe shaped from seed: (all red/pink)
'Ambition', 'L'Orient', 'Matador', 'Conservor'
(longish flask shaped)

Green onions
Allium cepa

The main types of green onion are the European 'salad' or 'spring' onion (*Allium cepa*), grown for the young green leaves and tiny bulbs, and the larger more robust oriental bunching onion (*Allium fistulosum*), a form of the hardy, perennial Welsh onion. These are adapted to both hotter and colder climates than ordinary bulb onions.

Spring onion (Salad or bunching onion, Scallion) *Allium cepa*

In these varieties of bulb onions the green leaves and stems, which are white in most varieties, but red in some, can be harvested within two months of sowing. Some are straight-shanked, others form tiny bulbs. Their refreshing flavour and colour are invaluable in salads. Recent hybridizing with *A. fistulosum* (the 'Welsh' and Japanese bunching onion group) is producing varieties with stronger, healthier leaves that remain green and erect far longer.

Cultivation For soil, cultivation, pests and diseases see bulb onions, p. 119. For the main summer-to-autumn supply, sow from early spring to early summer outdoors, making the first sowings under cloches or protection if necessary. Sow in succession every two or three weeks.

For very early spring supplies, sow hardier overwintering varieties in mid- and late summer. Where winters are mild and not too wet, sow in the open; otherwise sow under cover.

Sow either in single rows about 15cm/6in apart, or in roughly 10cm/4in wide drills, in both cases spacing seeds about 2½cm/1in apart. When the young onions reach a usable size, pull as required. Some of the bulb-forming varieties can be left to grow into larger bulbs.

Recommended varieties

(* = suitable for overwintering)
White: 'Eiffel' 'Elody', 'Feast' F1, 'Guardsman'*, 'Ramrod'*, 'White Lisbon';
Red: 'Apache', 'Red Beard', 'Reddy'

Welsh and Oriental bunching onion (Japanese bunching onion)
Allium fistulosum

The Welsh onion Welsh onion is a hardy, perennial, evergreen onion, long cultivated in northern Europe (it has nothing to do with Wales!). It can grow 50cm/20in tall, with fairly strong-flavoured, rather coarse, hollow green leaves, thickened at the base. Its value lies in the fact that it is useable all year round. It makes a good permanent edge to vegetable beds.

Propagate it by dividing established clumps every two or three years, replanting younger outer sections in a new site, 20cm/8in apart. Or sow seed *in situ* in spring or autumn, thinning to 20cm/8in apart.

Oriental bunching onion In Asia, over many centuries, a diverse group of milder onions has been developed from the Welsh onion. There are different varieties for harvesting at every stage: seedlings, young leaves, leafy stems and the imposing, leek-like, white shafts of the single-stem types, 2½cm/1in thick and 45cm/18in long.

Spring onions

Giant chives

Chinese
chives in bud

Standard
chives

Welsh onion

Some varieties have red-tinted stems. (For detailed cultivation, see Further Reading p. 274, *Oriental Vegetables.*)

Bunching onions grow best in light, fertile soil. Naturally healthy and vigorous, they tolerate a wide range of temperatures. Although perennial, they are best grown as annuals or biennials. For tender young salad leaves, sow *in situ* outdoors throughout the growing season, as for spring onions (see p. 124), making early and late sowings under cover. They can also be multi-sown in modules, planted 7½cm/3in apart. Pull for use at any stage from 5–15cm/2–6in tall, normally within five weeks of sowing.

For larger plants with slightly thickened stems, thin to 4cm/1½in apart; pull these, or cut single leaves, when 30cm/12in high, usually within three months of sowing.

In temperate climates, hardier single-stem varieties, which survive moderate frost, can be grown for winter and early spring. The leaves may be coarse but can be sliced finely into salads. Sow from spring to early summer *in situ*, in rows 30cm/12in apart, thinning to 7½cm/3in apart. Cut leaves as required. They often stand in good condition into spring and early summer, and are usable even after flower heads have formed.

Recommended varieties

Mainly for summer use: 'Laser', 'Parade', 'Savel', 'Summer Isle', 'Ishikura' (also for overwintering)

Chives
Allium schoenoprasum

Chives grow 23–30cm/9–12in high and both the slender leaves and tiny pink to purple flowers in the flower heads add a delicate onion flavour – and colour – to salads. 'Giant Chives' is a taller, handsome form. Chives tolerate light shade, but, as natives of damp meadows, do best in fertile, reasonably moist soil. They make excellent edges to vgetable beds, and can be grown in containers, provided there is plenty of organic matter in the pots and the roots do not dry out.

Cultivation Sow in spring in seed trays, or multi-sow about four seeds per module. Plant in clumps of about four seedlings, the clumps 23cm/9in apart. Lift and divide old clumps every three or four years in spring, replanting the younger, outer parts in clumps in a fresh site. Once they are established, cut foliage just above soil level.

Cut plants in sequence to allow them time to regenerate. Remove flower heads unless required for salads. In temperate climates, chives die back in mid-winter, but you can cloche or pot up a few and bring them indoors for early pickings.

Chinese chives (Garlic chives)
Allium tuberosum

Chinese chives have light green, flat leaves which emerge early in spring. They have a unique, part mild garlic, part chives flavour. From summer onwards the clumps produce a mass of starry, white flowers on 60cm/24in stems, fading into beautiful seed heads. Leaves, flowers buds and flowering stems are all edible. In China plants are covered after being cut with clay pots to produce a blanched crop of long, pale yellow, mild-flavoured leaves. (See Further reading p. 274, *Oriental Vegetables.*) Chinese chives are undemanding perennials, tolerating extremes of high and low temperatures.

Chinese chives in flower

Cultivation Chinese chives tolerate any well-drained, moderately fertile soil. Sow fresh seed in seed trays or modules from spring to early summer, planting seedlings in their permanent position in late summer/ early autumn when about 10cm/4in high. Plant in clumps of about six seedlings, the clumps 20cm/8in apart. They grow slowly.

In the first season after planting, cut sparingly when the leaves are 15cm/6in high and remove any flowering stems. Feed in spring with manure or a liquid feed. Keep the young plants well weeded, as it is hard to remove weeds once the clumps are established.

In spring in the second season rake over the plants to remove debris, then cut moderately, so they can build up their reserves. From the third year onwards they can be cut hard.

Chinese chives grow well in containers with at least 20cm/8in of soil, provided their roots don't dry out. Feed them regularly throughout the growing season with a dilute organic feed, or top-dress the container with garden compost.

Chinese chives can also be propagated by lifting and dividing clumps, as for chives. They are long-lived, and there is no need to divide them unless they are losing vigour. The leaves normally die back in mid-winter; bring plants into growth earlier by covering them with cloches in late winter.

127

Garlic
Allium sativum

The unique flavour of garlic is indispensable in many salad dishes and dressings. Mature bulbs are used fresh or stored; immature bulbs sold as 'green' or 'wet' garlic are superbly flavoured. In China, garlic is also cultivated for the young green leaves and flowering stem. (For this and more on garlic, see Further reading p. 274, *Oriental Vegetables*.)

Garlic is biennial, but if left in the ground, will perpetual itself and behave like a perennial. There are two distinct types, 'softneck' (*Allium sativum*), and 'hardneck', (*A. sativum* var. *ophioscorodon*), The 'softneck' type has soft leaves, and is most commonly grown in the West. It is also the most easily grown, the most productive, and stores well. The 'hardnecks' are characterized by developing a flower stalk, sometimes amazingly twisted, with a picturesque seed head of sterile seed. They produce fewer but larger cloves, which are only suitable for short-term storage. Their hard leaves make them impossible to braid. Connoisseurs, however, believe they are among the best flavoured.

There are numerous garlic strains, the sickle-shaped cloves being white, pink or purplish and varying in pungency. Garlic stores from six to twelve months, depending on variety. It is crucial to plant healthy, disease-free stock suited to your climate. Provided the cloves are healthy, you can save your own and replant for future crops.

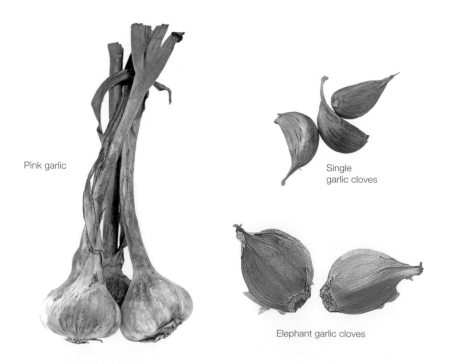

Pink garlic

Single garlic cloves

Elephant garlic cloves

Cultivation Garlic needs an open, sunny position, and grows best on moderately rich, light soil that is not freshly manured. Good drainage is essential. Bonfire ash can be incorporated when planting, as potash is beneficial. Lime acid soils. Garlic is hardy, surviving at least -10°C/14°F, and needs a long growing season. Although varieties differ in their requirements, most should be planted in late autumn. Otherwise plant in spring as soon as the soil is workable. Where winters are wet or the risk of slug damage is high, start off cloves singly in modules, planting out in spring when conditions improve.

Plant plump, healthy cloves split from mature bulbs, ideally 1cm/½in in diameter. The bulbs develop below ground. On light soils, plant up to 10cm/4in deep; on heavy soils plant more shallowly, but cover the cloves with at least 2½cm/1in of soil. Make sure the flat end is downwards: it is not always easy to tell. For optimum yield, space bulbs 18cm/7in apart each way. On wet ground, either plant on 10cm/4in-high ridges, or put coarse sand or potting compost beneath the cloves. Keep them weed-free and water in very dry weather early in the season. Cutting back the flower stalks of hardneck varieties two to three weeks before harvesting is said to increase the clove size considerably.

Harvesting Unlike onions, garlic must be lifted when the foliage starts turning yellow, or the cloves resprout. Dig them up carefully (they bruise easily) and dry them hung, or laid on trays, in a breezy situation – under cover in wet weather. Baking in full sun is not necessary. Store for winter like onions (pp. 120–121), ideally at 5–10°C/41–50°F.

Cloves accidentally left in the ground over winter may produce delicious shoots in spring, which can be used like chives.

Garlic rust (*Puccinia allii*) This disease, easily identified by the rust-coloured spores which occur on the leaves, can be serious but is very random in its attacks. The spores can be spread from overwintering alliums such as leeks and chives. It seems to be worst in humid climates and where winters are mild. If it is proving serious, try growing early varieties (such as 'Extra Early Wight' and 'Early Wight'). Harvest affected bulbs as soon as you can, and hang them in the kitchen for consumption. The rust won't affect their storage, but they won't be as large as healthy bulbs. Dispose of the rusted leaves in a waste system. Don't put them on the compost heap. Elephant garlic is less susceptible.

Recommended varieties:
Softneck: 'Early Purple Wight', 'Germidour', 'Solent Wight', 'Thermidrome', 'Vallelado' 'White Cristo', 'Extra Early Wight'
Hardneck: 'Carcassonne Wight', 'Lautrec Wight', 'Sprint', 'Sultop'

Elephant garlic
Allium ampeloprasum
Elephant garlic is a type of leek, which forms huge white, garlic-flavoured cloves. The flavour ranges from mild to fairly strong. Plant in autumn a month before frost is likely or in early spring, or start cloves in modules. Plant at least 2½/1in deep and 30cm/12in apart. Harvest as garlic above.

root vegetables

—

The root crops tend to play supporting roles in salad making, rather than grabbing the headlines. They are probably underrated: potatoes make superb salad dishes on their own as do beetroot and carrots. In small quantities, these, along with the great family of radishes and uniquely tasting turnips, contribute contrasting elements of flavour, texture and colour to all types of salad. They are especially prized in the winter months when the choice of fresh salad ingredients is far more limited.

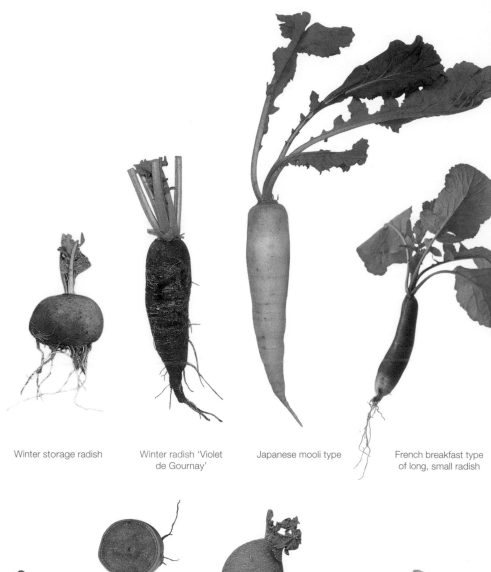

Winter storage radish

Winter radish 'Violet de Gournay'

Japanese mooli type

French breakfast type of long, small radish

Pink-fleshed Beauty Heart radish

Beauty Heart 'Green Goddess'

Typical round small radish

Radishes
Raphanus sativus

Countless children have been introduced to gardening by growing radishes. Not only are they fast growing and reliable, but they are a wonderfully varied and versatile salad crop. The familiar sharp flavour of radish roots is muted to refreshing subtlety in sprouted seeds, microgreens and in the highly productive baby leaf seedling crops. Perhaps the best-kept secret is the seed pods that develop after flowering. What a gastronomic treat, if picked young and green! In recent years the small radishes grown in the West have been joined by some of the large Asian radishes, such as the long white Japanese mooli and the spectacular pink- or green-fleshed Chinese Beauty Heart radishes. Most radishes are used raw in salads, but the larger types can be cooked like turnips. Mature leaves of some of the Asian radishes make pleasant cooked greens. Some varieties of radish are only available through heirloom seed libraries or suppliers of Asian vegetables.

Types of radish

Standard small radishes The most popular radishes are small and round, rarely more than 2½cm/1in diameter, or oblong or cylindrical in shape usually up to 4cm/1½in long, though there are other longer varieties. Typical of these is the scarlet-skinned, white-tipped French Breakfast. All have white flesh but the skin can be white, red, pink, yellow, purple to black or in bicoloured combinations – making for colourful salads. They are used fresh throughout the growing season.

Asian radish This diverse group of large radishes includes the white- or occasionally green-skinned Japanese mooli or 'Daikon', which are typically 30cm/12in long, weighing 500g/1lb; some giants reach 27kg/60lb (see Further reading p. 274 *Oriental Vegetables*). They are used fresh or stored, cooked or raw, mainly in summer and autumn. The various forms of the Beauty Heart types are round, oval or tapered, with mainly pink or green flesh. Rounded varieties are 5–10cm/2–4in in diameter; tapered green varieties up to 20cm/8in long. These decorative radishes are sweet and used raw in salads.

Storage and winter hardy radish These are fairly large radishes, with round and long forms, and black, pink, brown or violet skin. The round forms are 5–10cm/2–4in in diameter; the long types up to about 20cm/8in in length, They display varying degrees of frost hardiness. Some of mine have survived -10°C/14°F outside. They can be lifted and stored for winter use in boxes of moist sand. While they tend to be on the coarse side, they can be grated into salads, and also cooked, for example in stews.

Soil and site

Radishes grow best in well-drained, light, fertile soil with a neutral pH. Avoid freshly manured ground, which encourages lush leafy growth at the expense of the roots. They tolerate light shade in mid-summer. Adequate moisture throughout growth is essential. In hot, dry soils, growth is slow and there is a risk of radishes becoming pithy, woody, hollow and unpleasantly hot-flavoured. Rotate the larger, slow-growing types as brassicas. All radishes are susceptible to flea beetle attacks at the seedling stage; for control, see p. 229.

Cultivation of standard small radishes

These are normally ready three to four weeks after sowing, so are ideal for intercropping. For example small groups of seed can be sown between slow-germinating, station-sown parsnips, they can be broadcast in spring above recently planted potatoes, and children can have great fun writing their names in radishes, or making patterns by zigzagging them between established vegetables like cabbages or Brussels sprouts. Seed tapes are ideal for this purpose. These small radishes are easily grown in any kind of container.

For spring to autumn supplies

Sow 'little and often' at roughly ten-day intervals. Make the first sowings under cover in late winter, followed by outdoor sowings in spring as soon as the soil is workable. Make the earliest sowings in a sheltered spot, protect with cloches or fleece if necessary and use quick-maturing early varieties distinguished by having short tops. (See recommended varieties). Most of the small round radishes and French Breakfast varieties can also used for early sowings. Continue sowing outdoors until early autumn, making the last sowings under cover in mid-autumn.

Sow thinly *in situ*, broadcast, or in rows 15cm/6in apart, or in shallow wide drills. The commonest cause of failure is overcrowding: entangled lanky seedlings never develop properly. Aim to space seeds 2½cm/1in apart, or thin early to that, or slightly wider, spacing. Sow at an even depth of about 12mm/½in – slightly deeper for long-rooted varieties. This prevents seeds nearest the surface from germinating first and swamping those sown deeper. In dry weather, water weekly at the rate of 11 litres per sq. m/2 gallons per sq. yd. Pull radishes as soon as they are ready. Most varieties bolt rapidly on maturity, though some have good bolting resistance.

Mid-winter crops Certain small-leaved, slow-growing varieties, 'Saxa' for example, have been developed for winter culture in unheated greenhouses and polytunnels. Night temperatures should normally be above about 5°C/41°F. Sow from mid-autumn to late winter, thinning to 5cm/2in apart. Keep them well ventilated. They require little watering, except in sudden hot spells: leaves turning dark green indicate that watering is necessary. Give extra protection if colder weather is forecast. They will be ready in late winter/early spring.

Cultivation of Asian types

These large radishes respond to day length and low temperatures in the same way as oriental brassicas (see p. 69), so it is best to delay sowing until early to mid-summer. Bolt-resistant varieties of white mooli can be sown earlier, in late spring. Once ready, these types stand in good condition far longer than ordinary radishes.

They are susceptible to the normal range of brassica pests and diseases (see p. 65). Growing under fine nets gives excellent protection against cabbage root fly, which is particularly damaging.

Standard mooli These take seven to eight weeks to mature. Sow *in situ* 1–2cm /^{1}/$_{2}$–^{3}/$_{4}$ in deep; or sow in sunken drills 4cm/1^{1}/$_{2}$in deep and pull soil around the stems as they develop for extra support. Plants grow quite large, so it is advisable to sow in rows at least 30cm/12in apart – spacing varies from 7^{1}/$_{2}$–10cm/3–4in apart for smaller varieties to at least 30cm/12in apart for the largest; or you can sow mooli singly in modules and transplant. You can also pull some when immature, leaving the remaining plants to grow larger.

Beauty Heart types The pink-fleshed forms take ten to twelve weeks to mature. Delay sowing until mid-summer, partly to avoid premature bolting, but equally because the deep internal colour develops only when night temperatures fall to about 10°C/50°F in autumn. Sow *in situ*, spacing plants 20cm/8in apart each way, or 12^{1}/$_{2}$cm/5in apart in rows 30cm/12in apart. For more reliable results, sow in modules, singly or two seeds per module, and plant as one 30cm/12in apart, at the four-to-five-leaf stage.

Where summers are short, plant under cover to extend the season. These types tolerate light frosts, but if there is likely to be heavy frost lift them and store in cool conditions indoors, as hardy winter radish below. Internal colour intensifies with maturity and continues to deepen in storage.

Grow green varieties the same way, but as they mature faster they can be more closely spaced. They can be lifted sooner, as the pale green colour is constant.

Storage and hardy winter radish

These radishes are a valuable source of radish in winter and spring. Sow from mid- to late summer as for 'Beauty Heart' radish above. In temperate climates, you can leave them in the ground during winter; tuck straw around them to make lifting easier in frost. In more severe climates, or where slug damage is serious, lift the roots in late autumn, trim off the leaves and store in boxes of sand in cool conditions. They should keep sound until spring. Once cut, wrapped roots will keep in a refrigerator for several weeks.

Baby leaf/seedling radish

The fast growing nature of radish makes it a natural subject for seedling, baby leaf crops. While any of the small radishes can be used, their leaves tend to become hairy, and unpalateable, fairly fast, so are best picked very young before this stage is reached. Some of the Asian radishes have smoother leaves, and have proved excellent for cut-and-come again crops. Packs of these seedling radishes, known as 'Kaiware' are very popular in Japan. While most are white or green stemmed, some have very appealing pink tinged leaves and stems. They are a rewarding crop to grow for salads.

Radishes can be sown for baby leaves throughout the growing season. Very useful late sowings can be made under cover in early to mid autumn, the earliest sowings under cover in late winter, followed by outdoor sowings. Leaves can be cut within two to three weeks. For more on cultivation of baby leaves, see p. 235. Radishes are also being used as microgreens, see pp. 248–255.

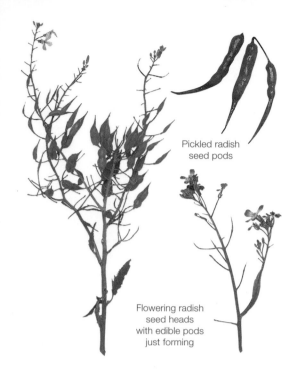

Pickled radish
seed pods

Flowering radish
seed heads
with edible pods
just forming

Radish pods

The immature seed pods of radishes have an
excellent flavour and crisp texture, and are
used raw or pickled. Allow a few plants to
run to seed for this purpose. The larger the
radish, the more succulent the pods seem to
be. A single hardy winter radish left in the soil
over winter will yield a huge crop of pods the
following spring. Pick pods regularly while they
are young and crisp to encourage production
over several weeks. Alternatively grow varieties
with exceptionally long pods, such as Bavarian
'Munchen Bier' and 'Rat's Tail'. Sow from
spring to summer, thinning to 30cm/12in
apart. Pollen beetle attacks can damage radish
flowers and prevent pods from forming. Where
the problem proves serious, plants will have to
be protected with fine netting.

Varieties

There is a huge choice: these are a selection
of recommended varieties. Mixtures of
different coloured types are often available.

**Standard round radish (most red
skinned)** 'Celesta' F1, 'Cherry Belle', 'Mars'
F1, 'Mondial' F1, 'Ping Pong' (white), 'Rudi',
'Rudolph', 'Sparkler' (white tip)
French Breakfast type 'Flamboyant-
Sabina', 'French Breakfast 3', 'French
Breakfast 4-Francis', 'French Breakfast –
Nelson'
Unusual skin colour *Purple:* 'Amethyst'
F1, 'Bacchus' F1, 'Purple Plum'
Pink: 'Juztenka', 'Pink Beauty'; yellow: 'Zlata'
Summer mooli (slow-bolting)
'April Cross' F1, 'Long White Icycle', 'Mino
Early', 'Minowase Summer Cross' F1.
Beauty Heart type 'Mantanghong' F1,
'Red Meat', 'Misato Green'
Large winter storage types 'Black
Spanish Round', 'Chinese Dragon' F1,
'Oriental Rosa 2', 'Violet de Gournay',
**Early short top varieties for early
outdoor crops, outdoor crops under
fleece, and winter crops in unheated
polytunnels/greenhouses winter**
'Fluo' F1, 'Poloneza' (improved Sparkler),
'Saxa', 'Short Top Forcing'
Leaf radish 'Minowase Spring Cross',
'Rioja' (mostly red leaf), 'Sai Sai', 'Sangria'
(red stem)

Carrot
Daucus carota

My long-standing dislike of grated raw carrot, probably dating back to school days, makes it hard for me to be enthusiastic about them as salad vegetables, although I love them cooked. I now realise that with a good dressing they can become a valuable salad ingredient. Any of the maincrop carrots can be used grated. For cultivation see *Further reading* p. 274, *Grow Your Own Vegetables*. Tailored to use raw in salads are what are now widely known as 'baby', 'finger' or 'mini' carrots – small, finger-thick carrots harvested at most 7½cm/3in long. These are sweet, tender and delicious raw, whether nibbled whole or sliced. Also clamouring to be used in salads are those with unusual coloured roots, which have become widely available in recent years. Only these two groups are covered here.

Cultivation of baby carrots

Carrots require deep, light, fertile, well-drained soil, with a pH between 6½ and 7½. Avoid heavy, compacted or clay soils, which prevent roots from swelling, and stony soils, which cause forking. Ideally dig in well-rotted compost or manure several months before sowing. Small carrots are excellent subjects for growing bags or large pots of potting compost. Carrots are cool-season crops, growing best at temperatures of 16–18°C/60–64°F. Seed germinates very slowly at temperatures below 10°C/50°F, so delay sowing until the soil has warmed up: lingering carrots are never succulent. Prepare a finely raked, weed-free seedbed, as carrot seedlings are easily smothered by weeds and awkward to weed.

Mini carrot production depends on growing appropriate varieties at dense spacing. In the past the varieties used commercially were developed from the slender Amsterdam types, and slightly broader Nantes types, which are both cylindrical, stump-rooted carrots traditionally used for forcing and early crops. Nowadays the distinctions between the different types are being eroded, and selections of Chantenay types

Baby carrots

137

are also being used. Varieties recommended below are fast-growing and smooth-skinned with a small central core – all factors making for tenderness. The small, round carrots, often recommended for shallow soils and for growing in containers, are also useful for baby carrots.

For a continuous supply, sow outdoors *in situ* from mid-spring to mid-summer, at two- to three-week intervals. Sow thinly in rows 15cm/6in apart, spacing seeds about 4cm/1½in apart so that thinning is unnecessary, or thin early to that spacing. Alternatively sow in shallow drills 10–15cm/4–6in wide, with seedlings about 2cm/¾in apart. Water sufficiently to prevent the soil from drying out. The carrots will be ready for pulling eleven to thirteen weeks after sowing.

Make earlier and later sowing under cover, in polytunnels for example. Protect early outdoor sowings by growing in frames, under cloches, or by covering with fleece. Unless the weather becomes very hot, small carrots can be grown under fleece to maturity. This also protects them from carrot fly.

Carrot fly can be a serious problem, though early sowings often escape attack. To overcome the problem either grow the carrots under fleece or nets like Enviromesh, or surround them with 60cm/2ft-high barrriers (of clear polythene for example) or grow them in containers raised off the ground to that height. This defeats the low flying, egg-laying flies. They are attracted by the smell of bruised foliage, so thin in the evening, burying thinnings in the compost heap.

Baby carrots can also be grown by sowing in modules, standing on soil, as described for 'pencil fennel' (see p. 93). Nantes varieties (eg 'Mokum', 'Romance') seem to do particularly well with this system.

Novelty carrots

Although we are conditioned to orange-fleshed carrots, heirloom European yellow and white carrots, often used as fodder crops, are surprisingly sweet-fleshed and well flavoured. More recently a range of colourful carrots has been developed. These include purple-skinned carrots, sometimes pure purple inside, sometimes blended with orange; creamy skin with creamy flesh; bright red skinned with pink flesh; yellow skin with yellow flesh. Although many of the currently available varieties are recommended cooked (preferably by steaming) and cold, as some have strong 'off flavours' when raw, it is certainly worth grating small quantities in salads for their unique impact. I once saw green-fleshed carrots in Tunisia, which were very palatable. If they become available, do try them! Different coloured mixes are now widely available.

Varieties

Especially recommended for baby carrots 'Adelaide' F1, 'Atlas' (round), 'Mokum' F1, 'Parmex' (round)

Other suitable varieties 'Amsterdam Forcing 3', 'Caracas' F1, 'Carson' F1, 'Cascade' F1, 'Flyaway' F1, 'Ideal Red', 'Maestro' F1, 'Nairobi' F1, 'Napoli' F1, 'Romance' F1, 'Sugarsnax' F1

Coloured carrots 'Cosmic Purple', (purple skin, orange and yellow flesh), 'Purple Haze' F1 (orange flesh), 'Purple Sun' F1 (purple skin and flesh), 'Red Samurai' F1 (red skin, creamy flesh), 'White Satin' F1 (white skin, creamy flesh), 'Yellowstone' F1 (yellow skin & flesh), 'Rainbow' (mix)

Heirloom 'Belgian White', 'Jaune Obtuse du Doubs' (yellow)

Beetroot

Beta vulgaris

Beetroot are available all year round – fresh during the growing season and stored in winter. They can be flat, round, tapered or cylindrical in shape, and while the textbook modern beet has evenly coloured, deep red flesh, there are older varieties with white or yellow flesh, and in the case of the Italian heirloom 'Chioggia' characterized by target-like rings of pink and white. These are all considered well flavoured.

Beet are normally cooked whole (otherwise the flesh bleeds) by baking in foil, steaming or boiling, and then used cold. Although not to everyone's taste, beet can also be grated raw into salads. The young leaves are edible raw or lightly cooked, the scarlet-leaved varieties being highly decorative and popular for baby leaves and microleaves. Small beet, about 5cm/2in diameter, make delicious pickles. 'Baby' or 'mini beet', roughly ping-pong-ball size, are probably the beetroot most worth growing for salad use: they develop fast, take least space and are arguably the best-flavoured. The long cylindrical beets, which grow well out of the ground, are ideal for slicing. (For cultivation of standard and storage beet, see Further reading p. 274, *Grow Your Own Vegetables*.) Sugar beet, incidentally, makes a very sweet-flavoured salad: a psychological drawback is its pale colour.

Cultivation of baby beet

For growing temperatures, soil and cultivation see Carrots, p. 137, though beet grow successfully on heavier soil than carrots. Beet withstand moderate frost, but risk premature bolting if young plants are exposed for long to temperatures much below 10°C/50°F. Early spring sowings should only be made with bolt-resistant varieties. Seed germinates poorly at temperatures below 7°C/45°F. A chemical inhibitor in the seed sometimes prevents germination; if so, soak seed for half an hour in tepid water before sowing. Beet 'seed' is actually a seed cluster, so several seedlings germinate close together and require thinning. ('Monogerm' varieties are single-seeded, avoiding the problem.) Beet is normally sown *in situ* as it does not transplant well, unless sown in modules.

For mini beet, sow *in situ* from mid-spring to mid-summer. Sow at two-to-three-week intervals for a continuous supply from early to mid-summer until autumn. Sow seeds 2cm/¾in deep, in rows 15cm/6in apart, thinning seedlings to 2½cm/1in apart. This will produce small, even, high-quality beets, ready for pulling on average twelve weeks after sowing. If larger beet are required, a few can be left to develop. The earliest outdoor sowings can be protected by sowing in frames or under cloches. Sowing under crop covers such as fleece, removed after four or five weeks, doubles the yields from early sowings.

Novelty beetroot

The striped, yellow, and white beets all lend themselves to artistic display in salads. Sow *in situ* from late spring to early summer, in rows 23cm/9in apart, thinning to 7½–10cm/3–4in apart; or multi-sow in modules, about three seeds per module.

If numerous seedlings germinate, thin to four or five per module before planting out 'as one' 20cm/8in apart. The highly coloured, red-leaved 'Bull's Blood' beet is a mainstay of my potagers, retaining its leaf colour late into winter; it has excellent beets. Plant a few under cover in early autumn for quality leaves until spring. It has also become very popular for baby leaves (see p. 235).

Varieties

For mini beet 'Action', F1, 'Bettolo' F1 'Boltardy' (bolt resistant), 'Bona', 'Boro' F1, 'Monodet' (monogerm), 'Pablo' F1 (bolt resistant), 'Red Ace' F1, 'Rubidus', 'Solo' F1 (monogerm), 'Subeto' F1, 'Wodan' F1
Long varieties for slicing 'Alto' F1, 'Cylindra', 'Taunus' F1
Novelty beet 'Albina Verdura' (white), 'Albino', 'Boldor' (yellow), 'Chioggia' (striped)
Red leaved 'Bull's Blood', 'McGregor's Favourite'
Mixtures of coloured roots also available.

Turnip
Brassica campestris Rapifera Group

While most turnips are too strongly flavoured for salads, small 'baby' or 'mini' turnips, harvested at ping pong ball stage, are pleasantly sweet, mild and crisp and can be grated raw in salads. Turnip seedlings are also suitable for cut-and-come-again baby leaf, microgreens, or sprouting. The seedling leaves are mild flavoured, but should be used at an early stage, as they soon develop hairiness. Some varieties of turnips have leaves which can be cooked as greens. For general cultivation of turnips, see Further reading p. 274, *Grow Your Own Vegetables*. For baby leaves see p. 235, and for sprouting and microgreens see pp. 248–255.

Cultivation of baby turnips

White Japanese varieties of turnip and some varieties with purple tops and white base, are the most suitable for baby turnips. Grow as baby beet (see p. 139), sowing from mid-late spring until late summer for early summer to mid-autumn use. They will be ready within seven weeks of sowing. Continue sowing in frost-free greenhouses or polytunnels until mid-autumn for a mid-winter crop. Harvest them when 2½–5cm/1–2in in diameter.

Baby turnips can also be grown by the method suggested for 'pencil fennel' (see p. 93). For this the varieties 'Purple Top Milan' and 'Sweetbell' have proved the most suitable. Baby turnips are an ideal crop for containers and growing bags.

Varieties recommended for baby turnips

'Market Express' F1, 'Oasis' F1, 'Primera' F1 (purple top), 'Purple Top Milan', 'Sweet Marvel' F1, 'Tiny Pal', 'Tokyo Cross' F1

Potato
Solanum tuberosum

There has been a sea change in the attitude towards potatoes since the first edition of *The Salad Garden* in the 1980s. The potato revolution in the UK was spearheaded by the late Donald MacLean. Not only did he set about cleaning up the virused stock of old varieties, but he made the public aware of the innate diversity of potatoes – how each has something unique to offer in terms of cooking quality, pest or disease resistance, flavour or appearance. Gardeners are now far more discerning and knowledgeable: hundreds attend the annual 'potato days' held by Garden Organic, the national centre for organic gardening in the UK, and relish the opportunity to learn more and buy a few tubers of unusual varieties. Garden suppliers have responded by producing specialist potato catalogues, offering a very wide choice. The best of the old are being augmented by excellent new varieties.

Where garden space is limited, it may seem logical to forgo potato growing. They are used in fairly large quantities, occupy a lot of space for a long period – nearly five months for 'late main' types – and are cheap to buy. Logic goes out of the window once you discover the superior flavour of carefully chosen varieties, freshly dug from your own garden. It is worth finding space for at least a few, more if possible. The less demanding early varieties can also be grown successfully in large containers. For general cultivation of potatoes, see Further reading p. 274, *Grow Your Own Vegetables*.

What makes a salad variety?

The texture of a potato largely determines how it is best cooked. At one end of the spectrum are potatoes high in dry matter: these become light and fluffy when cooked, and are best for baking, roasting and chips. At the other end are waxy potatoes, closer textured and low in dry matter. After cooking they remain intact without disintegrating, and keep firm if sliced or diced and mixed with dressings. These make the best salad potatoes. There are exceptions to every rule where potatoes are concerned, but waxy potatoes seem to have some of the best flavours, which are often brought out to the full when cooked and cold.

'Pink Fir Apple'

Cultivation

For practical purposes, potatoes are grouped according to the average number of days they take to mature, though the category chosen for a variety can be a little arbitrary. These are commonly used groupings: 'earlies' 75 days ('very early') to 90 days 'first earlies'; 'second earlies' – 110 days; 'early maincrop' – 135 days; 'late maincrop' – 150 days. What is significant is that the earlier, fast-maturing potatoes are initially lifted young as 'new' potatoes before the skins have set. (Within limits, the younger they are lifted, the better the flavour.) They are scrubbed whole before cooking.

Simply because they are small, firm and immature, new potatoes often make good salad potatoes, although they will not necessarily have the outstanding flavour of acclaimed salad varieties. They must be eaten fresh: the 'new potato' quality is soon lost and declines as the season progresses. You can also plant early varieties mid-season, to get small 'new' potatoes later in the year. Maincrop potatoes are slower-maturing but grow larger, have much higher yields and can be lifted and stored in frost-free conditions for winter use.

Most salad varieties are in the earlier maturing groups, with the exception of the old, long, knobbly European varieties such as 'Pink Fir Apple' (which stores well) and 'Ratte'. Salad potatoes are mostly yellow-, creamy- or white-fleshed, but an interesting group of heirloom varieties have deep blue or purple flesh. Their quality is often reasonable and they are highly decorative. Potato performance and flavour can vary enormously with local climate and soil conditions. It is worth trying many varieties to see which perform well in your garden.

'Anya'

Growing in containers

Successful crops of salad potatoes can be grown in containers. This is particicularly useful for early crops in an unheated greenhouse or polytunnel planted in early spring, or outdoors, in mid to late spring, provided there is no risk of frost. Early varieties, being the most compact, are generally the most suitable. All sorts of container can be used: half barrels, tubs, strong 'polybags', large pots. They need to be at least 45cm/18in deep and wide, with drainage holes in the bottom. Use good multipurpose potting compost, ideally mixed with well-rotted garden compost to increase fertility and moisture holding capacity. Tubers need to be planted about 30cm/12in apart.

The classic method was to put about 10cm/4in of compost in the bottom of the container, placing chitted potatoes on top, covered with another 10cm/4in layer of compost. When the stems are about 15cm/6in high, they are 'earthed up' with another 10cm/4in layer of compost, and this is repeated once more. The container must be kept reasonably moist (potatoes are thirsty plants), and fed with a seaweed based fertilizer roughly every ten to fourteen days once plants are showing. They are normally ready within about ten weeks. In many cases the flowering indicates readiness, but this is not infallible: if in doubt, poke your fingers into the bag and feel gently to gauge the size of the tubers.

A simpler alternative method which has been advocated recently is to fill a bag with good compost, up to about 2½cm/1 in below the brim and plant the potatoes at a depth of about 12cm/5 in below the brim. Water and feed as above.

Varieties

The supply of potato varieties is constantly changing. These are currently available and highly recommended for salads. Many can also be used for other purposes. (Consult catalogues and potato source for recommendations.)

* = especially recommended for early use in containers.

Early 'Amandine', 'Anabelle', 'Casablanca'*, 'Foremost', 'Juliette', 'Lady Christl'*, 'Maris Bard'*, 'Red Duke of York', 'Sharpes Express'*, 'Swift'*, 'Vales Emerald'*
2nd early 'Anya', 'Bambino', 'Carlingford', 'Charlotte'*, 'Gemson', 'Harlequin', 'International Kidney', 'Jazzy'*, 'Linzer

Delicatesse', 'Maris Peer', 'Milva', 'Nicola', 'Ratte', 'Roseval'
Maincrop 'Belle de Fontenay', 'Imagine', 'Pink Fir Apple'

'Nicola'

'Charlotte'

'Maris Peer'

Hardy roots
Brassica campestris Rapifera Group

The hardy root crops are a neglected group of nutritious, often sweet-flavoured vegetables, which are most useful during the winter months when there is a scarcity of leafy green salads. Some can be grated or sliced raw into salads, but their flavour is often brought out best when cooked and cooled. The more knobbly tubers can be difficult to peel. If so, scrub them, and steam for a few minutes – the skins then come off easily.

Most root crops do best in deep, light soil, with well-rotted manure or compost worked in several months before sowing. They are undemanding other than needing to be weeded in the early stages and watered to prevent the soil from drying out. Those included here normally survive temperatures of -10°C/14°F in the open. They can be lifted and stored in clamps (on a base of straw and covered with straw and/or soil) or in cool conditions under cover, but their flavour and quality often deteriorate. In most cases the leaves die down in winter, so mark the ends of the rows so you can find them in snow. Covering with straw makes lifting easier in frosty weather.

The following notes highlight their salad use. For cultivation see Further reading p. 274, *Grow Your Own Vegetables*.

Horseradish *Armoracia rusticana*
This vigorous perennial, with leaves up to 60cm/24in long, has stout roots that are used to make a strongly flavoured relish. They can be grated raw into a salad to add a wonderful piquancy. When about 5cm/2in long, the young leaves have a very pleasant flavour and can be used in salads. It is often found in the wild (see illustration, p. 163). The easiest way to acquire horseradish is to divide an established plant – but be aware it can be invasive.

Horseradish

Jerusalem artichoke *Helianthus tuberosus*
These tall, hardy perennials produce very knobbly, branched underground tubers, upwards of a hen's egg in size. They are nutritious, with a distinctive sweet flavour,

Jerusalem artichokes

and are excellent raw or cooked and cold.
The problem lies in scrubbing them clean!
The tall plants make good windbreaks and
their rugged, fibrous root system helps break
up heavy ground. The variety 'Fuseau' is
smoother than most.

Parsnip *Pastinaca sativa*

Parsnips have large, sweetly flavoured roots
up to 25cm/10in long and 10cm/4in wide
at the crown. They are excellent cooked and
cold, but unsuitable for use raw in salads.

Hamburg parsley *Petroselinum crispum* var. *tuberosum*

Hamburg parsley is a dual-purpose member
of the parsley family. The large roots
resemble parsnips and are used in the same
way. The dark glossy foliage looks and tastes
like broad-leaved parsley, but retains its
colour at much lower temperatures, making
it invaluable in winter. The young leaves
can be used whole or chopped in salads, or
for garnishing and seasoning. It is probably
easier to grow than parsnip or parsley, and
is tolerant of light shade.

Scorzonera (viper's grass) *Scorzonera hispanica*

Scorzonera is a perennial with black-
skinned roots and yellow flowers. Roots and
flower buds – both eaten cooked and cold
– flowers and young shoots or 'chards' are
all used in salads, and have an intriguing
flavour. (See Salsify right and flower
illustration on p. 158.)

Chinese artichoke *Stachys affinis*

These white, spiral-shaped knobbly tubers
are rarely more than 4cm/1½in long and
2cm/¾in wide. They have a crisp texture,
appealing translucent appearance and
delightful nutty flavour raw. They need
diligent scrubbing. Being small, the tubers
shrivel fairly soon once lifted. (For further
information, see Further reading p. 274,
Oriental Vegetables.)

Salsify (oyster plant) *Tragopogon porrifolius*

Salsify is a biennial, usually grown for its
long, brown-skinned, tapering roots, which
have a most delicate flavour when cooked
and eaten cold. Less well known is the
mysterious flavour of the plump flower buds
and light purple petals, which develop in
its second season, both used cooked and
cold in salads (see p. 161.) In the past salsify
was also cultivated for the young blanched
leaves, or chards, which develop in spring
and are tender enough to use raw in salads.
For chards, cut back the withering stems
just above ground level in autumn, and
cover with about 15cm/6in of soil, straw or
leaves. The chards push through in spring;
cut them when 10–15cm/4–6in long.

Chinese
artichokes

finishing touches

––

So often it is the finishing touches which
transform a salad from the mundane to
the unforgettable. It can be the brightness
of flower petals sprinkled over the top, the
subtlety of flavour conferred by herbs, or
the palate tickled with a garden weed or
even a wild plant.

Narrow-
leaved sage

Raripila mint

Spearmint

Sweet cicely

Apple mint

Variegated lemon
balm

Green lemon
balm

Ginger mint

Lovage

Winter savory

Curly
parsley

Broad-leaved
parsley

Pineapple
mint

Angelica
seed head

Angelica
leaves

Herbs

The deft use of herbs transforms a salad. Add a little chopped coriander or fenugreek to evoke the Orient; a few leaves of balm or lemon thyme for a hint of lemon; chervil or sweet cicely to create the subtle tones of aniseed. Or go for a more daring flavour with lovage, or a generous sprinkling of dill, or a little sage, tarragon or basil. Almost any culinary herb can find a role in salad making: experiment with what you have to hand. The only guiding principle should be that the stronger the herb, the more lightly it is used. The eminent twentieth-century gardening writer Eleanour Sinclair Rohde put this neatly: 'It is just the suspicion of flavouring all through the salad that is required, not a salad entirely dominated by herbs.' She would mix a teaspoon of as many as twenty finely chopped herbs to sprinkle into a salad.

Don't overlook the decorative qualities of herbs in salads. Many have variegated and coloured forms – marjoram, mint and thyme spring to mind – and many have leaves of outstanding beauty; the delicate tracery of salad burnet (see p. 166), sweet cicely, dill and the bronze and green fennels, for example. Add any of these, freshly picked, for a last-minute garnish.

It is a truism that fresh herbs are infinitely better-flavoured than dried or preserved herbs. In temperate climates most culinary herbs die back in winter, but chervil, caraway, coriander and parsley are some that can be grown under cover for use fresh in winter. Others can be potted up in late summer and brought indoors. Basil, thyme, mint, winter savory and marjoram can be persuaded to provide pickings from a winter windowsill.

Although many herbs can be preserved and are useful in cooking, only a handful, such as some mints, retain their true flavour. Several of the more succulent herbs, such as chives, parsley and basil, can be deep-frozen as sprigs or chopped into ice-cube trays filled with water. Thaw the cubes in a strainer when you need to use the herb. Otherwise herbs are usually preserved by drying. Pick them at their peak, just before flowering, and dry them slowly in a cool oven, or hang them indoors, covered with muslin to prevent them from becoming dusty. When they are completely dry, store them in airtight jars.

Herbs are worth growing for their ornamental qualities. Walls, patios, dry areas and spare corners can be carpeted with thymes, lemon balm or creeping mint. Ordinary and Chinese chives, parsley, hyssop and savory make effective edging plants, while mature plants of fennel, angelica and lovage are handsome features in their own right. So many are colourful when in flower. All in all, a salad lover's garden should be brimming with herbs.

Here are brief descriptions and cultural information for some of the most useful salad herbs, listed in alphabetical order by common name. For more detailed cultural information, see Further reading p. 274.

Angelica *Angelica archangelica*

A beautiful, vigorous biennial, growing up to 3m/10ft high when flowering, angelica is one of the first herbs to reappear in spring. The typical angelica flavour is found in the leaves, stems and seeds. All can be used in salads when young.

Angelica requires fairly rich, moist soil and needs plenty of space. Sow fresh seed *in situ* in autumn, thinning the following spring to at least 1m/3ft apart; very young seedlings can be transplanted. Angelica dies after flowering in its second season, but in suitable sites perpetuates itself with self-sown seedlings.

Basil *Ocimum* spp.

The basils are wonderfully aromatic tender annuals, used in many salad dishes but above all associated with tomatoes. They are in the main clove-flavoured. There are many varieties. Lettuce-leaved (Neapolitan) is the largest, growing up to 45cm/18in high with huge leaves; common, sweet or Genovese basil has medium-sized leaves; bush basil is a smaller plant with smaller leaves again, while the various forms of 'Greek', fine-leaved or miniature basil have tiny, strongly flavoured leaves and are exceptionally compact and low-growing. There are red-leaved forms, and many varieties with distinct flavours including cinnamon, anise, lemon and lime – the last two being outstanding.

Basils cannot stand frost or cold conditions. In cool temperate climates, grow them in a very sheltered, warm, well-drained site or under cover. Sow indoors in late spring, planting outdoors or under cover about 12cm/5in apart, depending on variety. To prolong the season, make a second sowing in early to mid-summer of bush or compact basil, potted into 10–12cm/4–5in pots. Bring indoors in early autumn. They may provide fresh leaf for several months.

Chervil *Anthriscus cerefolium*

Chervil is a fast-growing, hardy annual or biennial, about 25cm/10in high before seeding. The delicate leaves have a refreshing aniseed flavour, and can be chopped like parsley into many salad dishes. A great asset in temperate climates is that it remains green in winter.

Chervil is not fussy about soil. For summer supplies, sow *in situ* in spring in a slightly shaded situation, thinning to 10cm/4in apart. Keep the plants well watered. For autumn to early spring supplies, sow *in situ* in late summer, either outside or under cover for good-quality winter plants; or sow in modules and transplant under cover. Chervil can be cut several times before it runs to seed; if left to flower, it usefully seeds itself.

Coriander (cilantro, Chinese parsley) *Coriandrum sativum*

Coriander is an annual, 12cm/5in high in its leafy stage and over 45cm/18in high when seeding. The leaves, with their musty curry flavour, make a unique contribution to salad dishes, as do the flowers. It is also grown for the strong-flavoured seeds, commonly used in curries. Coriander grows best in cool conditions, in light soil with plenty of water throughout growth. It tolerates light frost, and stands well in winter under cover.

In temperate climates, it can be sown throughout the growing season, though it may run to seed rapidly in hot weather. Sow in succession outdoors from early spring to early autumn, *in situ*, either fairly densely to cut as cut-and-come-again seedlings or thinning to 15cm/6in apart for larger plants; or multi-sow several seeds per module, planting out

15cm/6in apart. The hard outer seed coat sometimes prevents germination: if so, crack the 'pods' gently with a rolling pin.

Earlier and later sowings can be made under cover, and early sowings can be grown to maturity under fleece. Cut leaves at any stage up to about 12cm/5in high. The flavour deteriorates once the plants start running to seed. Older varieties of coriander, such as 'Santo' and 'Leisure' are being joined by improved, larger leaved, slower bolting varieties such as 'Cadiz', 'Calypso' and 'Cruiser'. If you specifically want the seed, rather than leaf, for culinary use, leave a few plants to seed relatively early in the season, so they have time to ripen and dry. Some large seeded varieties, such as 'Moroccan', were traditionally used for coriander seed, but are no longer easily available. Coriander leaf can be frozen but does not dry well.

Dill *Anethum graveolens*

This feathery annual is grown for the seeds and seedheads, which are widely used in pickling cucumbers, and for the delicately flavoured leaves, easily chopped into salads The mature plant can be up to about 80cm/32in high.

Grow dill leaf like coriander (see opposite) using improved varieties such as 'Domino' and 'Dukat' where available. The problem with dill is its tendency to run to seed rapidly. Nor does it thrive in cold, wet conditions. So in cool climates the solution lies in sowing little and often, for example a small patch, or in a pot, in a greenhouse or polytunnel.

When grown as cut-and-come again seedlings, they will normally regenerate at least once after cutting.

For seed heads, and hence seeds for

culinary use, sow in early summer by broadcasting, or in rows 23cm/9in apart, thinning to about 15cm/6in apart.

Dill is very pretty at every stage from seedlings to seeding. Plants left in late summer will often reseed themselves.

Fennel *Foeniculum vulgare*

The herb fennel (unlike Florence fennel, p. 92) is a hardy perennial, growing up to 1½m/5ft high. The common green form has beautiful gossamer leaves, with a light aniseed flavour; the stunning bronze fennel (*F. v.* 'Purpureum') is milder-flavoured. The chopped leaves and peeled young stalks can be used in salads, as can the seeds.

Fennel tolerates most well-drained soils. Sow in spring *in situ* or in modules for transplanting, spacing plants 45cm/18in apart. Plants can also be propagated by dividing up clumps in spring. Plants tend to run to seed in mid-summer, but for a constant supply keep them trimmed back to about 30cm/12in high and remove flower spikes. Bronze fennel in particular can self-seed prolifically and become invasive – but deserves a place in every decorative potager. Renew plants when they lose their vigour.

Hyssop *Hyssopus officinalis*

Hyssop is a short-lived, shrubby, hardy perennial, about 45cm/18in high: it can be kept trimmed to make a neat, low hedge. The shiny little leaves have a strong, savory-like flavour, and remain green late into winter. Use the young leaves sparingly in salad: they combine well with cucumber and onions. The beautiful blue, pink or white flower spikes attract bees and butterflies.

Propagate hyssop by taking softwood cuttings from a mature clump in spring, or sow indoors in spring and early summer, eventually planting seedlings about 30cm/12in apart. Seeds need light to germinate, so should be sown on the surface covered lightly with perlite or vermiculite. Pinch back shoot tips to keep plants bushy, and prune back hard in spring. Plants need renewing every three or four years.

Lemon balm *Melissa officinalis*

This easily grown hardy perennial forms clumps up to 60cm/24in tall. Delightful lemon-scented leaves can be chopped into salad dishes. Lemon balm tolerates a wide range of soil and situations, and is an excellent ground-cover plant. Propagate by taking a rooted piece from an old plant; or sow seed indoors in spring, planting 60cm/24in apart. Cut plants back hard in the autumn. There are pretty variegated and golden forms.

Lovage *Levisticum officinale*

This handsome hardy perennial grows up to 2½m/8ft tall, and is one of the first to emerge each spring. The glossy leaves have a strong but superb celery flavour. Rub them into a salad bowl, or chop them sparingly into salads. The leaf stalks can be blanched like celery.

Lovage thrives in rich, moist soil and tolerates light shade. Sow fresh seed indoors in spring or autumn, eventually planting at least 60cm/2ft apart. (One plant is enough for most households.) Alternatively, divide an old clump in spring, replanting pieces of root with active shoots. Lovage often seeds itself, and young seedlings can be transplanted.

Marjoram and origanum *Origanum* spp.

There are many forms and varieties (and much confusion over naming) of these perennial Mediterranean herbs with gentle, aromatic flavours. Several compact forms are only 15cm/6in high, but taller varieties grow up to 45cm/18in. Gold-leaved, gold-tipped and variegated varieties may be less flavoured, but they are very decorative in salad dishes and in the garden. My favourites for salads are the half-hardy sweet or knotted marjoram (*O. majorana*) with its lovely soft leaves; gold marjoram (*O. vulgare* 'Aureum'); the hardy winter marjoram (*O. heracleoticum*) (there is some confusion over the name), which remains green in temperate winters, and the well-flavoured pot marjoram (*O. vulgare* or *O. onites*).

Marjorams grow best in well-drained, reasonably fertile soil in full sun, though golden-leaved varieties, which tend to get scorched in hot weather, can be grown in light shade. Some varieties, including sweet marjoram, can be raised from seed, sown indoors in spring and eventually planted 12cm/5in apart. Many others are propagated by softwood cuttings taken in spring, or by dividing established clumps. It is often possible to pot up plants for use indoors in winter. On the whole marjorams dry well.

Mint *Mentha* spp.

The majority of the many hardy perennial mints can be used, albeit sparingly, in salad dishes, imparting that special 'minty' flavour. My own favourites for flavour are apple mint (*M. suaveolens*), spearmint (*M. spicata*) and raripila or pea mint (*M. rubra* var. *raripila*). For their decorative quality, I grow the cream and green

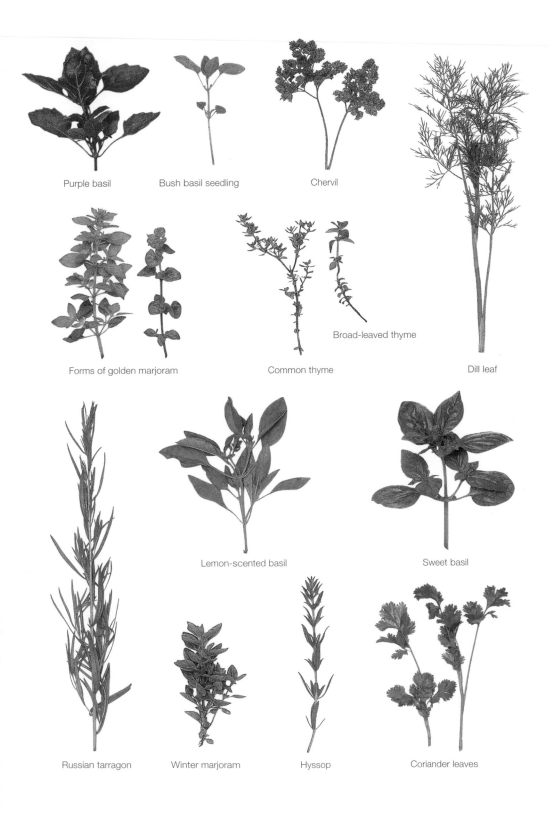

Purple basil

Bush basil seedling

Chervil

Forms of golden marjoram

Common thyme

Broad-leaved thyme

Dill leaf

Lemon-scented basil

Sweet basil

Russian tarragon

Winter marjoram

Hyssop

Coriander leaves

pineapple mint (*M. suaveolens* 'Variegata') and the variegated, gold and green Scotch or ginger mint (*Mentha* x *gracilis*). Each mint has its own subtly different flavour: yours to discover!

Most mints spread rapidly in moist, fertile soil and tolerate light shade. The easiest way to propagate is to lift and divide old plants in spring or autumn. Very few are raised satisfactorily from seed. Replant small pieces of root 5cm/2in long, laid horizontally 5cm/2in deep, 23cm/9in apart; or plant shoots with attached roots. Replant mints every few years in a fresh site if they are losing vigour. Plants die back in winter. In autumn, transplant a few into a greenhouse, or into pots or boxes: they will start into growth early in spring. Most mints retain their flavour well when dried.

Mitsuba (Japanese parsley, Japanese honewort) *Cryptotaenia japonica*

This hardy, evergreen perennial is a woodland plant, growing about 30cm/12in high. It has long leaf stalks and pale leaves divided into three leaflets, not unlike flat parsley in appearance. Stems and leaves are used raw in salads and have a delicate flavour, encompassing that of parsley, celery and angelica. The seeds can be sprouted. It does best in moist, lightly shaded situations. In the West it is mainly grown as single plants, often edging shaded borders. In its native Japan it is also grown densely, often in polytunnels, to get fine, virtually blanched, very tender stems.

Although perennial, mitsuba is best grown as an annual. Sow *in situ* from late spring to early autumn (optimum soil temperature is about 25°C/77°F), making successive sowings for a continuous supply. Thin plants to 15cm/6in apart. They will be ready for use within about two months. Alternatively, plant under cover in early autumn for use during winter. Plants left in the ground may seed themselves for use the following year.

Parsley *Petroselinum crispum*

Parsley is a biennial, growing 10–45cm/4–18in high. Its characteristically flavoured leaves are widely used in cooking and as a garnish. There are two types: curly, and plain or broad-leaved, of which 'French' and 'Giant Italian' are typical varieties. Curly parsley is more decorative, but the plain-leaved varieties are more vigorous, seem to be hardier and are more easily grown. Most chefs consider them better-flavoured.

Parsley needs moist conditions and fertile soil. For a continuous supply, sow in spring for summer use, and in summer for autumn-to-spring supplies. Sow *in situ* or in modules for transplanting when seedlings are still young. Failures with parsley stem from it being slow to germinate. Once sown, take care to keep the soil moist until seedlings appear. Thin or plant 23cm/9in apart. Parsley normally dies back in winter after moderate frost. Keep a few plants cloched or plant in a greenhouse in late summer/early autumn for winter-to-spring supplies. Cut off flowering heads to prolong the plant's useful life. If left, however, they often self-seed.

Sage *Salvia officinalis*

The sages are moderately hardy, evergreen perennials, growing 30–60cm/12–24in high. The large, soft, subdued grey-green leaves of common broad-leaved and narrow-leaved sage (*S. lavandulifolia*) are strongly flavoured. Only slightly less so but very decorative are gold sage (*S. o.* 'Icterina'), the less hardy, tricolor sage (*S. o.*

'Tricolor') with pink, purple and white leaves, and the red or purple sage (*S. o. Purpurascens* Group), frequently mentioned in traditional salad lore. See also Edible flowers p. 156).

Sages need well-drained, light soil and a sunny, sheltered position. For common sage, sow seed indoors in spring, planting out 30cm/12in apart the following spring. With other varieties, propagate from heel cuttings taken in early summer. To keep plants bushy, prune lightly after flowering in late summer and harder in spring. Sage flowers are edible, the beautiful red flowers of the tender pineapple sage (*S. elegans*) being deliciously sweet in salads.

Summer and winter savory *Satureja hortensis* and *S. montana*

Summer savory is a bushy annual that grows up to 30cm/12in high with fairly soft leaves, while winter savory is a more compact, hardy, semi-evergreen perennial, with narrow, tougher leaves. Both are almost spicy in flavour, and are said to enhance other flavours in cooking. Use them sparingly in salad dishes.

Savories need a sunny position and well-drained, reasonably fertile soil. Sow in spring indoors, but do not cover the seeds, as they need light to germinate. Plant 15cm/6in apart. Winter savory can also be propagated from softwood cuttings taken in spring. In late summer, pot up a winter savory plant for winter use indoors: they are very pretty when they burst into renewed growth in spring.

Sweet cicely *Myrrhis odorata*

Sweet cicely is an attractive, hardy perennial, often growing 1½m/5ft high; its leaves resemble chervil and have a sweet, aniseed flavour.

They are a delight chopped into salad or used whole as garnish, but pick them just before you need them, as they wilt almost instantly. The substantial roots can be boiled and sliced, and the immature seeds have a strong aniseed flavour, both a great contribution to salads. Sweet cicely starts into growth early in the year, dying back late, so has a long season of usefulness. It is sometimes found in the wild.

It grows best in rich, moist soil in light shade. Sow fresh seed outdoors in autumn, thinning to 8cm/3in apart, and plant in a permanent position the following autumn 60cm/24in apart. Or sow in modules, keeping them outside during winter. Plants can also be propagated by dividing roots carefully in spring and autumn. Replace plants only if they are losing vigour.

French and Russian tarragon *Artemisia dracunculus* and *A. d. dracunculoides*

French tarragon is a narrow-leaved, moderately hardy perennial, growing about 1m/3ft high, while Russian tarragon is larger, coarser and much hardier. The aromatic leaves of both have a distinct flavour, but the Russian is widely believed to be less strong. It is adequate for salad dishes, but French tarragon is preferable for flavouring vinegar and in cooking.

Grow tarragon in a well-drained, sheltered position, preferably on light soil. Russian tarragon can be raised from seed sown indoors in spring, but French tarragon rarely sets seed, so propagate it by dividing old plants or from root cuttings. Plant 60cm/24in apart. In cold areas, cover French tarragon roots with straw in winter. Plants decline after a few years and should be replaced.

Thyme *Thymus* spp.

The culinary thymes are pretty, creeping and low-growing herbs, sun-loving and mostly hardy perennials. Their tiny leaves can be added to salads, dressings and vinegars. The following are varieties I have found rewarding to grow for salads: the traditionally-flavoured common and large-leaved thymes (*T. vulgaris* and *T. pulegioides*); lemon-scented thyme (*T. citriodorus*); *T.* 'Fragrantissimus', which has an orange scent; and caraway thyme (*T. herba-barona*).

Grow thyme in a sunny spot on well-drained, but not particularly rich soil. Thymes thrive in dry conditions and do well in containers. Common thyme can be raised from seed sown in spring indoors, on the surface covered with perlite or vermiculite. The seed is tiny, so can be mixed with sand to make sowing easier. Space plants 30cm/12in apart. Propagate other varieties by dividing established plants in spring or autumn, or taking softwood cuttings in spring or summer. Trim back plants after flowering. Renew them every three years or so once they become straggly. They can be potted up for winter use indoors.

Flowers

Using edible flowers in cooking and salads is an ancient, universal tradition. They are often added just for their colour and fragrance, but some – nasturtiums, day lilies and anise hyssop, for example – have real flavour. In the past flowers were collected from the wild, but today the need to preserve wild species is paramount, so pick only where they are abundant and it is not illegal. Or grow your own.

Gather flowers early in the day, when the dew has just dried on them. Pick or cut them with scissors; handle them gently and carry them in a flat basket to avoid bruising.

Where flowers are invaded by insects (such as pollen beetle), lay them aside so the insects can creep away! If essential, wash flowers gently, lightly patting them dry with paper towelling. Keep them in a closed bag in a refrigerator until needed. Refresh them by dipping in ice-cold water just before use.

It is mainly petals that are used in salads. With daisy-like flowers, pull them gently off the centre. Small, soft flowers can be used whole, but large flowers may have rough, hard or strongly flavoured parts. Taste cautiously and remove these parts if necessary. Sprinkle flowers or petals over the salad at the last moment, after dressing, as dressings discolour them and make them soggy. Use either one or two types, or a confetti mixture, being careful not to overwhelm the salad. Charm lies in subtlety.

Very many cultivated and wild plants have edible flowers but there is only space for brief notes on a few of them. Be sure to identify plants correctly before eating the flowers; some common garden flowers – aquilegia, cyclamen, daffodils, delphiniums to name a few – can be toxic. (For identification and cultivation, see Further reading p. 274.) Plants are listed here under common names but alphabetically by Latin names.

Anise hyssop *Agastache foeniculum*

A hardy perennial about 60cm/24in high. The tiny flowers in the flower spikes have an almost peppermint flavour. The young leaves are edible raw. (Advisable to avoid when pregnant.)

Hollyhock *Alcea rosea*

These tall, cottage garden plants have beautiful red, yellow, rose and creamy flowers. Petals and cooked buds are used in salads. They are perennial but best grown as biennials to avoid infection with rust.

Blue flowored borage

Anchusa *Anchusa azurea*

A perennial growing 120cm/48in tall with bright, gentian-blue flowers which look superb mixed with red rose petals in a salad. After flowering in early summer cut back the main stem to encourage secondary shoots to prolong the flowering season.

Bellis daisy *Bellis perennis*

The many cultivated rose-, red- and white-flowered forms of the little white lawn or English daisy are all edible. Use the daintier, small-flowered varieties whole, but with the larger, double varieties, use only the petals. Treat them as biennials, sowing in autumn and spring for almost year-round flowers. Lawn daisies close quickly so pick just before use. (Daisy family flowers should be avoided by sufferers from hayfever, asthma or severe allergies.)

Borage *Borago officinalis*

This self-seeding annual grows about 120cm/48in high, typically a haze of sky blue flowers all summer though there is a less common, white-flowered form. The flowers are delightfully sweet, but remove the hairy sepals behind the petals before eating them. The flowers look wonderful frozen into ice cubes for drinks. We leave a few plants to seed in our polytunnel to give us early spring flowers. Finely chopped young leaves are edible raw in salads. (Avoid when pregnant or breastfeeding.)

Pot marigold *Calendula officinalis*

The petals of these vibrantly coloured annuals were traditionally used for seasoning and colouring cakes, cooked dishes and salads. Today's varieties are all shades of orange, yellow, bronze, pink and brown,

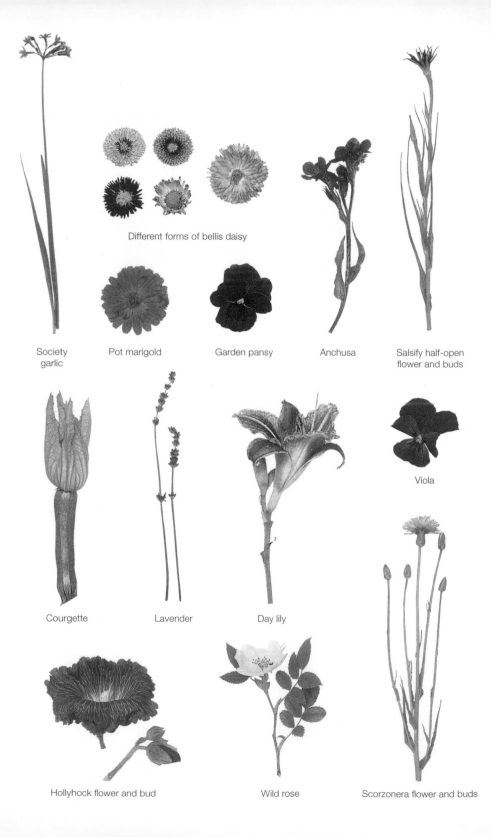

Different forms of bellis daisy

Society
garlic

Pot marigold

Garden pansy

Anchusa

Salsify half-open
flower and buds

Courgette

Lavender

Day lily

Viola

Hollyhock flower and bud

Wild rose

Scorzonera flower and buds

in single- and double-flowered forms. If regularly dead-headed they flower from early spring until the first frost. They often self-seed. Flowers can be dried for winter use, and in the past were pickled.

Chicory *Cichorium intybus*

Any cultivated or wild chicory plant left to seed in spring produces huge spires of light blue, occasionally pink, flowers. Use the petals or whole flowers in salads: they have a slightly bitter but distinct 'chicory' taste. The flowers close and fade rapidly, often by midday, but try picking early and keeping in a refrigerator. They can be pickled: the colour is lost but a faint flavour remains. (For cultivation, see Chicory p. 27.)

Courgettes, marrows, squashes, pumpkins *Cucurbita* spp.

The buttery yellow flowers of these and many oriental gourds have a creamy flavour and crisp texture. They can be cooked, but can also be used raw, whole or sliced, in salads. Pick the small male flowers once fruits are setting (leave a few for pollination) and any spare female flowers, identified by the tiny bump below the petals.

Carnations, pinks, sweet William *Dianthus* spp.

The raw flowers of these popular garden plants have varying degrees of fragrance and flavour, from mild to musky to a strong scent of cloves. The white heel at the base of the petals can be bitter and is best removed.

Garland chrysanthemum *Glebionis coronarium*

While various chrysanthemum flowers have been used for cooking in the past, the petals were often bitter unless given special treatment. This type, grown for its edible leaves, has mild-flavoured flowers which make a beautiful garnish. Only use the petals, discarding the bitter flower centre. For cultivation see p. 51. In China and Japan special varieties of the tender, perennial florist chrysanthemum are cultivated for culinary purposes.

Sunflower *Helianthus annuum*

The flower petals of this easily grown, highly popular annual are edible raw in salad and have a mild flavour, sometimes described as 'nutty'. The green buds can be blanched and eaten tossed in garlic butter.

Lavender *Lavandula* spp.

In the past salads were served on beds of lettuce and lavender sprigs but the flowers are strongly flavoured and should be used sparingly. There are blue-, purple-, pink- and white-flowered varieties.

Day lily *Hemerocallis* spp.

The flavour of raw day lily flowers varies widely. American writer Cathy Barash (see Further reading) believes the darker colours tend towards bitterness, while pale yellows and oranges are sweeter. My light orange variety (probably *H. citrina*), from a Chinese research station, has a superb, vanilla flavour

159

and crisp texture. Taste before use – and only eat in moderation! Dried day lily flowers are widely used in Chinese cooking.

Sweet bergamot (bee balm, Oswego tea) *Monarda didyma*

The colourful flowers of these perennials have distinct 'mint with hints of lemon' flavours. I love them mixed with borage in salads. Some F1 hybrid varieties are reputedly bitter. Dried flowers are used for a delicately flavoured tea.

February orchid *Orychophragmus violaceus*

The fabulous lilac flowers are stunning in winter and spring salads. For cultivation see p. 47.

Jacob's ladder *Polemonium caeruleum*

The sweetly scented flowers of the many species and varieties of these pretty hardy perennials are pleasantly flavoured and colourful in salads.

Primrose *Primula vulgaris* and Cowslip *P. veris*

In the past these mild-flavoured flowers were collected from the wild in spring. Today, they, and the many colourful hybrids, can be cultivated for salads. Primula flowers can be crystallised, and cowslip flowers were traditionally pickled.

Rose *Rosa* spp.

Most rose petals can be used in salads, but fragrant roses, especially the classic old roses – *R. rugosa*, the Apothecary rose *R. gallica*, and the Damask rose *R. damascena* – have the most flavour. Always try petals before using; some have a bitter aftertaste, often found in the white part at the base of petals.

Sage *Salvia* spp.

The blue, white or pink flowers of culinary sage (*S. officinalis*) have a pleasant subdued sage flavour, are fairly firm and stand well in salads. The colourful bracts of clary sage (*S. sclarea*) and painted sage (*S. horminum*) have a faint mint flavour. The sweet, scarlet flowers of pineapple sage (*S. elegans*) really do have a hint of pineapple in them. For cultivation, see p. 154.

Painted sage

Scorzonera *Scorzonera hispanica* and Salsify *Tragopogon porrifolius*

The plump flower buds are used cooked and cooled, and the more faintly flavoured petals – yellow in scorzonera, lilac in salsify – are strewn on salads. The flowers may open only briefly in the morning sunshine, then close firmly. If the petals are wanted later in the day try picking when open and keeping them in a closed bag in a refrigerator until needed.

Tagetes (Signet marigold) *Tagetes tenuifolia*

The sparkling little flowers of the 'Orange Gem', 'Tangerine Gem' and 'Lemon Gem' varieties have fruity, fragrant flavours. They are easily grown tender annuals with a long flowering season, making neat edgings to flower and vegetable beds.

Nasturtium *Tropaeolum majus*

These easily grown annuals, with trailing and dwarf forms, are of ancient use in salads. Buds and flowers are piquant, the leaves are peppery and seeds are pickled as capers. For salads grow the dainty, variegated-leaved *T.m.* Alaska series: their vibrantly coloured flowers retain a 'spur', which I think keeps them fresh longer once picked than modern spurless varieties. Also pretty is the red-leaved *T.m.* Empress of India'. Tuberous-rooted nasturtium (mashua), *T. tuberosum*, has edible flowers. Nasturtiums often reseed profusely.

Society garlic *Tulbaghia violacea*

This moderately frost-tolerant perennial has beautiful, fragrant, usually lilac flowers, with a mild garlic flavour. The leaves also are garlic-flavoured. For cultivation see Chinese chives p. 126 (which also has edible flowers).

Broad bean *Vicia faba*

The flowers are decorative and well flavoured. For cultivation see p. 115.

Pansy and violas *Viola* spp., Sweet violet *V. odorata*

All supply colour and texture, rather than flavour, to salads though in the past violet flowers were eaten with lettuce and onions! The tiny heartsease flowers, *V. tricolor*, are delightfully delicate. Winter-flowering pansies meet a need for colour in winter salads.

Yucca *Yucca* spp.

The white flowers of these handsome, moderately hardy perennials have a delicious sweet flavour and crunchy texture – a great addition, raw, in salads.

Nasturtiums with plain, red and variegated leaves

Wild plants and weeds

Our cultivated vegetables have all evolved from wild plants, so it is not surprising that the countryside is still a treasure trove of edible plants. Over the centuries some of these wild plants have invaded arable fields and gardens, becoming weeds. In this less competitive environment they grow lushly, providing tender pickings for salads. Many have wonderfully lively flavours that truly enrich a salad. They are probably best worked into mixed salads in small quantities, rather than made into a salad composed entirely of wild plants.

The golden rule with weeds and wild plants is to pick the leaves small and young, as most become tough as they mature. Peasant communities all over the world scour fields and mountains in early spring for those very first leaves. Wild plants have always been valued for their medicinal and 'health-giving' properties; we now know that many are rich in vitamins and minerals.

It is absolutely essential to identify wild plants accurately, as a few are easily confused with poisonous species. Identify them with a good botanical text or, if you have no botanical knowledge, be guided initially by an expert. You will soon get to know the common garden weeds and wild plants in your area. Never go just by a picture in a book. Two people I met did so, confused ground elder with dog's mercury, and found themselves in hospital as a result.

Seed of some wild plants is now widely available, so it is possible to grow your own. There is only space here for brief notes on a few of the many edible wild plants. They are listed by common name, in the alphabetical order of their Latin names as the common names are often misleading. For identification, see Further reading p. 274. There are few specialist seed suppliers, some wild plants and weeds can be found in herb and general seed catalogues.

Yarrow (Milfoil) *Achillea millefolium*
Very common weed, remaining green much of the year. Strongly flavoured.

Ground elder *Aegopodium podagraria*
Pernicious weed with a delightful angelica flavour. Do not confuse it with the similar but poisonous dog's mercury (*Mercurialis perennis*). In trying to eradicate ground elder Peter Harper, of the Centre for Alternative Technology, discovered that by cutting it back, then covering with 15cm/6in of sawdust or sand, the first leaves to grow through could be steamed for salad, and the blanched shoots below could be eaten raw. A second, weaker crop would follow.

Garlic mustard (Jack-by-the-hedge) *Alliaria petiolata*
Common hedgerow weed with an appealing, faint garlic flavour.

Wild garlic (Ramsons) *Allium ursinum* and *A.* spp.
The leaves have a strong garlic flavour. Leaves, stems, bulbs and flowers of many wild alliums

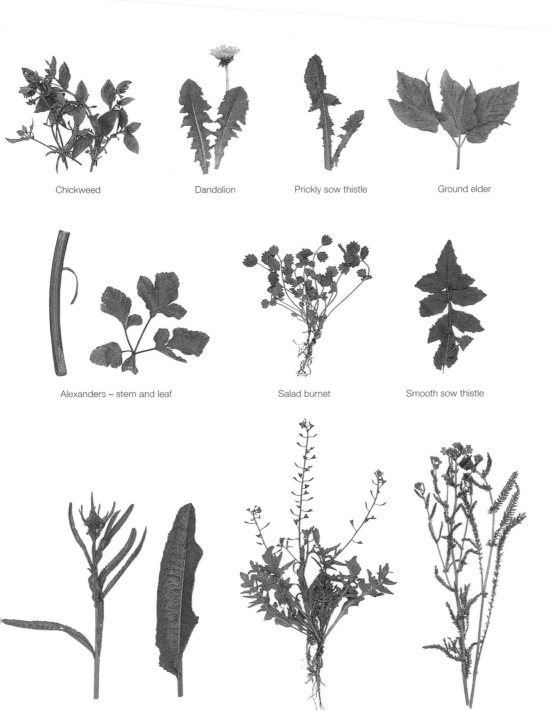

Chickweed

Dandelion

Prickly sow thistle

Ground elder

Alexanders – stem and leaf

Salad burnet

Smooth sow thistle

Horseradish

Shepherd's purse

Yarrow

have a mild to strong garlic flavour, including crow garlic (*A. vineale*), keeled garlic (*A. carinatum*) and sand leek (*A. scorodoprasum*).

Wild celery (Smallage) *Apium graveolens*

Grows in damp places. Chop leaves and young stems into salads. Do not confuse it with poisonous hemlock (*Conium maculatum*) or water dropwort (*Oenanthe crocata*).

Burdock *Arctium lappa* and Lesser burdock *A. minus*

Rampant plants, used all over the world cooked and raw. For salads, pick the leafy stems of young shoots in spring, strip off the peel and cut into 5cm/2in pieces. Intriguing flavour.

Horseradish *Armoracia rusticana*

For cultivation, see p. 144.

Shepherd's purse *Capsella bursa-pastoris*

Very common weed, green much of the year. Basal leaf rosettes and stem leaves are excellent raw; their distinctive flavour is due to sulphur. Cultivated in China for use raw and cooked. Said to be richer in vitamin C than oranges.

Hairy bitter cress *Cardamine hirsuta*

Very hardy, ubiquitous little weed appearing in autumn and spring. Cut the tiny, cress-flavoured leaves for salads. Seed pods explode when touched: thin out seedlings to get plants of a reasonable size. Cover them with cloches in autumn to increase their size and tenderness.

Lady's smock (Cuckoo flower) *Cardamine pratensis*

Plant of damp meadows; remains green late in winter. The leaves have a watercress spiciness and are excellent in salads.

Red valerian *Centranthus ruber*

Red-and white-flowered forms, found on dry banks and walls; often cultivated in gardens. Use young leaves and flowers.

Fat hen (Lamb's quarters) *Chenopodium album*

Very common arable weed, often found near manure heaps. It has a spinach-like flavour, and is excellent cooked like spinach or raw. American Indians made the seeds into cakes and gruel.

Ox-eye daisy (Marguerite) *Chrysanthemum leucanthemum*

The young leaves and flowers are used in salads in Italy.

Golden saxifrage *Chrysosplenium oppositifolium*

The *cresson des roches* of the Vosges mountains. Found in wet places.

Fat hen

Oyster plant *Mertensia maritima*
Pretty, seaside perennial. The fleshy leaves
are reputedly oyster-flavoured and excellent
in salads.

Watercress *Nasturtium officinale*
(Confusingly also called brooklime, the
common name for *Veronica beccabunga*, a
bitter but edible waterside plant.) Grows in
running water: never pick from stagnant,
contaminated or pasture water because
of the risk of liver fluke infection. It is
preferable to cultivate it (see p. 55). Older
leaves are more flavoured than young.

Evening primrose spp. *Oenothera biennis, O. erythrosepala*
The young leaves can be eaten raw; the roots,
lifted before the plants flower, can be eaten
after cooking.

Marsh thistle *Cirsium palustre*
A plant of damp places. Use young shoots and
the stalks after removing prickles and peeling.

Rock samphire *Crithmum maritimum*
Found on cliffs and shingle. Use the fleshy
leaves and stems cooked or pickled for salads.

Wood sorrel (Alleluia) *Oxalis acetosella*
The delicate, folded, clover-like leaves are
among the first to appear in woods in spring.
They have a sharp sorrel flavour.

Sea purslane *Halimione portulacoides*
Succulent grey-leaved plant of salt marshes.
Wash off mud carefully. The leaves can be
used fresh or pickled.

Field poppy *Papaver rhoeas*
Common red-flowered poppy. The leaves
are eaten in the Mediterranean, and the
seeds used to decorate buns. Don't confuse
it with the toxic red-horned poppy (*Glaucium
corniculatum*).

Woad *Isatis tinctoria*
The young leaves of this beautiful, easily
cultivated plant are pleasant in salads.

Red-veined sorrel

Redshank (Red leg) *Polygonum persicaria* and *Bistort P. bistort*

The leaves of redshank, a common arable weed, are used cooked or raw. Do not confuse it with the acrid water pepper (*Polygonum hydropiper*). The late Robert Hart of 'forest garden' fame used the young shoots and leaves of bistort in salads.

Common wintergreen *Pyrola minor*

Berried evergreen, found in woods, moors, rocky ledges and sand dunes. The young leaves are used in salads in North America.

Red-veined sorrel *Rumex sanguineus* var. *sanguineus*

Has elegantly colourful but coarse-textured leaves. Soften them by briefly blanching in hot water. Easily cultivated, but potentially invasive.

Glasswort (marsh or sea samphire) *Salicornia europaea*

Primitive-looking plant of salt marshes and shingle beaches. Gather narrow, succulent young leaves in summer. Excellent raw or pickled.

Salad burnet *Sanguisorba officinalis*

A low-growing, very hardy perennial of the chalklands. The decorative, lacy leaves have a faint cucumber taste and remain green for much of winter. Use the youngest leaves raw

Buck's horn plantain (Herba stella, Minutina) *Plantago coronopus*

A pretty perennial. The tough but tasty leaves are at their best in spring and autumn, remaining green well into winter. Blanch briefly in hot water to tenderize. Easily cultivated; sow in spring to late summer for an outdoor crop; sow early autumn under cover for a winter crop. Either grow single plants thinned or spaced 12cm/5in apart, or grow as cut-and-come-again seedlings. Cutting back flowers when they develop encourages further young leaves, but if flowers are left, it readily self-seeds.

in salads, but blanch tougher, older leaves in hot water. It is easily cultivated. Sow in spring, thinning to 10cm/4in apart. Remove flower stems.

Reflexed stonecrop *Sedum reflexum*

Succulent perennial found wild on walls and rocks. Use of the leaves of this and other sedums in salads is ancient. Easily cultivated in dry places.

Milk or Holy thistle *Silybum marianum*

Striking plant with beautiful white-veined foliage. Use young leaves and peeled, chopped stems raw, roots raw or cooked. Easily cultivated.

Alexanders *Smyrnium olusatrum*

Tall, striking plant, common in coastal areas. Use of buds, young leaves, stems and spicy seeds (a pepper substitute) in salads is ancient. The stems used to be blanched. Not to be confused with poisonous hemlock and water dropwort found in similar places. (See Wild celery p. 164)

Perennial sow thistle *Sonchus arvensis*, Prickly sow thistle *S. asper* and Smooth sow thistle *S. oleraceus*

Weeds found commonly on arable land. Pleasant taste, but trim off bristly parts.

Chickweed *Stellaria media*

Very common garden weed, growing almost all year round. Use refreshingly tasty seedlings or larger plants if still succulent. (They are often best if grown in the shade.) Cut with scissors and leave to regrow.

Dandelion *Taraxacum officinale*

For cultivation, see p. 58.

Field penny cress *Thlaspi arvense*

Very common weed with delicious, spicy leaves.

Field penny cress

garden practicalities

—

The pleasures and challenges of gardening lie in mastering the practicalities – everything from making best use of the site and building up its fertility to the basic skills of sowing and planting, to the many ways of protecting plants from the elements and pests, and lastly to the special techniques associated with salad growing – cut-and-come-again, blanching and seed sprouting.

Soil and site

Most salad plants are eaten raw, so it goes without saying that they must be succulent and tender. If they have to struggle for existence in poor soil, contend with alternating periods of drought and waterlogging, or be buffeted by cold and searing winds, they will inevitably become coarse and toughened. So in planning the vegetable garden four aspects hold the keys to success: fertile soil, good drainage, adequate water supplies and shelter.

The ideal site, as every gardening book tells you, is open, i.e. not overshadowed by buildings or overhung by trees, reasonably sheltered in that it is protected from strong winds, and reasonably flat. So where there is a choice, avoid exposed sites, frost pockets, steep slopes and deeply shaded situations. In practice one normally has little choice about the site. If it has shortcomings, it is a question of working around them and ameliorating them. If, for example, you are faced with a very steep sloping site, consider terracing at least part of it for a vegetable garden.

Soil

Vegetables can be grown on a wide range of soils, the 'perfect' soil being a medium loam, which generally means a well-drained mixture of soil types with a good level of organic matter in it. In practice, soils range from the extremes of very light sands to heavy clays.

Very light soil, being well drained, warms up rapidly in spring and is therefore excellent for early salad crops. On the other hand, its nutrients (plant foods) are washed out rapidly and in dry weather it is liable to suffer from drought. Clay soil, at the other extreme, is a cold, ill-drained soil in winter and may become baked hard in summer, but it is a rich storehouse of plant foods and can be very fertile once it has been worked and improved. Chalk soils tend to be light, warm and easily drained, but have varying levels of fertility.

For the practicalities of creating a fertile soil, see pp. 179–189. In essence, almost all soil types (an exception is very peaty soils) are improved by constantly working in 'organic matter', which is converted into humus, largely through the activity of earthworms. A key feature of organic matter is that it provides food for earthworms. They not only release the nutrients in the organic matter, but also in their burrowing and casting make 'cemented' burrows, which create vital drainage and aeration channels in the soil.

The main source of organic matter for gardeners is homemade compost and manure. The implication for planning is that all this heavy material has to be transported around the garden, in wheelbarrows or by some other means. The more accessible the garden and individual beds, the easier this will be.

Drainage

Good drainage is essential in vegetable growing. While a few salad plants, such as celery, Florence fennel and Chinese cabbage, originated in marshlands and can stand fairly wet conditions, for most waterlogged soil is the kiss of death.

A drainage problem is usually obvious. Classic signs are water lying on the surface of the soil for several days after heavy rain, or encountering water when digging down to, say, 30cm/12in. Absence of earthworms and soil that is greyish, bluish, blackish or mottled rather than brown are other indications of poor drainage.

Poor drainage can be improved, over several years, simply by digging in large quantities of bulky organic matter. This has been borne out by my own experience. When we first moved to our Suffolk garden the soil was sticky yellow clay and parts of the garden were waterlogged every winter. Constantly working in spent mushroom compost improved it beyond measure. Where the problem is more persistent it may be necessary to make drains to remove the excess water. The simplest form is a trench drain (see illustration below).

Make trench drains across the lower end of a slope, or on either side of a level site. You can even incorporate them into a path, meandering through the garden. Dig the trench about 30cm/12in wide and 60–90cm/2–3ft deep. Then fill the lower third with rubble, broken bricks are ideal, before replacing the soil. Where there is a very serious drainage problem clay or plastic drainage pipes can be laid in the trench which can be part of a network of drains emptying into an outlet such as a ditch, artificial soakaway or sump. Seek expert help on the type of drains to use, their layout, depth and spacing, and the gradient at which to lay them. A practical alternative to overcoming a drainage problem is to grow in raised beds (see p. 175).

Occasionally, poor drainage is caused by an underlying hard pan. This is an extremely compacted layer, which may occur at a depth of about 30cm/1ft. It can be due to a mineral deposit, or compaction resulting from the use of heavy machinery or continual rotovation at the same depth. Where this occurs, the only remedy is to break up the hard pan with a spade, pick-axe or small mechanical digger.

Water supply

Many salad vegetables have a high water content and may need frequent watering, especially during their 'critical' periods (see p. 210). Shortage of water restricts their growth and causes their quality to deteriorate. Under-watered radishes, to take one example, will be cracked, woody and unbearably hot rather than crisp and succulent. The oriental greens are more prone to premature bolting in dry conditions. In areas where water shortage is likely, bear this in mind when siting your salad crops: the shorter the distance that you have to carry cans or trail hoses, the better.

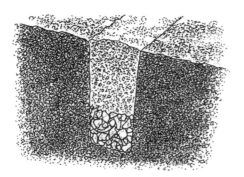

Trench drains are a practical way of improving poor drainage. To make a simple trench drain dig out a trench about 30cm/12in wide and 60–90cm/24–36in deep. Fill the lower third of the trench with rubble before replacing the soil.

Take measures to save rainwater for example, by collecting it off nearby roofs in water butts.

Shelter and windbreaks

Gardeners consistently fail to appreciate the value of shelter in vegetable gardens. Research has shown that sheltering vegetables from even light winds can increase their yields by up to 50 per cent. Salad plants are particularly vulnerable to the damaging effects of wind. So in gardens that are at all exposed it is worth erecting some kind of windbreak. In frost-prone areas, leave a gap at the lower end of a slope to allow frost to drain away.

The ideal windbreak should act as a filter to the wind, and should be about 50 per cent permeable. Wind tends to leap over a solid barrier, creating an area of turbulence on the leeward side. Hedges, lath fences (with gaps between the laths), hurdles and windbreak netting battened to posts all make effective windbreaks. In exposed situations it may be worth the expense of surrounding the entire garden. Factors to consider are that hedges compete with crops for nutrients, moisture and light, may create shade and require maintenance. Good modern netting lasts for several years, but it will have to take tremendous strain. Erect the posts securely, reinforcing the corner posts if necessary. In small gardens some kind of fencing, about 1½m/5ft high, may be more appropriate.

A windbreak is effective for a distance of roughly six times its own height, so a very large garden may require several windbreaks across the site. Where possible, site windbreaks across the path of the prevailing wind. In urban gardens, venomous winds often funnel through gaps between buildings. Any windbreak erected to close the gap should extend 1m/3ft beyond the gap on each side.

Within a garden you can put up smaller windbreaks to make it more sheltered. Strips of netting or hessian sacking about 30–60cm/12–24in high strung between beds or rows of vegetables cut down the wind very effectively. Even plants can make temporary windbreaks. Closely planted sweet corn or maize is grown as a windbreak in Holland; Jerusalem artichokes, sunflowers or a 'hedge' of cardoons can be used. Protective films, fleeces and nets, cloches, polytunnels and greenhouses are all devices that shelter plants and protect them from wind (see pp. 218–225).

Prime salad sites

For as long as salads have been cultivated, a premium has been put on the earliest crops, raised in sheltered sites on south-facing slopes. Enterprising market gardeners in the past even created slopes for early salads, while in the large walled kitchen gardens of the European gentry the earliest salads were grown in sunny beds at the foot of the walls… south-facing walls yielding the most prized spots. With ingenuity, warm fertile spots can be found or created in almost any garden, for growing early – and late – salads.

OPPOSITE Old greenhouse windows have been recycled to make shelter for tomato plants.

Bed design and cropping plans

The case for narrow beds

The layout of any vegetable garden is determined by the nature, size and shape of the beds. Whereas in the past vegetable gardens were laid out in large plots (wasteful in terms of space and resources), today the most efficient gardens are divided into small, permanent beds, narrow enough for the centre to be reached from the path. This 'narrow bed' system is widely adopted by organic gardeners.

Its salient feature is that it helps to preserve the fertility and structure of the soil (see p. 179). Good soil structure underpins soil fertility, but is a fragile quality, easily destroyed by digging heavy soil when it is wet, or simply by treading on the soil, again especially when wet. With narrow beds there is no need to walk on the soil, ever, either for cultivation or harvesting.

Another advantage of narrow beds is that all manures, compost and organic mulches are concentrated where they are needed: precisely where the plants are growing. In large beds much is wasted on ground that in practice has to serve as paths or access. It is much easier to build up and maintain fertility in narrow beds. This encourages plants to be deep rooting, which increases their resistance to drought.

Narrow beds lend themselves to the kind of intensive planting that suits the small size of contemporary gardens. Instead of widely spaced rows (where much of the space between rows simply invites weeds to grow), plants are grown at equidistant spacing. Among many benefits (see p. 230), their mature leaves form a blanketing canopy over the soil, inhibiting weed growth. The exception is plants with narrow, upright leaves, such as onions, leeks and garlic, which do not blanket the ground, though they still benefit from equidistant spacing.

Bed size, shape and height

Narrow beds can be various sizes and shapes. Rectangular beds are probably the easiest to manage and can be any length. Square beds must be kept reasonably small, or it becomes impossible to reach the centre from the paths. Beds can also be round, curved, crescent-shaped, triangular or any irregular shape. One of the charms of the potager approach is the scope for grouping beds of any shape into aesthetic patterns. A practical width for beds is 90–150cm/3–5ft. The important point is to choose a width that feels comfortable to you. I personally like a width of about 120cm/4ft; this is also a convenient width for the hoops we use for low polythene and net tunnels (see pp. 223–5).

Beds can be level or raised above the ground. Level beds are the easiest to establish though salad plants at ground level tend to get muddied. Flat beds in a kitchen garden can be edged with plants – herbs such as chives, parsley, marjoram and thyme are a common choice – or with hard materials.

OPPOSITE Raised beds enable the gardener to concentrate manures where most needed, and to overcome underlying problems of poor soil or bad drainage.

ABOVE The 75cm/30in high raised beds in my West Cork potager provide comfortable access and keep the encroaching grass at bay.

These tend to take less space and, where salad plants are concerned, help to keep them clean. Bricks, tiles, stones, recycled plastic and various forms of timber are all commonly used. For lasting boards use durable timber or pressure-treated boards – they can be stained with weatherproof preservatives or painted to add a colourful touch. If scrap wood is used, frequent repairs will be necessary.

Raised beds can be anything from 10 to 90cm/4 to 36in high; the higher beds are often made on a brick or concrete foundation to provide access for disabled gardeners. Free-standing raised beds are usually made by excavating the soil from the path area on either side on to the beds. The beds should be slightly tapered to make them stable. A bed 125cm/4ft wide at the base should be about 90cm/3ft wide at the top. The surface can be flat or rounded. Where beds are oriented in an east–west direction, the south-facing rounded surface (in the northern hemisphere) will attract increased sunlight and radiation. If you are making raised beds to overcome serious soil problems, such as contaminated or very badly drained soil, you will have to import good-quality soil. The soil in the final bed needs to be at least 30cm/12in deep.

Raised beds are frequently made with permanent edgings: raised bed kits, made from timber and recycled plastic, are widely available. Railway sleepers are still widely used. However they are large and bulky. In our new garden in West Cork we made a 'raised bed potager' with recycled plastic – which is thinner, neater and very durable. There are many options, as for edges for ground level beds above.

Paths

Paths are an important element in any vegetable plot. They should be at least 38–45cm/15–18in wide, with occasional wider paths at least 60cm/24in wide, so that you can manoeuvre laden wheelbarrows comfortably. The choice of surface ranges from bare soil and grass to permanent paths of brick, stone, gravel, stone or paving slabs. Brick paths, perhaps combined with stones or pavers, can be laid in imaginative patterns, making a feature of a practical element. Lay them on a base of sand and black polythene film (see illustration opposite). Our original kitchen garden paths were bare soil, covered with heavy-duty, weed-suppressing but permeable black fabric, disguised, wherever feasible, with a light layer of bark chippings. It made a serviceable, firm, clean and well-drained surface.

Bed direction

In the northern hemisphere, to make maximum use of sunshine, beds should theoretically be orientated from north to south for summer crops, and from east to west for early and late crops. In practice this is difficult to carry out. Site tall plants such as sweet corn and climbing beans so that they do not cast shade on low-growing plants.

Cropping plans

To get the most out of the garden, it is worth planning carefully. The traditional starting point is the rotation plan. Rotation is the practice of grouping together closely related vegetables and growing them in a different bed, or different part of the garden, over at least a three-year cycle.

This is to prevent the build-up of those serious soil pests and diseases that attack a limited range of plants in the same botanical family. In practice, many soil pests are fairly mobile, so there is little point in simply moving a crop a few metres away. Moreover some species of eelworm and diseases such as clubroot, can remain in the soil for up to six or seven years, so rotation would have to be practised over a long cycle to be really effective. This is obviously impractical in small gardens.

Nevertheless, without being a slave to rotation theory, it is sound preventive medicine to try to rotate the main groups below over a three- or preferably four- or five-year cycle. It is easier to work out a flexible rotation plan where a garden is divided into several small beds rather than two or three large ones. In the absence of a rotation plan, at least try to follow each crop with one from an unrelated group; and never replant a piece of ground with a crop that is the same as, or closely related, to the crop that has just been cleared.

Main rotation groups:
- Solanaceae – potatoes, tomatoes, aubergines, peppers.
- Leguminosae – peas, beans, leguminous green manures such as field beans, clover, winter tares.

To make a path, excavate a depth of 10cm/4in, then line it with heavy black polythene film to prevent weeds from germinating.

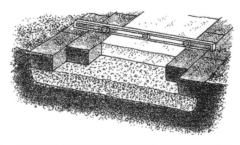

Level the base with a 5cm/2in layer of sand over the film, and lay bricks and pavers on top.

- Brassicas – cabbages, cauliflower, broccoli, radishes, mustards, turnips, swedes, kohl rabi, oriental greens, green manure mustard.
- Alliums – onion, leeks, garlic.
- Fit in the many other vegetables wherever there is space.

Detailed planning At the outset, draw up a plan of your beds and decide how many and which to allocate to the main rotation groups. Write on the plan the vegetables you are growing in those groups, with a note of how many months they are likely to be in the ground. (For a year-round 'saladini' plan, see p. 272). Where space and time allows, follow or precede them with another crop. For example, in the potato bed, you could plant lettuces or cucumbers when you lift the early potatoes in June or July. It is worth putting aside a part of the garden, or a couple of beds, for perennial vegetables such as asparagus, globe artichokes, rhubarb, sorrel and some of the larger, perennial herbs like lovage and sweet cicely.

Keeping the pot boiling

One of the challenges of planning is to have something fresh from the garden all year round. Gluts, so often partnered by shortages, are a waste of space. Bolting lettuce is depressing, however fond you are of lettuce soup.

What you can grow successfully is largely determined by the climate, but you can do a lot to extend the natural season.

- Choose varieties (of lettuce or cabbage, for example) to span the growing season. Make use of varieties that fill gaps: for example autumn-planted onion sets mature in the 'onion gap' in early summer.
- Sow 'little and often', especially salads such as hearting lettuce and summer radish which run to seed or deteriorate soon after maturing. As a rule of thumb, make the next sowing when the previous one has germinated.
- Stagger planting. Plant a crop over several days, so that the plants mature in sequence. Alternatively select seedlings of different sizes when planting; they will mature at diffeerent times. Raising plants in modules (see p. 200) produces excellent plants, which can be held back without damage.
- In cold climates use to the full all forms of cover, from light fleeces laid over outdoor crops, to greenhouses and polytunnels (see pp. 218–225). A 0.5°C/1°F rise in temperature is equivalent to moving 160 kilometres/100 miles south (in the northern hemisphere). In spring, sow early cut-and-come-again seedling crops and make early sowings of outdoor crops under cover. In summer, grow heat-loving crops such as peppers and tomatoes. In autumn and winter, use their sheltering effect to improve the quality of winter salads.

Soil fertility and manuring

The soil is essentially the plant's larder, supplying the elements or nutrients a plant needs and absorbs through its roots. The three major elements are nitrogen (N), potassium (K) and phosphorus (P). A plant needs several other elements in smaller quantities, and 'trace' elements, such as iron, in minute quantities. Broadly speaking, N is important for leaf growth (leafy crops such as brassicas require large amounts), P for early growth, and K for general plant health and ripening. Nitrogen is always the nutrient most likely to be in short supply, as it is very soluble and washed out of the soil in winter; most soils have reasonable reserves of P and K.

The nutrients come from three sources, the first being the mineral particles of sand, silt and clay in the soil, produced over the centuries by the weathering of rocks. The second source is organic matter in the soil. This, through the action of micro-organisms, is broken down into humus, from which the elements are 'released' in forms plants can use. Thirdly, nitrogen is obtained from atmospheric nitrogen in the soil, which is 'fixed' for plant use by soil bacteria.

So soil micro-organisms play a vital role. However, they only flourish in soils of suitable acidity/pH (see below), with an adequate supply of oxygen and water. The soil's ability to meet these requirements depends on its structure – that is, its network of soil 'crumbs' and the spaces between them.

In a good soil the mineral particles and humus join together to form tiny but very stable crumbs of varying sizes. The crumbs are separated by air spaces which link to form a network of aeration and drainage channels. After heavy rain, water drains away through the large spaces, which then fill with air, but a crucial reservoir of moisture is retained in the smaller spaces. Soil quickly becomes waterlogged and airless without these drainage channels. The significant fact for gardeners is that humus is a key agent in crumb formation: it both coats sand and silt particles so that they form crumbs, and facilitates the breakdown of large clay clods, ultimately into crumbs. It also absorbs and retains moisture.

Earthworms, who are enormously beneficial in the soil, feed on organic matter. As they plough through the soil, it passes into their bodies, where it is intimately mixed with soil and gums and lime from their bodies. This kickstarts the crucial process of converting organic matter into humus.

For all these reasons, adding organic matter to the soil is the basis of soil fertility. Hence the maxim at the heart of organic gardening: 'Feed the soil, not the plant.' The main sources of organic matter are bulky animal manures, compost and green manuring.

Manure and fertilizers

The terms 'manure' and 'compost' imply bulky 'organic' substances, derived originally from plants or animals. The best-known forms are farmyard manure and garden compost. They improve soil fertility

179

ABOVE Grass clippings can be used to mulch a fallow bed over winter, suppressing weeds, adding nutrients and protecting the soil from winter rain.

chemicals. They will give quick results and high yields, but should be seen as a form of 'force feeding'. The resulting lush growth is 'soft', and prone to pest and disease attacks. It is also easy to give an overdose, damaging the soil and the plant. These are some of the reasons why they are not used in organic gardening.

Organic matter in the soil breaks down fairly fast, especially in hot and wet conditions, so must be regularly replenished to maintain soil fertility. Aim to work some into every piece of ground every year. As a very rough guide, think in terms of 2¾–5½kg per sq. m/5–10lb per sq. yd, the higher figure being for poorer soil. If you start with poor soil, it will of course take a few years to raise the fertility to a satisfactory level. Home-made liquid fertilizers, and seaweed-based stimulants and organic fertilizers can be used to supply extra nutrients where growing conditions are below par, and to boost growth for hungry crops such as tomatoes.

Finding supplies of organic manure is not as easy as it used to be, especially in urban areas. Don't be shy of collecting vegetable waste from greengrocers and city markets: it all makes excellent compost.

as outlined above, and also supply some plant foods.

A 'fertilizer' is a concentrated liquid or solid, such as granules, which contains plant nutrients but is of little benefit to the soil. Typical 'organic' fertilizers are liquid comfrey, seaweed extracts and proprietary products made from various animal and vegetable sources. Traditional organic fertilizers, which are less widely available today, include 'hoof and horn' (a source of nitrogen), and 'fish blood and bone' (a general source of nutrients). All these have their uses where an extra 'boost' seems advisable, but are relatively slow acting.

'Inorganic' or 'artificial' fertilizers are soluble, fast-acting, manufactured

Sources of organic matter

Apart from garden and household waste which can be composted (see opposite) the following are the main sources of organic matter which can be brought into the garden.

Farmyard and manures from large animals Ideally the manures should be mixed with plenty of straw or litter, which, as they absorb the animal urine, are a valuable source of nutrients.

Fresh manure should be composted in a covered heap for anything from two to six months before use. This reduces potentially damaging levels of ammonia, and helps to kill weed seeds. Manure mixed with sawdust or wood shavings should be composted eighteen months before use. (Faeces from pets should not be used.)

Poultry, pigeon and rabbit manures These are very concentrated, so work them into a compost heap in small quantities.

Spent mushroom compost Over the years this excellent product has improved the fertility of our Suffolk garden with its heavy clay soil and solved its drainage problems. It is sterilized, so free of weed seed. The high chalk content is beneficial in clay soils, but makes it unsuitable for alkaline (chalk) soils. Do not use it continuously on the same ground.

Straw and hay Both are good sources of organic matter. Stack fresh material in layers 15cm/6in thick, watering each layer unless it is moist. Keep the heap covered with tarpaulin or old carpeting until required. Hay must be very well rotted to kill the grass seed. We had excellent results in our polytunnel by mulching the paths with straw in summer, prior to converting them into beds for winter salads. The worm population increased dramatically beneath the straw.

Seaweed A rich source of nutrients and can be used fresh, dried or incorporated into a compost heap. If you spread it on the soil, it may attract flies while decomposing; to overcome this, cover lightly with soil. In any case, the flies and their grubs soon disappear without any ill effects.

Recycled municipal waste and treated sewage sludge More of these products are becoming available. They

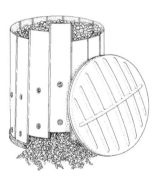

ABOVE A patented compost bin is useful for small households, through its capacity is generally too small to generate enough heat to break down very coarse material. Waste is put in the top and several months later removed from the base.

RIGHT A pair of purpose-built compost bins are durable and efficient. See p.183-4 for construction details.

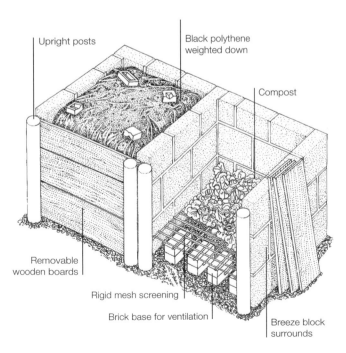

Upright posts

Black polythene weighted down

Compost

Removable wooden boards

Rigid mesh screening

Brick base for ventilation

Breeze block surrounds

can be excellent. Just make sure they are guaranteed free of heavy metals.

Garden compost

I would strongly advise gardeners to make their own compost from their garden and household vegetable wastes. There is a great deal of discussion about how to make compost and what constitutes 'perfect' compost, but, as an eminent soil scientist told me years ago, all compost is valuable. Even when the end product is only partially decomposed it still provides food for the earthworms, and that is the key to maintaining soil fertility.

Compost can be made in simple heaps, or in purpose-made bins, which can be home-made or purchased. Bins accelerate the decomposing process. A huge range of proprietary compost bins are now available, many suitable for small gardens, or where only small quantities of compostable waste are produced.

Compost heaps This is the simplest way to make compost. Pile suitable waste materials into a heap up to about 1½m/5ft high, then cover it with black polythene sheeting. In temperate climates it will be ready for use in about a year. To get the best end product, mix different types of material into the heap. Anything of plant origin, that will rot, can be

used including small quantities of the organic matter sources mentioned above. Shred or chop up coarse or woody material, such as cabbage stalks. Just avoid having a solid mass of any one substance, such as lawn mowings or autumn leaves. Do not use diseased plant material, weeds that have gone to seed, or roots of perennial weeds such as ground elder or couch grass, unless they have been killed by drying them off thoroughly. They should otherwise be buried, or if feasible, taken to a green waste recycling centre, where all potentially toxic organisms are destroyed in the composting systems used.

The disadvantage of this method, apart from being slow, is that it does not generate high temperatures, so weed seeds and disease spores may not be killed; nor will coarse material be completely rotted. Nevertheless, organic matter is eventually returned to the soil, and that is what matters.

Compost bins As well as keeping garden waste tidy, the object of a purpose-built bin is to generate high temperatures, so that waste decomposes rapidly, killing weed seeds and disease spores. The end product is homogenous, and looks like soil. High temperatures are generated only with a relatively large volume of waste material, so the larger the bin the better. The minimum size for a home-made bin would be 1m/3ft wide and 1m/3ft high, though they can be any length. They should be well insulated. If you make two bins side by side, one can be maturing while the other builds up. A bin is normally a permanent construction, sited in an out-of-the-way place on well-drained soil.

The bin must be strong, as the raw material is heavy and bulky. The side and back walls can be constructed of insulating

OPPOSITE LEFT Comfrey is easily grown and can be made into a liquid fertilizer or used as a mulch. It should be cut before it flowers, but leave a few for their beauty, and for the bees.

OPPOSITE RIGHT This compost heap has been invaded by a free-loading squash taking advantage of its nutrients, but adding an aesthetic touch in return.

ABOVE Seaweed can be used as a mulch, added to your compost heap, or made into a liquid fertilizer.

material such as breeze blocks, bricks, timber or straw bales (these, of course, would need to be replaced annually). The front can be made of loose boards slipped behind upright posts. This enables you to build up and dismantle the heap in stages.

If feasible, raise the base of the heap 10cm/4in off the ground for ventilation and drainage. Use a layer of brushwood, rubble, clay drainage pipes or double rows of bricks with 5cm/2in gaps between them. Heavy mesh screening can be laid over the drainage base to hold the compost in place (see illustration on the right, p. 181).

The best way to fill the bin, although it requires discipline, is to pre-mix the

materials in a plastic sack, balancing leafy (nitrogenous) and fibrous (carbon) material. Either add a sack at a time, or wait until there are enough sackfuls to make a layer about 20cm/8in deep. The general recommendation is to aim for a heap with about two-thirds, by bulk, of material which is a source of carbon (stems, strawy material, roots) and one-third a source of nitrogen (leafy green material.)

The micro-organisms that bring about decomposition need air, moisture and a source of nitrogen, which is found naturally in leafy green material or animal manure. There will be plenty of nitrogen in a summer heap, but in autumn and winter supplement the nitrogen by adding a bucket of chicken or animal manure, or seaweed extract or proprietary compost activator (at the rates recommended by the manufacturer) to each layer or to pre-mixed wastes.

Nutrients are easily washed out of compost by rain, so when the bin is full cover it with black polythene sheeting, punctured with 2½cm/1in diameter holes about 30cm/12in apart for ventilation. Either weight this down, or cover it with permeable but insulating material, such as 7½cm/3in of soil, matting or a layer of straw.

In temperate climates a heap made in summer is normally ready in two or three months, in winter in eight or nine months. Turning the heap 'sides to middle', into a second bin, accelerates the process.

Leaf mould Leaves decompose very slowly and are best composted separately. Pile fallen leaves into a wire-netting enclosure at least 60–90cm/2–3ft high, sited in a dry, shady place, or keep them in airtight, black plastic bags. They take about two years to turn into a mould that can be used in potting composts or for mulching.

Worm compost is made by recycling organic wastes in a home-made or patented 'wormery' or bin, using worms such the red brandling worm, which feed exclusively on decaying organic matter. It is an efficient form of composting, which can be done indoors. With care, worm composting systems can handle small quantities of processed food and meat, which should not be put into a compost heap. The fertile end product can be used as a fertilizer, or mixed into potting composts.

Home-made liquid fertilizers

These simple 'brews' can be used, like proprietary organic fertilizers, to stimulate growth or as a general purpose fertilizer.

'Black Jack' Suspend a sack of well-rotted animal manure mixed with grass clippings in a butt of rainwater. It will be ready a few weeks later. Dilute the liquid to the colour of weak tea before use.

Liquid comfrey Comfrey (*Symphytum* x *uplandicum*) is an easily grown, hardy perennial. Use the productive variety 'Bocking 14'. Make the liquid in a barrel or bin, raised off the ground on bricks. Insert a tap near the bottom, or drill a 1cm/½in hole in the base, putting a container beneath to catch the liquid. Stuff the barrel with comfrey leaves, weight them down, then cover the barrel with a lid. Within a few weeks the concentrate will drip through. Use it diluted with 10–20 parts of water. It is rich in potassium, making it an excellent feed for tomatoes. Just be aware that it is liable to smell.

Nettle manure Nettles are a rich source of minerals, and can be integrated into a compost heap, or made into a liquid feed, ideally using young nettles picked in spring. Either use the method for comfrey above, or simply half fill a bucket with compacted nettles and cover with water. The late Robert Hart, advocate of 'Forest Gardening', used the resulting liquid without dilution 'once it started to smell'.

Liquid seaweed Seaweed products are valuable growth stimulants. Liquid seaweed is easily made by filling any kind of container, from a bucket to an empty oil drum with seaweed, and covering it with water. Stir it regularly, and drain off the liquid when it is a dark colour. It can be diluted 50:50 for using as a feed. Use the residue seaweed as a mulch or integrate it into a compost heap.

ABOVE Fast growing green manure *Phacelia tanacetifolia* can be dug in within three months. Leave a few to flower, as the beautiful flowers attract pollinators.

It shoud be said that a lot of guesswork is involved in deciding on dilution rates for home-made liquid feeds: no one mix will be the same as the next. Watch your plants to see how they are responding. Be reassured that there's a wide margin of error compared with the use of inorganic fertilizers!

Green manuring

Green manuring is the technique of growing crops (often called 'cover crops') that will be incorporated dug into the ground to improve soil fertility. Different plants are used for different situations and purposes. Fast-growing leafy crops such as mustard and *Phacelia tanacetifolia* give a quick nitrogen boost when turned in or allowed to rot on the surface; fibrous rooters such as 'grazing' rye increase the organic matter in the soil; various legumes (field beans and clovers, for example) can fix atmospheric nitrogen in the soil. Hardy green manures such as winter tares and field beans can be sown in autumn, protecting the soil and preventing the loss of nutrients in winter. Green manures should never be the sole form of manuring, but sowing even small patches can make a valuable contribution to fertility.

Incorporating bulky organic matter into the soil

There are several options when it comes to incorporating bulky manures and compost into the soil. They are either dug into the soil, or spread on the surface, depending on the soil and the state of the manure. Well-rotted manure and compost can be spread on the surface, allowing the worms to work it in gradually. In most cases, with average garden soil, it is probably best to apply it in late winter or early spring, as otherwise nitrogen and potassium will be leached out by heavy rains.

If the manure is very 'strawy', there can be a temporary 'locking up' of nitrogen, due to a rapid increase in microbial activity, as it is broken down. In this case it is probably best applied in late autumn.

Traditionally heavy soils were dug in the autumn – so that frost action could break up the clods – with manure dug in at the same time. The soil was forked over lightly in spring if necessary. This may not make optimum

DOUBLE DIGGING

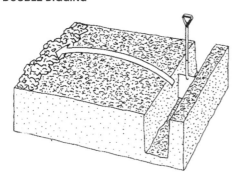

Make a trench one spade deep and about 38cm/15in wide across the bed, and remove the soil to the far end of the strip. Keep the manure handy in a wheelbarrow.

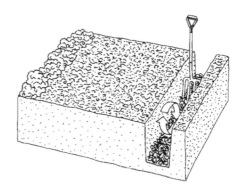

Fork the soil at the bottom of the trench, then put in a good layer of manure or garden compost, or whatever you are using.

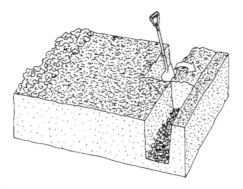

Fill the trench with soil from the next strip, then fork soil and manure together so that the manure is spread evenly through the soil.

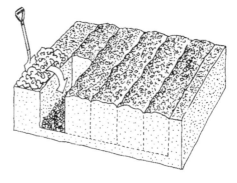

Continue in this way to the end of the strip, then fill the last trench with soil from the original trench. Double digging is normally necessary only one year in four.

use of the organic material (see above) but ultimately gardeners need to choose a system that fits in with their own conditions.

An alternative method for heavy soils is to ridge them up in winter, and cover the ridge with well-rotted manure or whatever mulching material is being used. In the 90cm/36in-wide beds in our original garden in Suffolk I first forked down the centre of the bed, then spaded the soil from each side on to the middle, making a single central ridge. This was usually covered

with a thick layer of mushroom compost. The ridges ensured good drainage while exposing a greater surface to frost action. By spring, the soil had has a beautiful crumbly surface and usually only needed light forking.

Light, well-drained and sandy soils are best covered with well-rotted manure or some form of bulky organic matter in winter, but dug over in spring. This protects the soil surface from winter rains, which destroy soil structure and wash out nutrients

187

in the soil. In most years it is adequate simply to fork the soil to the depth of a spade (one spit deep).

Double digging

In the early days in a difficult garden with heavy soil, and even occasionally in established gardens (say every four years) digging more deeply can be very beneficial. 'Double digging' (see illustration on previous page) breaks up any hard pan that may be forming in the soil and impeding drainage. Compaction can develop at the lower levels even in relatively well worked gardens. Double digging enables manure to be worked in at a deeper level, encouraging plants to root more deeply – the best insurance against drought.

Soil acidity

Soil acidity is another factor affecting soil fertility. It is related to the amount of calcium (lime or chalk) in the soil, and is measured on the pH scale. This ranges from 0 to 14, the neutral point being 7. Soils with a pH below 7 become progressively more acid, those with a pH above 7 more alkaline. The change from one pH level to the next represents a tenfold increase in acidity or alkalinity. Most vegetables grow best on a slightly acid to neutral soil, with a pH of about 6–6.5.

In extremely acid or alkaline soils plant nutrients become 'locked up' and unavailable to plants, soil micro-organisms cease to function and earthworms move out. In humid climates soils become increasingly acid, as rainfall washes calcium out of the soil. This is most marked on light, well-drained soils and where there is atmospheric pollution.

Don't worry about acidity unless plants are growing poorly, or there are few worms, or the soil looks sour with moss growing on the surface. In these circumstances test the soil with a simple soil analysis kit or pH meter. If the soil is acid, raise the pH level to around 6.5 by adding lime over several successive seasons. Organic gardeners should use ground limestone or dolomite rather than the faster-acting gardener's lime. Apply it in the autumn, but never at the same time as manure. In practice, regular additions of organic matter tend to prevent, and correct, soil acidity problems.

RIGHT Most garden and kitchen waste can go on the compost heap, from vegetable peelings to tea bags. Avoid meat (which will attract rats), pet wastes, diseased plants and perennial weeds, unless they've been dried out first.

Plant raising

Seed

Is it worth going to the trouble of raising your own plants, rather than buying them ready for planting out? The answer must certainly be 'Yes, if you can.' It's fun, satisfying, you avoid the risk of introducing soil-borne pests and diseases – such as vine weevil and clubroot – into your garden, but, above all, it gives you a far greater choice of interesting varieties. Until recently garden centres and nurserymen invariably supplied only the most popular varieties. However that is changing, with mail-order seed companies, and some suppliers geared to organic gardeners, now offering a far wider range of plants. If you have limited space and facilities, it makes sense to take advantage of these opportunities. (See Seed suppliers p. 275).

The majority of salads are raised from seed; the better the seed quality, the greater the chances of a good crop. In most Western countries minimum standards of purity and germination are laid down for the main vegetables, so you can be fairly sure of buying seed that was of reasonable quality when it was packeted. However, seed deteriorates with time and, in adverse conditions, loses its viability (ability to germinate).

Wherever possible, buy seed in hermetically sealed foil packets. These safeguard viability much longer than paper packets, but once the packet is opened normal deterioration sets in.

Be wary of packets that have obviously been subjected to damp or very dry conditions: they are unlikely to germinate well. My heart sinks when I see the sun beating down on a shop's seed rack.

Storing seed

Seed should be kept dry and cold. Many germination failures stem from using old seed or seed that has been kept in damp garden sheds or hot rooms. Ideally, seed should be stored at temperatures below freezing: for every 5°C/9°F rise above zero, the storage life of seed is halved.

Keep seed in an airtight tin or jar in a cool room, or, if you have space, in a domestic refrigerator. An additional safeguard is to put a cloth bag or dish of silica gel in the container to absorb atmospheric moisture. Silica gel will need to be dried out periodically. 'Indicator' silica gel, which changes colour when it gets damp, can be bought on line. An alternative, suggested to me by the UK Vegetable Gene Bank, is to use grains such as wheat or rice. Dry them initially for about an hour on a metal tray in a low oven (to drive out any moisture), then cool them somewhere dry. This is best done in an airtight jar. Seed can then be stored in paper packets in the same jar.

The natural viability of vegetable seed varies according to the species, and is affected by a range of factors. Tomato and legume (the family that includes peas and beans) seed can, under good conditions, keep for up to ten years; brassicas, lettuce, endive and chicory will normally last four or five years, but may fall off after a couple of years; the onion and leek family deteriorate after the second year; root vegetables such as parsnip, salsify and scorzonera lose viability rapidly, so it is advisable to use fresh seed each year.

If in doubt, do a germination test before making your main sowing. Put a piece of foam rubber (to retain moisture) in a dish, cover it with a double layer of paper towelling, lay the seeds on top and put it somewhere warm. If they have not germinated within a couple of weeks, cut your losses and buy fresh seed.

Saving your own seed

Home gardeners are usually advised against saving their own seed, as it is unlikely to match the quality of purchased seed. Nevertheless, it can be worth saving seed of salads used as cut-and-come-again seedling crops, not least because you will need far more seed than the average seed packet contains. You may also want to save seed of unusual varieties that are difficult to obtain, or of an outstanding plant of your own. Never save seed of F1 hybrids, as they will not come true.

Save seed from only the very best plants, never from diseased plants or those running to seed prematurely. If possible, keep the plants isolated from other varieties to avoid cross-pollination. Keep them well watered while they are flowering and forming seed heads, but stop watering once the pods are formed. Ripening plants may need staking to prevent them from falling over and soiling the seed pods. It is best to let the seed pods dry naturally on the plant, but in persistently damp weather uproot the plants and hang them under cover until completely dry.

When the pods are brittle, the dry seed can be shaken out on a newspaper and stored in envelopes or jars. I sometimes leave garden cress and salad rocket seedheads in the greenhouse, crumbling the seed pods directly on to the ground when I want to sow.

Seed saving is most successful where the climate is dry when the seed is ripening. Cress, salad rocket, corn salad, chervil, radish and chicory are amongst the easiest to save. To be sure of maintaining quality, it is advisable to start again with commercial seed every few years.

Choosing varieties

In common parlance gardeners still talk about 'varieties', although the correct term today for 'varieties raised in cultivation' is cultivars.

For keen salad growers, the widest choice of varieties is generally found in mail-order seed catalogues. There are some useful indicators of quality and performance.

F1 hybrid seed Most new vegetable varieties are 'F1 hybrids'. These are bred by crossing two parent lines, each of which has been inbred for several generations. The parentage is known only to the breeders, so they cannot be reproduced by others. Compared to standard 'open-pollinated' varieties, the resulting hybrid seed is generally notable for its vigour, evenness and reliability, often with useful pest or disease resistance. Their widespread use commercially has tended to erode, and lead to the loss of, some heritage varieties. F1 hybrids are usually considerably more expensive than open-pollinated varieties.
Awards of merit As a result of assessment in formal trials, outstanding cultivars are

---

LEFT Harvesting coriander seed into a paper bag.
RIGHT Radishes are easy to harvest; snap the pods open when they are dry and brittle to collect the seed.

given the Award of Merit (AM) by the Royal Horticultural Society in the UK, and Gold, Silver and Bronze medals in the All America Awards Scheme (AAA) in the USA. This is a useful indication of quality.

'Organic seed' This indicates that seed has been produced organically, and the varieties chosen are often suitable for organic production. In the 1980's trials were conducted in the UK to assess a variety's performance in an organic system. The main qualities looked for were natural vigour (not least to outstrip weeds), and pest, disease and weather resistance. These trials have been discontinued, though the results were included in my book, *Grow Your Own Vegetables* (See Further reading p. 274). Seed catalogues sometimes indicate seed is 'suitable for organic gardeners' when the variety has good pest or disease resistance. Incidentally, strictly organic gardeners would not use dressed seed, although these chemical treatments undeniably protect seed in the vulnerable early stages of germination.

Forms of seed

Besides ordinary or 'naked' seed, seed is available in various forms.

Pelleted seed Individual seeds are coated with an inert protective substance, making each seed into a small, round ball. This makes them easy to handle and sow with precision. The coating breaks down in the soil, but the pellets must be kept moist until this point, or they may not germinate. Softer-coated pellets, known as 'pills' or 'split pellets', are sometimes available. They are mainly sown under cover, and should be sown shallowly.

Chitted (pregerminated) seed The seeds have already germinated, to the stage of an incipient radicle (root), or with the first 'seed leaves' developed (the first tiny leaves after germination, before the next 'true' leaves). They are posted to customers in airtight sachets, and are pricked out on receipt. The technique is used for seeds that are difficult to germinate.

Primed seed The seeds are brought to the point of germination, then dried before being packeted. Once sown, the seed germinates exceptionally fast – a useful characteristic for early sowings in adverse conditions. Primed seed is advocated for early sowings of carrots, onions and parsnips. Seed has to be sown soon after receipt.

Seed tapes, sheets and mats Evenly spaced seed is embedded in soluble tapes or paper-like sheets, which are 'sown' on the ground or in a seed tray, covered lightly with soil and kept moist until germination. The predetermined spacing means that little, if any, thinning is required.

Where to sow

There are two main options for sowing vegetables, depending on climate, season and the nature of the crop.

'Outdoors' implies sowing either *in situ* – that is, in the ground where plants will mature, or in a seedbed from which they will be transplanted into their permanent positions. Sowing outdoors is suitable for robust vegetables that germinate easily, for vegetables that dislike being transplanted and for seedling crops that are sown thickly and harvested young.

'Indoors' is a loose term to describe sowing in some kind of seed tray or pot in

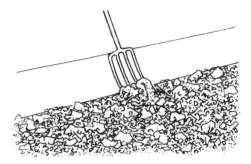

The first stage in preparing a seedbed is to break up any clods of earth with a garden fork.

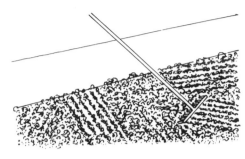

To prepare a tilth rake backwards and forwards in different directions.

a protected environment, which can range from a windowsill to a cloche to a greenhouse. Sowing indoors enables plants to be given a head start when conditions outdoors are still unsuitable for sowing or planting. The first lettuces, for example, may be sown indoors early in the year and planted out as soon as conditions allow. In areas with a cold or short growing season, the only chance of growing tender crops like tomatoes and peppers to maturity is to start them indoors, planting outside when they are well developed.

Sowing outdoors

Choosing the right conditions for sowing and preparing the seedbed well are crucial to success when sowing outdoors. A lot of good seed fails to germinate because it was sown when the soil was too cold, too wet, too dry or too lumpy.

The seedbed

The term 'seedbed' is used ambiguously both for the surface of any piece of ground where seed is sown and for an area put aside for raising seedlings that will later be transplanted.

The latter, 'nursery' seedbed is primarily a means of saving space for vegetables that have a long growing season or take up a lot of space when mature. In their early stages they can be grown relatively close in the seedbed, during which time you can use the ground they will eventually occupy for another crop.

A nursery seedbed should be made in an open position. Resist the temptation to use an out-of-the-way corner, perhaps near a hedge. This is likely to result in sad, drawn seedlings deprived of light and moisture. The soil does not need to be rich but it must be well-drained and, if possible, weed-free. Where the soil is likely to be full of weed seeds, prepare the seedbed first, then leave it a week or so for the main flush of weed seeds to germinate. Hoe them off before sowing.

Preparing a seedbed

The surface of the seedbed needs to be free of clods, lumps and stones, and raked to a fairly fine tilth – with the soil particles about the size of breadcrumbs. A fine tilth is important for sowing small seeds, but larger seeds, such as peas and beans, can cope with a rougher surface. The soil should be reasonably firm:

where feasible, leave it to settle for a few weeks after it has been dug.

The mechanics of making a seedbed depend on the soil. Sandy and light soils are easily raked down into a good surface in spring, but clay and loam soils are naturally much lumpier. (Some clay soils are unsuitable for seedbeds but can be improved by working potting compost and sand into the surface.) These heavier soils should be dug over in autumn and exposed to winter frosts, which help break down the clods. Once the soil has started to dry out in spring, you can start work on making a seedbed.

It is important to choose the right moment to do so. If the soil sticks to your shoes, wait a few days until it has dried out. Covering the soil with cloches or clear film will make it dry faster. If the soil is too dry, water it before working on it. Start by breaking down large remaining clods with a garden fork or the back of a rake. If this proves difficult, fork the soil over lightly first. Then rake it smooth (see illustration opposite), removing small clods and stones.

When to sow

Most vegetables have an optimum temperature for germination. As a rule, the higher the temperature, the faster they germinate, although some seeds (butterhead lettuce and onion, for example) germinate poorly at temperatures above 24°C/75°F. You can measure the soil temperature with a soil thermometer; to obtain a correct reading, insert it 5–7½cm/2–3in deep in the soil. Otherwise simply feel the soil. If it feels cold to your touch, delay sowing. There is little to gain by sowing prematurely in cold soil: the seed is likely to rot or become diseased. If you are unable to sow immediately after preparing

the seedbed, cover it with a light mulch of straw or dried leaves to protect it from strong, drying spring winds or heavy rainfall until you are ready to sow.

Methods of sowing

Seed can be sown in drills, broadcast or sown individually.

Sowing in drills A slit made in the soil, normally in a straight line (see illustrations overleaf). Sow at an even depth, which helps prevent erratic germination. The depth depends on the size of the seed. As a rough guide, seeds need to be covered by at least twice their depth. A 'wide' drill, often used for sowing peas or cut-and-come-again seedling crops, is usually up to about 10cm/4in wide, made using the broad blade of an onion hoe or similar tool.

Spacing seeds evenly along the drill is essential, both to prevent overcrowding when the seedlings first germinate, and to minimize subsequent thinning. 'Station sowing', where three or four seeds are sown in a group together, at regular intervals or 'stations' along a drill, makes this easier. Where plants will eventually be thinned to stand 20cm/8in apart, station sow at half that distance – that is, 10cm/4in apart. Pelleted seed is very useful for station sowing. Not only does station sowing simplify thinning, but it enables a fast-growing crop to be sown between stations as markers for a slow-growing one (see Space-saving systems, p. 230).

Sowing in adverse conditions Seeds germinate poorly if sown in very dry conditions. A useful technique to overcome this is to make the drill and carefully water the bottom of the drill (not the ground surrounding it) until it is almost muddy.

Use the point of a trowel or hoe to 'draw' the drill at an even depth.

Space seed thinly and evenly along the drill, so the seedlings are not overcrowded.

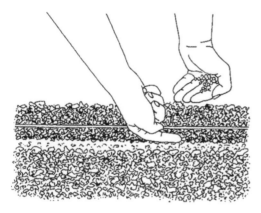

After sowing, press the seeds gently into the bottom of the drill, using a finger or the back of the trowel or hoe.

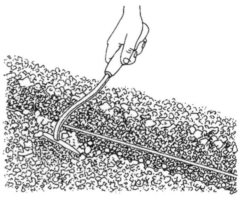

Cover the seed with soil using the hand or the blade of a hoe. Finally firm the soil gently with the hands or trowel.

Then sow the seed, press it into the drill, and cover it with dry soil. The dry soil acts as a mulch, preventing evaporation, so the soil remains moist until the seed has germinated. (This tip, which I heard on a radio programme, has saved me from countless fruitless sowings.) To further encourage germination in dry weather, cover the seedbed after sowing with a light mulch or with clear polythene film, removing it as soon as the seedlings break through the surface.

To counteract very wet conditions, line the drill with sowing or potting compost, or with well-rotted leaf mould, to make a dry bed on which the seed is sown.

Broadcasting This is the old-fashioned method of sowing by scattering seed over the surface. It is still very useful for seedling crops that require little or no thinning, and for fast-growing salads such as radishes or early carrots, and for some green manures. It is economical with space.

Prepare the seedbed as described above, taking special care to ensure that it is free of weeds. Then scatter the seed over the surface as evenly as possible. Crops used at a very young stage, such as garden cress, can be sown thicker than, say, radishes or Sugar Loaf chicory, for which individual seedlings will eventually need more space to develop.

After sowing, cover the seed by raking gently first in one direction, then at right angles. Because the seed is so near the surface, there is a greater risk than normal of it drying out in hot weather, in which case cover the bed with a thin mulch or polythene film until the seed has germinated. Alternatively, sprinkle fine soil, potting compost or sand over the surface.

You can achieve much the same effect by making parallel drills very close together. Make narrow drills about 5–7½cm/2–3in apart, and wider, 10cm/4in-wide drills (to take one example) about 10–15cm/4–6in apart. These will be easier to weed than a broadcast patch.

Sowing large seeds individually Very large seeds, such as peas, beans, cucumbers and sweet corn, can be sown by simply making a hole in the soil with the point of a small dibber and dropping the seed into it. Make sure the seed touches the bottom of the hole and is not suspended in mid-air. Sow two or three seeds per hole, thinning to one seedling after germination. For early sowings, you can use a jam jar as a 'mini cloche', placed over the planted seeds to help warm the soil (see illustration above). Early sowings can also be made under cloches.

Sowing under fleeces and transparent films To give extra protection against the weather early in the season, sow seeds under

A jam jar can be used as a 'mini cloche' to give seeds an early start. Sow large seeds singly or in a group of two or three, thinning to the strongest after germination. Remove the jar during the day as soon as the seeds are through.

fleeces and polythene films (see p. 224–5). Sow the seed in slightly indented drills, with the films laid over the top. This will prevent the films from slumping on to the germinating seedlings if wet weather ensues.

Thinning

Seedlings grow very rapidly, and if they are overcrowded they become diseased and fail to develop properly. Thin them as soon as they are large enough to handle, either when the ground is moist or having watered gently beforehand. To minimize disturbance to the remaining seedlings, simply nip off unwanted seedlings just above soil level. It is best to thin in stages, each time thinning so that every seedling stands clear of its neighbour (see illustrations p. 200). Be sure to clear away surplus thinnings, as their scent may attract the plant's enemies.

Sowing indoors

Raising plants indoors is best seen as a multi-stage operation in which certain phases may be omitted or merged with others. The key phases are:

To avoid damaging seedling roots, thin by nipping off surplus seedlings just above soil level.

Thin so that each remaining seedling stands clear of its neighbour. Firm back the soil after thinning.

Sowing Seed is sown in a small container, in fine-textured 'compost' or a special growing medium. It is put somewhere warm to germinate.

Pricking out The crowded seedlings are transplanted individually into a larger container with richer, coarser compost. They are spaced out so that they can grow rapidly.

Potting on The by-now small plants are moved into individual pots of richer compost.

Hardening off Plants destined to be grown outside or at lower temperatures are gradually acclimatized before being planted in their permanent positions.

With modern composts and propagators it is deceptively easy to germinate seedlings, and at this stage they take up little space. Once they are pricked out and/or potted on, they need more room, good light and some warmth. It may be difficult to meet these conditions unless you have a greenhouse or polytunnel. It can be several weeks from sowing before soil conditions and temperatures are suitable for planting outside, so beware of sowing more plants than you have room for. If they are kept in overcrowded conditions with inadequate light or heat, they will deteriorate and be prone to disease. If this is the case, consider buying some of the plants you need from garden centres or mail order seed companies, many of whom now supply plants.

Sowing containers

Seed trays are the most widely used containers for sowing seeds. They need to be deep enough to hold about 2½cm/1in of growing medium. You can use all sorts of things, from small clay or plastic horticultural pots 5–7½cm/2–3in deep to the wide range of containers used in the take-away industry. Whatever the container, it must have some means of drainage (make holes in the base if necessary) or be naturally porous, like cardboard egg boxes.

Modules In recent years the concept of sowing in 'modules' has gained ground and is highly recommended. In essence, a module is any container or 'cell' in which a single seed is sown and grown on until it is ready for planting. This eliminates the need for the pricking-out stage and, because the seedlings have no competition from neighbouring seedlings, results in plants of excellent quality.

The module-raised plant is planted out intact, so there is virtually no root disturbance. Fibre pots are planted out whole, as roots will grow through them. The robustness of seedlings grown in modules means you can often plant them under conditions where planting normal 'bare-root' transplants would be impossible. They are also less likely to deteriorate if for any reason you have to delay planting. Plants raised in modules are often known as 'plugs'.

Modules are a useful means of raising a range of plants or a sequence of varieties where garden space is limited. For example, you could sow a dozen or so lettuce modules every week or ten days to provide continuity, or, in theory, sow a large, forty-celled module tray with something different in each cell, or more likely several different varieties or crops. In this case try and choose ones that are likely to germinate at roughly the same time, or you will run into logistic problems over hardening off, with half empty trays occupying precious space in the propagating area.

The most common type of modules are seed trays of moulded plastic, divided into cells. A unique form of deeper module is the 'Rootrainer' system, originally developed for raising tree seedlings. The sets of plastic cells open up for planting so there is minimal root disturbance. They last for several years.

You can convert standard seed trays into modules with interlocking plastic dividers – home-made if necessary. Small pots, if seeds are sown in them individually, are in effect modules. Another form of module is the 'soil block', made by compressing specially formulated potting compost into a compact cube with a block-making tool. The freestanding blocks can be aligned in a standard seed tray.

Blocking tools and compost are currently hard to find, so the system, valuable though it is, has fallen out of use. I mention it here in case it reappears in future.

TYPES OF SOWING CONTAINER

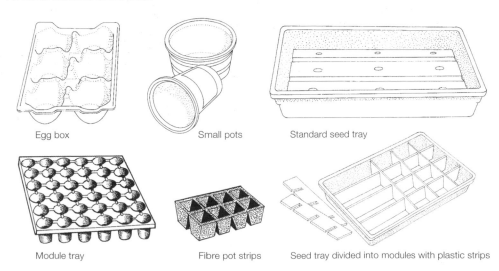

Egg box

Small pots

Standard seed tray

Module tray

Fibre pot strips

Seed tray divided into modules with plastic strips

Sowing and potting compost

Ordinary garden soil is unsuitable for raising plants indoors, as it is too coarse and likely to be full of weed seed. Various light-textured sowing and potting composts have been developed for the purpose; most are sterile, so there is no problem with germinating weeds. Sowing composts are very fine-textured, and contain few plant nutrients, so they cannot sustain plants beyond the seedling stage. An experienced grower has found that their performance is improved, and more robust seedlings are produced, by incorporating perlite or vermiculite at a rate of 25–50%.

Potting composts are coarser with a higher level of nutrients, so they can support plants until they are potted on or planted out. In practice, most salad plants can be sown direct into a potting compost or 'multipurpose' compost, unless the seed is exceptionally fine. Alternatively, seed can be germinated successfully in an inert medium such as coarse sand, perlite or vermiculite, or even sifted leaf mould; these have no nutritive value, so seedlings need to be transferred into a stronger compost soon after germination. 'Garden' compost, incidentally, is unsuitable as a growing medium: it is too rich and using it would result in sappy, disease-prone seedlings.

In the past, two main types of composts were widely used: the soil-based composts made to the John Innes formula, and peat-based composts. Both incorporate chemical fertilizers and both utilize peat. As peat is a diminishing natural resource, its use is discouraged in organic gardening. Finding

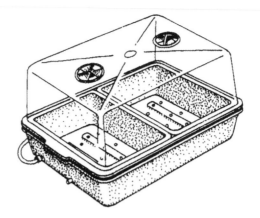

A simple domestic plug-in propapagator, in which the heat source is an electric light bulb beneath the tray. The cover helps retain moisture, while the small ventilators prevent the build-up of condensation, which may lead to damping-off diseases. Otherwise remove the cover daily, wiping off any moisture.

satisfactory substitutes has been a problem. However, alternative composts are being developed from various sources: coir (the natural coconut waste product), worm-worked compost, green waste from household recycling sites, wood waste and others. Use them whenever possible. Buy good quality potting compost: don't be tempted by cheap offers. I am a firm believer in the benefit of watering sowing or potting composts with a weak solution of seaweed extract. It seems to stimulate healthy growth, as well as providing nutrients for the developing seedlings.

Propagators

Most seeds germinate best in warm soil, a soil temperature of 13–16°C/55–60°F being suitable for the majority of salad plants. Propagators are a means of supplying 'bottom heat' below the seed tray. They range from very simple units heated with an electric light bulb, to electrically warmed plates or coils placed beneath or within a seed tray, to elaborate automated, self-watering units.

OPPOSITE Plants raised individually in modules develop exceptionally strong root systems and suffer minimal disturbance when planted out.

A propagating unit can also be installed on a greenhouse bench using insulated electric cables buried in sand. Get professional advice if making a home-made system. Propagators can be designed to run in conjunction with gas, oil and paraffin greenhouse heaters.

A propagating unit should have a cover to retain atmospheric moisture and prevent the seed trays from drying out. As space in a propagator is always at a premium, try to choose containers of a size that will fit into it neatly.

Sowing in containers

Fill the containers as in illustration (1) below, with moist but not wet compost. Some types of compost are difficult to re-wet when dry; if so it may be easier to fill the container with dry compost and stand it in a tray of

SOWING IN CONTAINERS

1. Fill the seed tray to within 12mm/½ in of the top, levelling the surface with a piece of board.

2. Sow seeds very thinly on the surface. Here a piece of glass, with the tip moistened, is used to pick up individual seeds, and space them 1–2½cm/½–1in apart.

3. Sift a thin layer of potting compost, coarse sand, perlite or vermiculite over the seeds to cover them. Press it smooth after sowing.

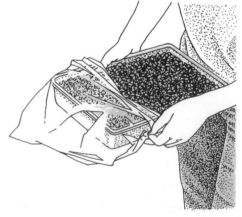

4. Slip the seed tray into a plastic bag to keep the compost moist until the seed germinates.

water for an hour or two or even overnight to absorb moisture. See what works best with the materials you have. Once you have filled the container, tap it a couple of times to settle the compost, then smooth the surface with a piece of board or, for a round container, with the bottom of a flower pot or something similar.

Sow the seed thinly on the surface, trying to space seeds at least 1–2½cm/½–1in apart. Large seeds can be handled between the fingers; with small seeds it is easier to push them gently off a piece of paper. A useful method of sowing individual seeds is to tip them into a saucer, and to pick them up singly on the moistened point of a piece of broken glass (see illustration (2) opposite). Dangerous though this sounds, it works beautifully, the seed dropping off as it touches the compost. You can pick up seed on the tip of a darning needle or bodkin, but it does work best with broken glass!

Cover the seeds with sifted compost, coarse sand, or a thin layer of perlite or vermiculite, which seems to reduce the risk of damping-off (see illustration (3) opposite). If the surface is dry, water gently with a fine rose on the can, or for very small seeds, use a mister. To prevent the compost drying out, put the container into a covered propagator or plastic bag (see illustration (4) opposite), or cover it with a sheet of glass. Some seed trays have a plastic dome or cover for this reason.

Sowing in modules

Use the same method to sow in modules, but, with the exception of multi-sowing below, aim for only one germinated seedling in each module. To this end either sow one seed per cell, or sow several seeds and nip out all but the strongest after germination. If you are uncertain about the viability of the seed, do a germination test before sowing (see p. 192). Sow the seed in a small indentation in the centre of each module, made with the finger or a miniature dibber.

Multi-sowing There are cases where several seedlings can be sown in a module, left unthinned and planted out 'as one'. This saves space and time when sowing and planting. The modules are planted slightly further apart than normal to compensate for the number of plants at each station. Onions, turnips, kohl rabi, leeks, and round beetroot all respond well to multi-sowing. The wider spacing enables intercropping in the early stages, such as small lettuces between rows of multi-seeded onions.

Germination

After sowing, put the containers somewhere warm to germinate – in a propagator, in an airing cupboard, above but not directly on a radiator, or on a windowsill (in which case keep them out of direct sunlight). Examine the seeds daily, removing the covers for a few minutes to let air circulate and wiping off condensation. This helps prevent damping-off diseases.

Post germination Most vegetable seeds germinate within four to ten days, and once germinated, tend to grow rapidly. Bring seeds that have been germinated in the dark into the light immediately, or they will become weak and etiolated and rarely develop into strong plants. Turn seedlings on a windowsill half a circle daily, so that growth is even. Germinated seedlings need good light (but not direct sunlight) and warmth: in most cases temperatures 3–6°C/5–10°F lower than those needed for germination will suffice during the day; at night, aim to keep them at

First water the seedlings thoroughly. Fill the seed tray or module into which they are being moved with moist potting compost and level the surface. Use a small dibber to ease out the individual seedlings, holding them by their leaves to avoid damaging the root hairs.

Make a small hole in the compost just large enough for the seedling's roots. Insert the seedling so that the lower leaves are just above the surface.

Firm the soil gently around the base of the stem. Space most seedlings about 4cm/1½in apart and keep them out of direct sunlight until they are well established.

least frost-free. At this stage remove covers on the containers wholly or partially to give the plants adequate ventilation. Keep the compost moist but do not overwater.

Pricking out

Never allow seedlings to become overcrowded. As soon as they are large enough to handle, generally when they have two or three small leaves, prick them out into potting or multi-purpose compost. They are normally pricked out into seed trays that are about 4cm/1½in deep, or into modules. (For the method, see illustrations above.)

Potting on

Many salad plants – lettuce and endive, for example – can be planted out direct from the seed tray after hardening off (see opposite page, bottom right) once they have developed a good root system and four or five healthy leaves. Plants such as tomatoes, which need to remain under cover longer, or will be grown to maturity in a large pot, need to be potted on. Never move a plant directly from a small into a very much larger pot: pot it first into a pot of an intermediary size.

Standard potting compost is normally used for potting on, but home-made mixtures can be satisfactory. I often make my own, mixing roughly equal quantities of good soil (taken from near the compost heap), well-rotted garden compost, and well-rotted leaf mould or commercial potting compost to lighten the mixture. If using a soil-based compost, fill the bottom third of the pot with drainage material, such as broken crocks, covered with dried leaves or coarse fibrous material (this is unnecessary with proprietary composts, which are well drained). Plants may need supplementary feeding after a few weeks in pots (see p. 242).

Hardening off

Before they are put outside, plants need to be gradually acclimatized to colder, more exposed situations, preferably over a two- to three-week period. Start by increasing the ventilation indoors; then move the plants into a sheltered position outside during the day,

POTTING ON

Water the plant that is being moved, then ease it out of its container. Holding it so that the bottom of the stem is 2½cm/1in below the rim of the new pot, pack potting compost gently around the roots. Tap the pot on the bench to settle the compost, and finally firm around the stem with the fingertips. Water gently after planting, using a fine rose.

bringing them in at night. If you have a cold frame, simply remove the frame lights during the day and replace them at night. Finally leave the plants out day and night before planting. 'Stroking' or 'brushing' is a method of hardening off which avoids the need to move plants or manipulate their conditions (see illustration right). Hardening off is especially important when plants are raised in peat-based composts, which encourage lush, soft growth, making plants more susceptible to checks, pests and diseases after planting.

Planting

Planting is inevitably a shock and setback to a plant, so whatever you are planting, whether small plants from a seedbed or seed tray or a pot-grown plant, try to minimize the disturbance.

Plants vary in their optimum size for planting. Some, such as Chinese cabbage, transplant badly, though the use of modules helps overcome the problem. Within reason, the younger plants are when transplanted, the better. Root crops such as carrots and parsnips, though normally sown *in situ*, can be transplanted when very small before the taproots develop. Always plant in dull weather or in the cool of the evening.

Having already dug over and prepared the ground, rake it smooth. The soil should be pleasantly moist, so in dry conditions, water several hours prior to planting. Similarly water the seedbed or container well in advance. Dig up the plants with a trowel, holding them by the leaves or stem so the delicate root hairs are not damaged. Remove plants in pots by upturning the pot and tapping it sharply. Make a hole in the ground large enough to accommodate roots without cramping them. Holding the plant in the hole, replace the soil around its roots (see illustration overleaf). Firm

'Stroking' or 'brushing' is an alternative method of hardening off developed by the Japanese to save moving the plants outdoors. Using a piece of paper or cardboard, brush the seedlings backwards and forwards for up to a minute a day. It can be done twice a day. This equates to the 'toughening' effect of exposure to the elements.

When planting, hold the plant by the stem, while filling in the soil around its roots. Both the original container and the soil where it is being planted should be watered well in advance.

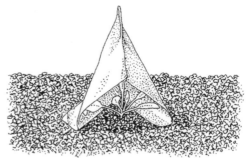

In hot weather plants benefit from shading immediately after planting. Make a simple shading cone from newspaper or a heavy-duty envelope, stapled to a short cane. Small pieces of shading net can also be used.

the soil around the stem and check that the plant is firmly anchored by tugging a leaf. If the plant wobbles, replant more firmly. If necessary, water and mulch after planting, provided the plants would not be swamped by the mulch.

In hot weather shade the plant for a few days: simple shades can be made from paper (see above right). Leafy plants that are naturally vigorous but wilt in heat, like chicories and spinach, can be trimmed back to a couple of centimetres after planting to minimize water loss.

Weeding

The salad lover looks upon weeds with a kindlier eye than most gardeners because many weeds, especially in the seedling stage, make tasty, nutritious additions to a salad. But they compete with other vegetables for water, nutrients, light and space, so must be kept under control. Weeds are either perennial or annual.

Perennials live on in the soil from one year to the next. They may have invasive creeping root systems, such as couch grass (*Agropyron repens*) and ground elder (*Aegopodium podagraria*), or deep, stubborn tap roots, such as the broad-leaved dock (*Rumex obtusifolius*) and dandelion (*Taraxacum officinale*). Use a good wild-plant book (see Further reading p. 274) to identify your perennial weeds, and dig them out without mercy. Remove even small pieces of root, and expose them to the sun to wilt before composting them. Most perennials decline when ground is cultivated regularly. Where there is a serious problem, in a previously neglected garden for example, the only solution other than using chemical weedkillers is to blanket the ground with heavy-duty black film, cardboard or old carpet. If necessary, leave this for up to a year, though it may be feasible to start planting sooner through a film or cardboard mulch.

Annual weeds germinate, seed and die within a year, in some cases having several generations a year. A single plant can produce an enormous number of seeds, and some remain viable in the soil for very many years. So in weed-ridden soils there is a huge reservoir of seed, waiting for favourable conditions to germinate.

The most important factor in the war against annual weeds is to prevent them from going to seed in the first place. There is considerable truth in the old adage, 'One year's seeding, seven years' weeding.' Shallow cultivation disturbs weed seeds near the surface, destroying about half as a result, either when they germinate and are hoed off, or through exposure to birds or bad weather. After several years' cultivation their numbers will be markedly reduced. Deeper cultivation brings up seed from lower levels, so in weedy soil confine cultivation to shallow hoeing.

When previously undisturbed soil is cultivated, there is a great flush of weeds in the first year. Hoe them off and, if you have time, let a second crop of weeds germinate before sowing or planting.

Where the ground is obviously still harbouring reserves of weed seeds, it is best initially to avoid direct sowing in favour of planting: plants will have a head start over weeds. Minimize cultivation during the growing season or only cultivate shallowly to avoid bringing up deeper weed seed. Keeping crops mulched (see p. 213) is a very effective means of preventing weeds from germinating. Growing plants at equidistant spacing (see p. 230) rather than in rows also prevents weed germination.

Research has shown that weeds between rows pose much more competition to

ABOVE An onion hoe enables you to weed closely between plants. In hot weather the weeds can be left on the surface to wilt.

growing crops than those within rows, so remove them first. Where crops are sown as opposed to planted, weeds start to become competitive about three weeks after the crop has germinated. If time is short, postpone weeding until that point: remember though, that by then it is urgent! My favourite tool for weeding in an intensively cultivated salad garden is a small hand or onion hoe, which enables you to get really close to the plants.

Watering

Plants require a constant throughput of water, taken in through the roots and evaporated through the leaves. They need enough water to keep the leaves turgid – growth is checked once they start to wilt – but it is a fallacy to assume that the more watering the better. Water washes nitrogen and other soluble nutrients out of reach of the roots; it encourages shallow, surface rooting, rather than the deep rooting that enables plants to utilize deeper reserves of nutrients and moisture; and I am personally convinced it reduces the flavour of vegetables such as tomatoes.

Water mainly stimulates leaf growth, which is what you want for leafy plants such as lettuce and cabbage. With root and bulb crops, radish and onions for example, overwatering may result in excessive leaf growth at the expense of the roots. Requirements also vary according to the stage of development: there are 'critical periods' for watering (see opposite).

Conserving water

In regions where water is an increasingly scarce resource, do everything you can to conserve it. The following practices all work towards this end:

- Dig in as much bulky organic matter as possible, as deeply as possible. This increases the water-holding capacity of the soil, and is particularly beneficial on light, fast-draining soils.
- Keep the soil surface mulched to prevent evaporation (see p. 213). Far more water is lost through evaporation than drainage.
- On sloping ground, cultivate across rather than down the slope (see illustration right).
- In dry weather, cultivate as little as possible and only very shallowly; deeper cultivation brings moisture to the surface, which then evaporates. Once the top few centimetres of the soil have dried out, they act as a mulch and the rate of evaporation is slowed down.
- Keep the ground weed-free. Weeds both compete for water and evaporate

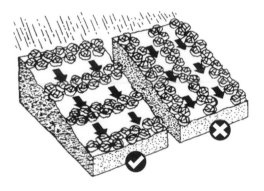

In a sloping garden, plan beds and crops to run across, rather than down, the slope. This cuts down water loss through surface run-off, and helps to prevent soil erosion from becoming a problem.

moisture through their leaves.
- Wind increases the rate of evaporation, so especially in exposed gardens erect artificial windbreaks (see p. 172).
- Collect water from conveniently sited roofs, with a down pipe leading to a lidded rain butt, barrel or suitable container.
- Where water is scarce, concentrate watering on the critical periods (see opposite).

How to water

The golden rule is to water gently and thoroughly. Large water droplets destroy the soil surface and damage fragile plants and seedlings. Water these with a fine rose on the can, the rose turned upwards for the gentlest spray.

The most common fault is to underwater. Even when it looks wet, the soil is often still surprisingly dry. Soil becomes wet layer by layer, and until the top layers are thoroughly wet, the root zone beneath will remain dry. To test how far water has penetrated, push your finger into the soil after watering. It is often far drier than you imagined it would be. Generally speaking, heavy but infrequent watering is far more beneficial than frequent, light watering. However, light soils need to be watered more frequently than heavy soils, though less water is required at each watering.

With established plants, direct water to the base of the plant. Where plants are spaced far apart, confine watering to a circular area around each, leaving the soil between them dry to discourage weed germination. Water large plants such as tomatoes and courgettes by sinking a clay pot into the ground near the plant and watering into the pot.

Plants grown close together make heavy demands on soil water and need generous watering. In very arid conditions plants are spaced far apart for this reason. Intensively grown cut-and-come-again crops also need plenty of water.

Wherever possible, water in the evening to minimize evaporation, but allow time for leaves to dry before nightfall. This is particularly relevant in greenhouses and polytunnels, to prevent diseases exacerbated by high humidity.

A method of watering while away is to make 12mm/½in wide wicks from twisted soft material (such as wool, string or cloth). Place one end in a bucket and the other on the soil. Water seeps along the wick keeping the plant moist.

Critical periods for watering

Germination Seeds will not germinate in dry conditions, so water ground destined for sowing in advance.

Transplanting This is a delicate stage for plants. Transplant them into moist but not waterlogged soil, and keep it moist until they are established. Root hairs on bare-root plants (as opposed to plants raised in modules) are often damaged by transplanting, so the plant can only absorb a little water at a time initially. Water gently – daily in dry weather – applying no more than 140ml/¼ pint each time.

Leafy vegetables Leafy vegetables such as brassicas, lettuce, endive, spinach, celery and courgette require a lot of water throughout growth. In the absence of rainfall, they will benefit from about 9–14 litres per sq. m/2–3 gallons per sq. yd a week. Where regular watering is difficult, limit watering to a single, very heavy watering – about 18 litres per sq. m/4 gallons per sq. yd – 10–20 days before you estimate the plant is ready for harvesting.

- **Fruiting vegetables** For tomatoes, cucumbers, peas and beans – all vegetables grown, in botanical terms, for their fruits – the critical time for watering is when the plants are flowering and the fruits start to swell. Heavy watering at this stage increases their yields appreciably. (Approriate rates for each crop are given pp. 16–167.)
- **Root crops** These need enough water for steady growth, but too much water encourages lush foliage rather than root development. In the early stages, water only if the soil is in danger of drying out, at the rate of at least 4½ litres per sq. m/1 gallon per sq. yd a week. They require more water in the later stages as the roots swell.

Watering equipment

In small gardens, a watering can, with a fine rose for watering seedlings, is sufficient. In larger gardens, a hose with a spray nozzle can be used, or semi-automatic systems, which potentially save time and water. In these, various types of hose or tubing are connected directly to a tap or garden hose running from a tap. They gently water a strip up to 50cm/20in wide. Reasonable water pressure is necessary for them to work well. Overhead sprinkler systems are not recommended. They waste water (much evaporates or falls on bare soil), and plants are more prone to disease when water is directed on to leaves, rather than to the roots.

The following are systems currently marketed to home gardeners.

Perforated polythene 'layflat' tube This cheap, flexible, but not very durable hose is laid on the ground between plants. Water seeps out through small holes in the tube. Systems made from stronger materials are also available.

Porous pipe/soaker hose These robust hoses are permeable over their whole surface. They can be buried 10–15cm/4–6in deep in the soil in permanent beds or, where more flexibility is wanted, laid on the surface. Covering them with mulch prevents evaporation and the build-up of scale in hard-water areas.

Trickle or drip irrigation Water is delivered to individual plants through nozzles or emitters in fine tubes. Networks can be designed to water large areas, greenhouses and containers such as growing bags and hanging baskets. Some drip irrigation systems can work from a water butt reservoir without need for mains water. On a large scale, get professional advice and good-quality equipment. Smaller systems are available from garden suppliers and garden centres.

Mulching

Mulching is the practice of keeping the soil covered with some kind of material. The mulch can be an organic material, such as compost, leaf mould or even recycled paper, cardboard or the more recently developed biodegradable films, all of which eventually rot into the soil. It can also be an inorganic material, such as polythene film, or even stones, gravel and sand – traditional mulching materials in hot climates.

The main purpose of a mulch is to conserve moisture in the soil. This is important, not only because plants need water, but because they can only extract soluble nutrients from moist soil. However, mulches have many other beneficial effects. They help control weeds, both by inhibiting weed seed germination and suppressing subsequent growth; weeds that do germinate are easily pulled out of a mulch. Mulches improve soil structure by protecting the soil surface from heavy rain and desiccating winds, and by lessening the impact of treading on the soil. Most organic mulches are a source of nutrients and provide food for worms which, in turn, contribute in many ways to soil fertility. Mulches beneath sprawling plants such as cucumbers help keep the fruit clean, and prevent disease spores from splashing on to the foliage and fruit. Small mats made of materials such as flax fibre are sometimes sold for the purpose. White reflective mulches can be used to encourage fruit ripening in tomatoes. Some mulches are used to deter insects.

Mulches keep the soil cooler in summer and warmer in winter. This slows down frost penetration, making it easier to dig vegetables out of the ground. Stone, gravel and sand mulches in greenhouses radiate heat at night, raising the air temperature.

Types of organic mulch

The many suitable materials for organic mulches include animal manures, garden compost, seaweed, old straw, spent mushroom compost, cotton waste, wilted green manures, wilted comfrey, lawn mowings, leaves, coir and cocoa shell. Various other materials can be used, provided they will rot down and are fairly loose-textured. This makes them easier to spread close to plants and allows rain to penetrate gently.

Fresh lawn mowings can form an impenetrable sticky mat – so for mulching during the growing season are best partially dried first. As a general rule mulching materials should preferably be wilted or partly rotted, or nitrogen will initially be taken from the soil as decomposition starts.

Avoid materials that are likely to be a source of diseases or weed seeds, or have been treated with weedkillers. It is best to avoid using wood derivatives, such as sawdust, wood shavings, and pulverized and shredded bark, and tough leaves such as pine needles on vegetable beds unless they have been composted for several months, alone or mixed with animal manures. They are excellent, however, as path mulches. Newspaper, cardboard, recycled paper and carpet, though of low nutritive value, can be used in appropriate situations for mulching

vegetables. Use them like polythene mulching films (see below). The remnants of most organic mulches can be dug in at the end of the season, although by then earthworms will often have done the work.

When and how to mulch

A key fact about mulching is that it maintains the status quo of the soil. So don't mulch when the soil is very cold, very wet or very dry – all conditions which discourage plant growth – because the soil will stay that way. Mulch when the soil is warm and moist: the soil temperature should be at least 6°C/43°F and preferably higher.

On the whole, the most suitable time to mulch is when planting. But if planting in spring, make sure that the soil has warmed up before mulching; in summer, water well after planting and then mulch to cut down on subsequent watering. Either plant through the mulch, or mulch after planting. In his book *Square Foot Gardening*, Mel Bartholomew suggests drilling holes in a pile of newspapers or carpet squares and slipping them over growing plants. Or make a carpet mulching pad by cutting a slit from the perimeter to a hole in the centre; you can then ease it around a plant.

It is inadvisable to mulch with loose organic materials immediately after sowing, as birds are likely to scratch around, disturbing seeds and seedlings. Mulch seedlings in stages once they are through the soil, taking care not to swamp the small plants.

As to thickness of mulch, with the exception of films and similar materials, the thicker the mulch the more effective it will be in conserving moisture and suppressing weeds. In most circumstances a mulch 2½–5cm/1–2in deep is adequate, though tall plants like tomatoes grow well with a mulch 15–20cm/6–8in deep.

Mulching Films

There is a wide range of mulching films, with new forms being regularly introduced.

Impermeable, light, black polythene films These suppress weeds in the short term, but don't allow rainfall to penetrate. They tend to make soils cool. Use them as a short-term weed mulch in vegetable beds. Early potatoes are often grown under black film to avoid earthing up.

Biodegradeable mulching films These are manufactured from various materials, such as jute, recycled paper, and corn starch and vegetable oil. They are used to suppress weeds, conserve moisture and keep crops clean. They generally last for about 3–4 months, depending on the product. When the crop is harvested, the remnants can be dug in or composted.

Perforated, light, black polythene films These have masses of tiny perforations, allowing some water and air to penetrate. This makes them suitable for longer-term mulches, usually on perennial crops such as strawberries.

Perforated, clear polythene films Primarily used as crop covers, these can also be used to warm up soil.

Impermeable, clear polythene films Use these to warm up the soil in spring.

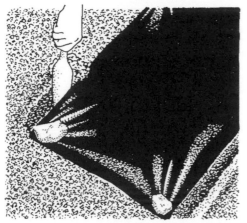

Lay the film on the bed with a little spare film on each side. Use a trowel to make slits in the soil about 10cm/4in deep on each side of the bed.

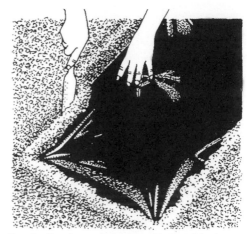

Bury the film edge, replacing the soil to keep it in place. The film should be smooth but not too taut.

Cut crossed slits (about 8cm/3in long) in the film at suitable intervals for the plants.

Ease the slits open and plant through them.

They retain moisture, but will not prevent weed germination.

Opaque, white polythene films These reflect light and warmth upwards, so are used to mulch ripening tomatoes, melons, etc. They help retain soil moisture, but do not suppress weeds very effectively.

Double-sided black and white polythene films These dual-purpose films are used as opaque, white films above.

The black surface is laid downwards to suppress weeds, while the upper white surface reflects light, and therefore heat, up to ripening fruit.

Permeable woven polypropylene black films These heavy-duty films suppress weeds, and are excellent for mulching paths. Their permeability prevents paths from becoming waterlogged. They can be used to mulch large plants, but are apt

ABOVE Salad plants can be kept very clean by mulching with polythene film.

to chafe them. Weeds and plants eventually grow through them: disentangling them from the fabric can be tricky. 'Mypex' is the best-known brand.

Permeable, black fabric This lightweight fabric is warm and soft to the touch. It suppresses weeds, allows some moisture to penetrate, and has a warming effect. It is excellent for mulching winter crops under cover, but can also be used outdoors. It is more expensive than polythene films, but should last several seasons. 'Permealay' is one brand name for this material.

Chequered and coloured films
Various films deter specific insect pests, but are currently not widely available.

The above films can be anchored into a slit in the soil (see illustration opposite), pinned with metal 'tent pegs' or plastic pins, or weighted down with bags of soil or sand (see image on p. 224). When mulching individual plants, it is usually easiest to lay the film, then to plant through a cross or semicircle cut in the film (see illustration opposite). Alternatively plant first, unroll the film, cut openings over the plants and ease them through. Large seeds like sweet corn can be sown through holes punched in film, easing the leaves through when large enough. I should add a warning: polythene films attract slugs. But at least you know where to look for them!

217

Protected cropping

Greenhouses, walk-in polythene tunnels (polytunnels), garden frames, cloches, low polytunnels and the various kinds of 'crop covers' are all means of growing 'under cover' or 'protected cropping'. Essentially, this means giving plants shelter, and nothing increases yields and productivity as markedly as shelter from the elements (see p. 172). Moreover with salad plants, it is the combination of low temperatures and high winds that is potentially lethal. If they are protected from wind, they will survive much lower temperatures than would otherwise be the case, and the leaves will remain palatable instead of becoming tough.

Uses of protection

In cool temperate climates, protection is the main tool for extending the salad season, with a view to having fresh salads all year round. Most plants start to grow when temperatures rise above 6°C/43°F in spring, and stop growing when they fall below 6°C/43°F in autumn. The days between these two points are termed 'growing days': their number determines which crops can be grown successfully in any area. Soil protected with glass or polythene warms up sooner in the year and remains warm later, potentially extending the growing season by at least three weeks – twenty-one 'growing days' – at either end of the season.

For example, in spring the very first salads can be cut-and-come-again seedlings from early sowings under cover (see pp. 234–239). Many summer vegetables can be started under cover in seed trays or modules, for planting outside as soon as soil conditions and temperatures allow. Where the growing season is short, this head start is crucial for the success of heat-lovers such as tomatoes, peppers and cucumbers, which cannot be sown or planted outdoors until all risk of frost is passed. These crops can also be grown to maturity in greenhouses and polytunnels – along with tender herbs such as basil. Towards the end of summer, marginally hardy salads such as Chinese cabbage, pak choi, Florence fennel, red chicory, endive and winter purslane can be planted under cover for winter and spring use. So can hardier salads such as oriental mustards, along with cut-and-come-again seedling sowings of kales, spinach, corn salad, chervil, coriander, salad rocket, Sugar Loaf chicory and so on. All will be far more productive and better-quality when grown under cover.

Heated greenhouses and polytunnels are very costly, and outside the scope of this book, though where facilities are available they can be turned to excellent use in winter and early spring. Garden frames are relatively easy to heat with electric soil-warming cables. However, in my experience in the UK climate, a wide range of winter salads can be grown satisfactorily in unheated forms of protection.

It has to be appreciated that unheated glass and polythene structures will not keep out frost. This can only be guaranteed by heating them: winter temperatures under cover will be only marginally higher than those outside. The benefits of these structures lie in their

ABOVE Rows of carrot, red mizuna, komatsuma and mizuna in a cold frame for a winter crop.

sheltering effect. Incidentally, if plants, either under cover or in the open, have been affected by frost, shade them or spray them with water the following morning, before the sun reaches them. This allows them to thaw out slowly and may prevent serious damage.

In hot weather, temperatures under cover can soar, encouraging the rapid build-up of greenhouse pests such as red spider mite and whitefly. So greenhouses and polytunnels must have good ventilation. In hot conditions they should be 'damped down' once or twice during the day when temperatures are at their highest. Lightly sprinkle plants, the ground and paths with water to increase humidity and lower the temperature. It is most easily

done with a finger on the end of a hose pipe, breaking up and directing the jet. Good air flow is also important in winter, as disease builds up in stagnant conditions. Overall, the value of good ventilation under cover, especially for organic gardeners, cannot be over-emphasized.

Protected ground is a precious resource, and should be treated as such. Bring the soil to a high state of fertility by working in plenty of well-rotted organic matter. I personally avoid using farmyard manure in permanent structures, as it may introduce soil pests, such as symphilids, which are hard to eliminate. Weeds germinate and grow rapidly under cover and soil dries out quickly, so keeping the soil mulched is highly recommended to control them (see pp. 213–217). Most forms of protection have to be watered by hand, unless a semi-automatic watering system is installed (see p. 212).

There have been notable developments in the protected cropping field in recent years, with a huge range of options now available to amateur gardeners. Indeed the distinctions between polytunnels and greenhouses, and even garden frames, have been eroded. Polytunnels are available in a variety of shapes and sizes, some with pitched roofs not unlike greenhouses, while the widely acclaimed 'Keder' greenhouses are made with steel frame hoops clad with bubble film.

Some so-called garden frames are almost mini tunnels. They are an invaluable resource for salad growers.

Broadly speaking, what do the different types of protection have to offer?

Greenhouses

Traditional greenhouses are expensive, permanent structures, but as glass transmits light well and traps heat efficiently at night, they create excellent growing conditions. They can accommodate tall crops such as tomatoes, and plants can be grown in the ground or in containers. As solid structures, they are easily ventilated.

Their main drawback is 'soil sickness', a build-up of serious soil pests and diseases which develops where tomatoes and related crops in the Solanaceae family (peppers, aubergines and potatoes) are grown continuously in the same soil. Unless the soil is sterilized or replaced – both laborious procedures – subsequent crops have to be grown in fresh soil in containers or in soilless systems such as ring culture (which uses bottomless pots filled with compost mix,

standing on an inert base such as shingle). Where possible rotate the Solanaceae crops around the greenhouse to prevent the problem developing.

Walk-in polytunnels

Polytunnels are less sophisticated than greenhouses but a fraction of the cost. Their great advantage is that they need no foundations, so can be dismantled relatively easily and erected on a fresh site, so avoiding soil sickness. Hoops can also be concreted into the ground, which is recommended where space is limited, or where netted side vents are fitted at ground level.

The typical, basic, walk-in polytunnel is a structure about 1¾–2m/6–7ft high, made by anchoring polythene film over a frame of galvanized tubular steel hoops. The hoops are slipped into foundation tubes in the ground. Once the frame is erected, the film is secured either in a trench about 45cm/18in wide, which is dug around the base, and backfilled with soil. Or, the more modern system, attached to a wooden or steel base rail. Where polytunnels are erected on a hard surface such as concrete, or flag stones, they need to be secured to base rails attached to special steel plates, which act as 'feet'. (For detailed guidance on erecting polytunnels follow manufacturer's instructions; see also Further reading p. 274.)

There is a wide choice of films today. The better quality the film the longer it will last. Commonly used now are 800-gauge films with a five-year guarantee, though many will last much longer. Always use film treated with an ultra-violet (UV) inhibitor, which extends its life. Films treated with an anti-

A typical modern aluminium-framed greenhouse on concrete foundations. Plants are grown in the soil or in containers. In cold areas greenhouses are used in summer for tender crops and in winter for a range of high-quality salads. They are very easy to manage.

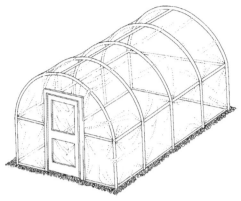

A walk-in polytunnel or hoop tunnel is made by anchoring polythene film over galvanized steel hoops. Polytunnels are cheap and versatile, and are easily moved to a fresh site to avoid the development of soil sickness. They can be used to grow salad crops all year round.

condensation or anti-drip agent increase light levels and reduce the risk of disease. 'Diffuse' films enhance light transmission. 'Thermic' films trap heat inside the tunnel; bubble polythene increases insulation.

Film life is prolonged by insulating the outer curved surfaces of the metal hoops with adhesive 'anti-hot-spot' tape. This protects the film from direct contact with the hoops, which can become very hot and burn the film. Always fit the film as smoothly and tightly as possible: the first tears arise where film is flapping or rubbing against a rough surface – though with modern tapes even extensive damage can be repaired. It really pays to cover the hoops initially on a warm day, when the film is limp and easily pulled taut.

Polytunnels are difficult to ventilate. They tend to overheat in summer and become humid in winter, with the attendant risks of pests and disease. Always build in as much ventilation as possible with a means of through ventilation, such as a door at each end with a ventilation panel in at least the top half of each door. Long tunnels are now often fitted with netted side vents at the lower edge: polythene covers can be rolled down over them in cold weather. A primitive method of ventilation, which we used in our original 6m/20ft polytunnel, was to cut semi-circular 'porthole flaps' of 30cm/12in diameter about 45cm/18in above ground level along the length of the tunnel; these could be taped back down in cold weather.

As an organic gardener, I advocate siting polytunnels in a north–south, rather than east–west direction, to minimize the exposure of the long flank to the sun. This helps to keep summer temperatures down and lowers the risk of pests. Not everyone agrees!

With the technical advances in polytunnels, the more sophisticated systems can be costly and even daunting. Don't be deterred: polythene film can be used imaginatively to cover all sorts of structures from wooden frames to derelict outbuildings. It is astonishing the benefits which stem from the even simplest of sheltered structures.

221

Garden frames

A frame is essentially a miniature greenhouse, covering a couple of square metres/yards of ground. Traditional frames were permanent with solid brick or wood sides and a glass 'lid' or 'light'; they were well insulated. The typical modern frame is portable, and made of aluminium and glass or polythene film; it has less insulation but light is more evenly distributed. Free-standing and lean-to frames are easily made from wood and other materials.

The height of the frame determines what can be grown. A clearance of about 23cm/9in is adequate for lettuce, endive and low-growing salads; about 45cm/18in height is necessary for horizontally trained cucumbers, celery, fennel, bush tomatoes or peppers; upright tomatoes can only be grown in a lean-to frame. However, the lights from standard frames can be removed to give maturing plants more room. Ventilation is adjusted by raising or removing the lights.

Besides being used in spring for raising seeds, and for early sowings of carrots, beet, lettuce and radish, frames are ideal for hardening plants. An additional use in winter is for forcing Witloof chicory and blanching endive (see also Uses of protection, p. 218).

Cloches

Cloches are small units made from a wide range of materials including glass, fibreglass, rigid and semi-rigid plastics and polythene film. They vary in size from low, 'tent' cloches, only suitable for low-growing salads, to the classic, high-sided 'barn' cloches, which can accommodate larger plants such as tomatoes,

dwarf beans and peppers, at least in the early stages of growth. Cloches can be used over single plants or placed end-to-end to cover a row. Never leave them open-ended, or winds funnel through, damaging the plants. If no endpieces are supplied, improvise with panes of glass or rigid plastic, held in place with upright canes.

The main advantage of cloches is their mobility. Glass cloches apart, they are lightweight and easy to move around the garden. To some extent, this is also their drawback, as they have to be moved for cultivation, watering and harvesting. To minimize handling, try to plan the garden so that you only need to move them between adjacent strips of ground – a technique known as strip cropping. (See Further reading p. 274 *Grow Your Own Vegetables*.)

When choosing cloches, consider the following factors:

Materials Glass cloches are the most expensive, provide the best growing conditions, are the most stable and, breakages apart, are the most durable. They are however increasingly rare. Opaque corrugated plastics create diffuse light, in which plants seem to grow well. Most plastic materials break down and discolour with exposure to sunlight and should be stored under cover when not in use.
Size The larger the cloche, the more useful it is. Some have extensions which can be raised as the crops grow, or a removable roof. These enable plants that have outgrown the cloche to continue benefiting from side shelter. Large cloches have better air circulation.
Strength Cloches must be robust enough to withstand regular handling and wind. Lightweight cloches may require anchorage

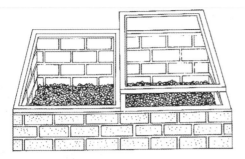

A traditional, permanent, brick-sided frame, with glass lights. It has good insulation.

A portable modern aluminium and glass frame, notable for good, evenly distributed light.

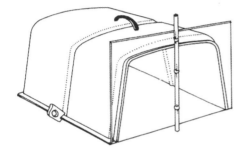

Rigid plastic cloche with end pieces made from glass held in place with a cane.

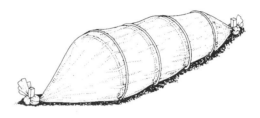

The cheapest form of protection, a low polythene tunnel of thin film laid over wire hoops.

of some kind – such as metal pins through a basal flange.

Ventilation Temperatures rise rapidly under cloches, so removable or built-in ventilation panels are useful. (Some have netting beneath the panels to protect crops against birds when the panels are removed.) Otherwise move cloches apart to ventilate them, removing them completely during very hot weather.

Low polytunnels

In practice low polytunnels, or cloche tunnels as they are also known, are superseding cloches. This cheap form of protection originally consisted of light polythene film (about 150-gauge) over low wire or steel hoops,

the film tied at either end to angled stakes in the ground. They were rarely more than 45cm/18in high at the ridge. Increasingly sophisticated kits have come on the market, utilizing more robust and longer-lasting films and covers, anything up to 1m/3ft height and 2m/7ft width, with end pieces or base frames to anchor the film securely. There are also pegs for attaching the film to the hoops.

Inexpensive low tunnels can be improvised with hoops of plastic electric conduit tube or alkathene water pipe. The sides of the films tend to be blown up in windy conditions, so they may need additional anchorage. There are several options: bury the ends and one side in the soil (leaving the other open for access); run strings or fine wires from side to

223

ABOVE Fine netting laid over hoops, shown anchored with weights, two types of plastic pegs and tent pegs.

ABOVE Fleece anchored with strong plastic bags filled with sand, which will not damage the delicate fabric.

side over the top and attach them to the hoops at ground level; weight the sides in any of the ways used for mulching films (see p. 215). Very light (about 150-gauge) films can only be expected to last two seasons; heavier films will of course last longer.

Unless the film is well anchored, low tunnels offer less protection than more solid cloches. But they are easily worked. For cultivation and ventilation simply push the film back to one side. In some countries they are ventilated, like walk-in polytunnels, by cutting ventilation flaps along their length.

Uses of cloches and low polytunnels

Within the limitations of their height, cloches and low polytunnels are useful means of extending the salad season and improving salad quality. Like frames they can be used for hardening off and for early outdoor sowings. They are easily moved to wherever required: in spring on to ground that needs to be warmed before sowing; in summer over maturing crops like onions or tomatoes to hasten ripening; in autumn and early winter over outdoor salads

to prolong their useful life. They can also be used inside greenhouses and walk-in tunnels, in winter and early spring, as an extra layer of protection for salad crops.

Crop covers

Also known as floating mulches or floating films, these very light films are laid directly on a crop, mainly in the early stages of growth. Their varying degrees of elasticity allow plants to push them up as they grow. They also give some protection against pests. Films are usually put over plants after planting, and anchored by any of the means used for mulching films (see illustrations above and p. 215). They are normally removed four to eight weeks later. Do so in dull conditions or in the evening, to lessen the shock of sudden exposure on the 'soft' plants. These films are generally unsuitable for exposed sites, unless very carefully anchored.

The main types are clear, perforated polythene films and spun-bonded, polypropylene fleeces. With careful handling they will last a couple of seasons. Buy films with reinforced edges where available.

Perforated polythene films These low-cost films are perforated with small holes or slits, allowing air and some water to penetrate. They give no frost protection, but warm the soil and air quickly. Lay them over the crop with a little slack to allow for plant growth. Restricted ventilation means that once temperatures rise plants can deteriorate rapidly; watch the plants carefully and remove the films if they show signs of stress. You can also use the films over low hoops to cover taller crops like tomatoes, but remove them or slit them open once flowering starts to allow insect pollination.

Fleeces These soft fabrics are gentle in action, and more permeable to air and water, so can be left longer on a crop – up to about eight weeks in some cases. Light fleece (17g/½oz) protects against slight frost, heavier fleece (30g/1oz) down to about -6°C/21°F. To increase frost resistance, fleeces can also be covered with the fine nets normally used for pest control. Lay fleece fairly taut over the crop, but with the edges folded so that more fabric can be released as plants grow. Fleeces are used on early salads, potatoes and carrots, on overwintering salads outdoors, and as extra frost protection in greenhouses. In cool conditions carrots are sometimes grown to maturity under fleeces, which also protect them from carrot fly. A drawback is the difficulty in seeing the crop beneath the fleece.

ABOVE It is sometimes simplest to lay Enviromesh directly over a crop to protect against insects. Anchor it along its length and at the corners with pegs, weights or plastic bags filled with sand.

Insect proof mesh nets

Organic gardeners make extensive use of insect-proof mesh nets, of which 'Enviromesh' was the prototype, to protect vegetable crops from a wide range of insect pests. The net is generally laid over low hoops, and well anchored so there are no gaps for insects to enter. Sometimes it is laid directly over the plants. Apart from protecting against pests, the net has a very useful secondary role as a windbreak, effectively sheltering plants and creating a well-ventilated but benign environment for plant growth. Temperatures would not be raised as high as they would under film-clad low tunnels, but for practical purposes, they can be used for much the same uses.

Pests and diseases

The better plants are grown, the fewer problems there will be with pests and diseases. Time and again it is overcrowded or starved plants, those sown too early or at the wrong time, or grown in the wrong situation or an unsuitable climate, that succumb to attacks which well-grown plants resist or outgrow. So I am not going to dwell on pests and diseases, other than the few most likely to occur in the salad garden. It is far more important to create conditions that encourage healthy growth.

This is especially true for organic gardeners, as there are only a few pesticides which have no long-term damaging effects on the soil or environment, and are therefore considered permissable in organic gardening. There are also very few measures which can be taken against disease – such as the 'damping-off' which affects seedlings – other than creating good germination conditions. However, there are alternative remedies for organic gardeners, such as biological controls, where a pest's natural enemies are introduced to control it, and preventive measures such as fine nets, which act as physical barriers against insects. A very important weapon in the gardener's armoury is using varieties bred with resistance to pests or disease. Check in seed catalogues for the latest introductions.

'Best practice' to avoid problems

Make your garden as environmentally friendly as possible; this will encourage the natural enemies of pests. Wasps, incidentally, are great caterpillar predators.

- Practise rotation to prevent the build-up of soil pests and diseases.
- Practise intercropping where appropriate; it confuses and deters pests. (See pp. 231–2).
- Delay sowing or planting outdoors if the soil is cold or wet. Far better to wait a week or so: the plants will catch up. Use cloches or transparent film to warm up the soil.
- Sow thinly and thin early. Overcrowded seedlings are most vulnerable to seedling diseases. If losses from direct sowings in the ground are high, use plants instead, raised indoors, ideally in modules, or purchased.
- When buying-in plants, choose the sturdiest with dark, healthy leaves; examine them carefully for any signs of disease, such as clubroot swellings on the roots of brassicas.
- Grow plants 'hard'. Coddling and overfeeding produce 'soft', vulnerable plants. Remember the organic maxim: 'Feed the soil, not the plants.' Forgo the first tomato in the neighbourhood in favour of a later but healthier crop.
- In summer, keep greenhouses on the cool side: over-ventilation is far healthier than under-ventilation.
- Inspect plants regularly for signs of trouble. It is easy to squash caterpillar eggs or a clutch of newly hatched caterpillars; far harder to track them when they are foraging deep in a plant.
- Dispose of or bury diseased plants. Clear away debris, weeds and old brassica stalks, which may harbour overwintering pests that emerge in spring. Keep water tubs and tanks covered; wash pots and seed boxes after use.

OPPOSITE LEFT A mock bird of prey hopefully deterring pigeons. **RIGHT** Intercropping both confuses pests and looks lovely, while flowers attract beneficial insects.

Handle storage vegetables such as carrots, garlic and onions gently. Storage rots almost invariably start with cuts and bruises, which may be invisible to the naked eye.

Grow appropriate plants for your conditions. For example, if your overwintered lettuce always gets mildew, grow endives instead, which are more tolerant of winter conditions.

'Organic' control measures
Manufactured products

Most have to be applied frequently: their effectiveness is short lived, and they must be applied directly on the pest. There is always some risk of harming beneficial insects and natural predators. The following products are currently available:

Pyrethrum and related products To control greenfly, whitefly, thrips, caterpillars, flea beetle.

Insecticidal soaps (fatty acids) Mainly to control aphids, whitefly and red spider mite.

Vegetable oils (eg rape seed oil) To control aphids, mealybugs, whitefly, blackfly, scale insects, red spider mite.

Ferric phosphate slug pellets Reasonable control of slugs.

Potassium bicarbonate To control powdery mildew on cucumbers and courgettes, applied at first signs of disease.

Plant stimulants and growth promoters Various products, some microbe based, some garlic derivatives, claim to increase root growth and plant vitality, so increasing resistance to disease.

Biological controls

These are particularly successful against greenhouse pests, but the range of pests controlled is continually extending. There are practical restraints on implementing biological controls, relating to temperature, moisture levels and timing. It is important to identify the pest correctly, and follow the supplier's instructions. They are relatively expensive.

Greenhouse biological controls

Live predators or parasites control whitefly, aphids, red spider mite, mealy bugs. Sticky, yellow glue traps can be hung in greenhouses to monitor pest levels, as a guide to introducing controls.

Biological controls using nematodes

Applied as solutions watered on plants or the soil, mainly to control soil pests including, slugs, vine weevil, leather jackets, chafer grubs, carrot root fly, cabbage root fly.

Net and fleece barriers

Nets of different dimensions are often the most effective way of protecting plants from pests. To keep out insects they must be securely anchored without gaps at soil level. (See Mulching films p. 215). For short-term crops they can be laid directly on the plants; for longer-term crops it is more practical to lay nets over low hoops, which makes access easier. When laid directly on crops adult butterflies may lay eggs on the nets allowing the caterpillars to crawl through. The following and similar products are currently widely available:

Enviromesh Gives protection against carrot fly, cabbage root fly, egg-laying butterflies, birds, rabbits plus incidental protection from rain, hail and light frost. It is strong and lasts at least seven years.

Ultra Fine Enviromesh Protects against flea beetles and diamondback moth. The very fine mesh restricts ventilation so it is unsuitable for long-term use, although it is strong and durable.

Envirofleece Primarily laid on seedlings and

young plants to create a sheltered environment in their early stages, it also gives protection against pests such as flea beetle and carrot root fly. It is lightweight and not very durable. Heavier grades are available for frost protection.

Bird netting Many types are available: they can be erected over hoops of varying heights or temporary or permanent cages.

___

Common salad pests

Birds Small birds, eg sparrows, attack seedlings and young plants like lettuce, spinach and beetroot. Protect seedlings with a single strand of strong, black cotton thread 5cm/2in above the row, or use mesh or bird nets. Larger birds damage peas and brassicas. The many deterrents include humming wire stretched over the beds about 1¼m/4ft high, and bird scaring hawks. Birds get used to most devices unless moved frequently. A permanently netted cage may be the only solution to serious problems.

Slugs and snails No. 1 enemy for salad growers. No measures are foolproof: see what works best for you, and concentrate protection on young vulnerable plants. Controls against slugs include potassium bicarbonate pellets and nematode biological control (effective up to six weeks but only in damp soil). Deterrents, include copper tape, anti-slug plant collars, plastic containers with the base cut out put over plants, slug traps (which must be 2½cm/1in proud of the ground to prevent beneficial ground beetles falling in.) My principal method is collecting them at night by torchlight. Less productive, but easier, is placing pieces of wood or heavy black plastic among vegetables, and gathering hiding slugs and snails in daylight.

Soil pests Various soil pests, eg wireworm, cutworm and leatherjackets, are immature forms of flying insects. They attack roots and stems, often nipping off plants at ground level. They tend to be more active in spring and on freshly cultivated ground and generally diminish with regular cultivation. Many are night feeders and can be caught by torchlight like slugs and snails. If young plants wilt unexpectedly, dig them up, inspect the roots carefully, and the responsible pest can often be found. Biological controls can be used in some cases.

Caterpillars The larval forms of moths and butterflies are most serious on brassicas. Destroy eggs and caterpillars by hand or grow crops under Enviromesh or fleece.

Aphids Various aphids attack a wide range of outdoor crops; mealy aphids and whitefly attack brassicas. Squash early infestations by hand, or use the sprays above.

Flea beetles These tiny insects nibble small round holes in seedling leaves in the brassica family, particularly radish and salad rocket. Protect crops for four to five weeks under ultra fine Enviromesh or fleece. Keeping the soil moist discourages attacks.

Root flies Most serious are carrot root fly and cabbage root fly, which attacks all brassicas. Eggs are laid at ground level, and the hatching maggots burrow into the stem and severely damage the plant. Protect large brassicas with 12cm/5in-diameter collars made from rubberized carpet underlay. Cut a hole in one side to the centre, and slip these around the stems at soil level when planting. Or slip a plastic cup or bottle with the base removed over the plant, pushing it into the soil. For measures against carrot fly see carrots p. 138.

Greenhouse pests Glasshouse whitefly and red spider mite are the most serious, affecting common greenhouse crops. Use the appropriate biological controls when necessary.

Salad techniques

Vegetable gardens in the twenty-first century are smaller than in the past, many would-be gardeners, especially in urban areas, having to make do with the tiniest of plots. This was brought home to me when I visited community gardens in the USA. In some a piece of ground the size of an average desk was considered 'large'. It was inspiring to see what was produced in these minute gardens. Salad plants have much to offer where space is at a premium, and lend themselves to space-saving techniques such as equidistant spacing and all the forms of intercropping.

Space-saving systems
Equidistant spacing

Scientific research has now demonstrated the inefficiency, in most cases, of the traditional method of growing plants close together in rows, with the rows spaced far apart. Within the rows plants compete fiercely for the limited resources of nutrients and moisture, and in so doing deprive each other of sunlight. Yet in the space between the rows, where there is no competition, weeds flourish.

You can overcome this problem with equidistant spacing. Think of each plant as the centre of a circle, from which it draws its nutrients and moisture, the radius varying with the size of the plant and its demands. A cauliflower, for example, draws from a far greater area than a lettuce. The most economic way of utilizing the soil – the storehouse of both nutrients and moisture – is to space plants so that when fully grown their 'circles' just overlap. You can achieve these effects by planting in staggered rows with equidistant spacing in both directions – that is the same space between the plants in each row as there is between the rows themselves (see illustration above). The mature plants, each more or less touching their neighbours, form a leafy canopy over the soil. This proves an effective means of weed control,

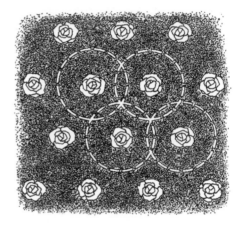

Equidistant spacing makes optimum use of the ground. Here the spacing between the plants is the same as the spacing between the rows. The dotted circles indicate the area the full-grown plant will occupy, and from which it draws its nutrients and moisture.

as few weed seeds germinate when deprived of light. The main exception is narrow-leaved plants like onions. In this case keeping the soil between the plants mulched (see p. 213), will control potential weeds. Broad-leaved plants can be mulched in their immature stages before they cover the soil.

Spacing as a tool

For the most widely grown vegetables, researchers have established the optimum spacing to get the highest yield from a given area. You can also use spacing as a tool, to control the size and quality of vegetables, and the speed with which they mature. With onions, for example, close spacing will produce pickling onions, moderate spacing small cooking onions and wide spacing very large onions. The same principle holds true for carrots, cabbages, leeks and many other vegetables. The quality of calabrese heads and self-blanching celery stalks will, to some extent, be improved by close spacing; tomatoes will mature earlier when grown relatively close.

The most extreme example of close spacing is seedling crops, and the slightly more mature stage known as 'baby leaves'. The archetype seedling crop is garden cress, grown by generations of children on blotting paper (superseded in more recent times by paper towelling) on a windowsill and cut about 4cm/1½in high. When cress is sown in ordinary soil rather than on paper towelling or blotting paper it will grow up to 30cm/12in high, and after it has been cut, it will resprout. In fact, depending on the conditions, you can often make several cuts from one sowing.

For the space- and time-saving technique of multi-sowing, where several seedlings are sown together in a module and planted 'as one', see p. 205.)

Intercropping

The underlying principle of intercropping is that some plants, typically brassicas such as cabbage and Brussels sprouts, grow much more slowly than others. They will not occupy their allotted 'circle' until they have been in the ground for several months. In their early stages, when they are still small, it is possible to grow a fast-growing crop alongside or around them, which will be ready for use and harvested before the entire space is required

TOP Lettuce and early summer cabbages, interplanted together in spring.
ABOVE Cress intersown beween young kohl rabi plants.

by the slower-growing plant.

In much the same way, it is not always necessary to wait for a crop to be cleared before sowing or planting its successor. There may be space to sow or plant alongside. By the time the second crop needs more space, the first will be ready for harvesting. For example, towards the end of summer in my polytunnel, I sneak drills of winter cut-and-come-again seedlings between the last of the basil plants.

Intercropping takes various forms. The 'intercropper' can be sown or planted, within existing rows, between rows, or simply around another plant. It has to be said that intercropping is easier to manage when plants are grown in conventional rows rather than when they are at equidistant spacing.

231

Intercropping is a great tool for creating beautiful patterned effects in the salad garden.

In-row intercropping In this case slow-growing root vegetables such as parsnips, are station sown (see p. 197), and a few seeds of a fast-growing crop such as radish, spring onion, salad rocket or a small lettuce are sown between each 'station'. A slightly less precise method is to mix seeds of fast growers with slow growers (such as maincrop carrots or parsnips) and sow them together in the row. The fast growers will act as row markers for the slower-developing carrots or parsnips (see also Mixed patches opposite).

Sowing between rows and around plants A quick crop can often be sown between rows of onions, shallots or leeks, whose narrow leaves require little space when first planted. Similarly, where celeriac, beet and brassicas are grown in rows, intercrops can be sown between them in the early stages. Where the main crops are grown at equidistant spacing, there will be room, when they are first planted, to sow a quick-growing crop around them. I often sow salad rocket, radishes, cress or red seedling lettuce in figure-of-eight patterns around Brussels sprouts and cauliflowers. The intercrops must all be harvested before the brassicas overcrowd them. This may seem like stating the obvious, but I have found that it requires quite a lot of will power to uproot the intercrops if they are still being reasonably productive.

An interesting method of double cropping – you might even call it 'top cropping' – is to sow a seedling crop in the ground above potatoes, after they have been planted. You can usually make at least one cut before the potatoes burst through.

Planting between rows and plants Some of the smaller salad plants can be planted between rows, or between individual plants, of

Climbing plants such as beans and cucumbers that are trained up tepees will shade the ground beneath them when they are fully grown. However in their early stages they can be underplanted or undersown with salad plants like lettuce.

relatively slow-maturing vegetables. Appropriate interplants are lettuce, small pak choi, summer or winter purslane, chrysanthemum greens, mizuna greens (if kept cut back hard), corn salad and land cress. All will normally provide a picking or two before they are encroached upon by the main crop. Corn salad, land cress, winter purslane, red and Witloof chicory can be planted between Brussels sprouts in the autumn in mild areas, and will grow there happily until spring. They probably even benefit from the extra shelter.

Undercropping This is a form of intercropping where tall plants are combined with ground-hugging or trailing crops. Sweet corn is one of the most amenable plants for undercropping. The leaves create only light shade, so you can plant the ground beneath with a range of crops, some of which will remain in the ground long after the corn is harvested in late summer (see Intercropping guidelines,

ABOVE Spicy salad mix seedlings making good use of an old sink.

p. 234). Asparagus is another plant with airy foliage that casts little shade, so you can use the ground beneath for small plants like corn salad and seedling crops. I have found that parsley does well in an asparagus bed: a few plants left to seed more or less perpetuate themselves.

There is sometimes scope for undercropping climbing vegetables in their early stages, for example climbing beans, the smaller squashes and cucumbers. One year I grew the round South African squash 'Little Gem' (also available as 'Little Gem Rolet') up a tepee of four canes, each set at the corner of a 1m/3ft square. I sowed the squashes under jars to help germination, one at the foot of each cane; at the same time I planted a dozen lettuces in the square. While the squashes germinated and started to grow up the canes, the lettuces grew steadily. They were ready for cutting before the squashes had clothed the cane structure and blocked out the light. The foliage of 'Little Gem' squash and of some trailing marrows has pretty, grey markings and makes a striking garden feature.

Natural coexistence This is another form of intercropping. It was the late Rosemary Verey, the well-known gardener, who showed me how chervil and dill work well in tandem. Both, once established, self-seed and so keep going on the same spot. The chervil naturally germinates in autumn, normally remains green in winter, and runs to seed in late spring. Just when it is dying down the dill germinates and carries on throughout the summer. Parsley can be allowed to establish itself on an asparagus bed, leaving a few plants to self-seed. They co-exist harmoniously.

Mixed patches The concept of mixing different seeds and sowing them together is ancient, the idea being that they mature in turn, making optimum use of a piece of ground. The seventeenth-century diarist John Evelyn suggested mixing lettuce, purslane, carrots, radish and parsnips. A simple traditional mixture is radishes and carrots. A common Chinese practice is to mix carrots and pak choi: the pak choi is harvested at the seedling stage, leaving the carrots to mature. (This works well with a ratio of two teaspoons of carrot seed to one of pak choi.) A trick I was taught long ago is to mix carrots and annual flowers such as love-in-a-mist, nemesia and scabious. The annuals flower colourfully, and all the while the carrots are growing inconspicuously (hidden from carrot fly), ready for pulling at the end of the season.

Mixing your own cocktail of seed is something of a gamble, but premixed selections are widely available. Among the most popular are variations of the traditional salad mixes, which we first encountered on our European travels, known as mesclun in France, and misticanza in Italy. They are now often sold as 'saladini'. These mixtures can contain up to a dozen salad plants, typically several types of lettuce and chicory, salad rocket, chervil, endive and corn salad. They can give a continuous supply of salad over many months, different plants maturing in succession. Similarly, 'stir fry' mixtures, mustard mixes and blends of oriental greens such as 'Oriental saladini' make lovely salading when cut young.

Intercropping guidelines

Slow-growing plants that can be intercropped in early stages Brassicas: e.g. cauliflower, cabbage, broccoli, Brussels sprouts, kales, kohl rabi; parsnips, Hamburg parsley, salsify, scorzonera; onions and shallots; celeriac, leeks, beetroot; perennials: e.g. globe artichokes, cardoons.

Tall plants that can be undercropped (climbers in early stages only) Sweet corn, climbing squashes, marrows, cucumbers and climbing beans – all on supports.

Fast-maturing plants suitable for intercropping, and undercropping climbers in early stages Summer radishes; small lettuces such as 'Tom Thumb', 'Little Gem'; early turnips; all cut-and-come-again seedling crops.

Low-growing plants suitable for undercropping Sweet corn (as it does not form a dense canopy), trailing marrows, cucumbers and gherkins, red and Witloof chicory, endive, corn salad, land cress, salad rocket, mizuna, chrysanthemum greens, dwarf French beans, parsley and all cut-and-

come-again seedling crops, all fast-maturing crops above.

Last word on intercropping

Once tuned into the concept of taking a quick 'catch crop' in a piece of ground that is currently under-utilized, you will find endless opportunities to do so, making great use of salad plants. For help in working out intercropping combinations, see the lists on the left and the Cut-and-come-again seedling chart on p 236. Base your schemes on your observations of how plants grow in your garden. But be careful not to overdo it. In areas with high rainfall or low light conditions, excessive intercropping may result in rampant, jungle-like growth and an increase in disease. Both sets of crops must have enough space, light, moisture and nutrients to develop fully, and there must be room for necessary cultivation and harvesting. These factors are sometimes overlooked in the excitement of 'getting in as much as possible'. The soil must be fertile and well watered to sustain such intensive use. Once crops are established, it is advisable to water well, then mulch the plants to retain moisture, stifle weeds and keep the plants clean.

Cut and come again

People tend to think of vegetables as 'one-offs': they are picked or cut when ready, and that's that. But many leafy salad vegetables and some others, if they are not uprooted when cut, will regrow, allowing two or even three more cuts.

'Cut-and-come-again' is a useful umbrella term for this happy ability to resprout, which saves the gardener much time, space and effort. Depending on the plant, cutting can be carried out when plants are at the seedling stage, half-grown or mature.

Seedling crops

A seedling crop is one where seeds are sown relatively thickly and the very young leaves are cut, generally between 2½cm and 10cm/1in and 4in high (often marketed as 'baby leaves'). They are not only succulent, tasty and wonderfully fresh-looking, but also highly nutritious: they can have twice the vitamin content of mature leaves. Seedlings can be cut just once or, where conditions allow, used as cut-and-come-again crops.

The use of seedlings goes back a long way. Over 250 years ago, the English writer Richard Bradley, in his book *New Improvements of Planting and Gardening*, gave advice on the cultivation of seedlings, or 'small herbs cut in seed leaf' as he called them. He listed a wide range of plants grown for their seedlings: lettuce, chicory, endive, several types of cress, spinach, radish, turnip, mustard, salad rape – even the seedlings of oranges and lemons, which were much in vogue in the seventeenth and eighteenth centuries. These seedlings, often forced on hot beds of fermenting manure in frames or in greenhouses, kept the gentry supplied with fresh 'salading' from winter to spring. People with ample supplies of fresh manure can still make hot beds for early crops, but today heating frames with electric soil-warming cables is a more likely approach.

Where and when to sow seedlings

Seedlings can be grown inside or outdoors, according to the time of year. Richard Bradley remarked that those grown outdoors were better-flavoured; I'm not so sure, but would suggest that they are more tender if grown under cover, especially in winter.

Seedling crops are probably best value in autumn, winter and spring, when salad greens

ABOVE Cut and come again leaves growing in a flower pot, convieniently close to the back door.

are most scarce. In high summer, unless sown in light shade, many have a tendency to run straight to seed, quickly becoming coarse and, in the case of mustards and salad rocket, very hot-flavoured. For a continuous supply, a good rule of thumb is to make the next sowing when the previous sowing has emerged through the soil. See also the cut-and-come-again seedling chart on p. 236.

Seedlings are an excellent means of utilizing ground that is left idle under cover after the summer crops have been harvested. Patches of fast-growing cress, salad rape or salad rocket, sown in late autumn, may allow one cutting before low winter temperatures stop their growth. They will probably look miserable by then, especially if they have been touched by

CUT-AND-COME-AGAIN SEEDLING CHART

Use this chart to plan for a continuous supply of young salad leaves, and to plan intercropping.

	GERMINATION TIME	NO. OF CUTS	LASTS (MONTHS)	WHEN TO SOW
Amaranthus spp. Leaf amaranth	❄	2	2–3	W
Atriplex hortensis Orache	❄ ❄	3	3	●
Beta vulgaris var. *cicla* Perpetual spinach	❄ ❄	3+	6+	●
Brassica carinata Texsel greens	❄ ❄	2	2–3	C
B. juncea Red mustard	❄	2	2–3	●
B. napus Salad rape	❄	3–4	3–4	●
B. oleracea Acephala Group Curly kale	❄ ❄	2–3	6–8+	C
B. oleracea Acephala Group Fine-leaved kale ▶	❄ – ❄ ❄	2–3	6–8+	●
B. rapa Chinensis Gp Pak choi	❄	2–3	2–4	C
— Rosette pak choi	❄	2	2–4	C
— *B. rapa* v. *nipposinica* Mibuna greens	❄ ❄	2	3+	C
— Mizuna greens	❄ ❄	2–3	4+	C
— *B. rapa* var. *perviridis* Komatsuna	❄ – ❄ ❄	3	4+	●
Cichorium endivia Curled endive	❄ ❄	2–3	3–4	●
C. intybus Sugar Loaf chicory	❄ ❄	2–3	3–4	●
Eruca sativa Salad rocket	❄	3	2–3	● C
Lactuca sativa Salad Bowl and cutting lettuce	❄ ❄	2+	3–4	●
Lepidium sativum Garden cress	❄	2–4	1–2	C
Medicago sativa Alfalfa (lucerne)	❄	2–4	12+ ▶▶	●
Montia perfoliata Winter purslane	❄ – ❄ ❄	2	2–3	C
Plantago coronopus Buck's horn plantain	❄	2	6–8	●
Portulaca oleracea Summer purslane	❄ ❄	2	2	W
Raphanus sativus Leaf and seedling radish	❄	2	1–2	●
Spinacia oleracea Spinach	❄ ❄	2–3	2–5	●
Valerianella locusta Corn salad	❄	2–3	3+	C
Oriental saladini mix ▶▶▶	❄	2–3	2–5	C
Saladini/mesclun mix ▶▶▶	❄ ❄	2–3	3–4	●

KEY

KEY

Germination time

✳ = less than a week
✳ ✳ = 2–3 weeks
✳ ✳ ✳ = 3 weeks
This is the average time (under favourable conditions) before the seedling appears above ground. Most are then large enough to eat within 2–3 weeks

Number of cuts

The average number of cuts from one sowing. This will vary according to the season. Most cut-and-come-again crops run to seed rapidly in hot weather, and grow more slowly in cold weather, limiting the number of cuts

Lasts

The average period in months during which the crop can provide tender leaves

When to sow

● = can be sown throughout the growing season
C = best sown in cool conditions
W = requires warm conditions

Notes

▶ e.g. 'Pentland Brig', 'Hungry Gap', 'Red Russian'
▶▶ Alfalfa is perennial, but leaves become coarse unless plants are cut back regularly
▶▶▶ Performance will depend on the actual seed mixture

Other seedling crops

Brassica campestris Rapifera Group Turnip, see *Brassica napus* Salad rape

Brassica oleracea Acephala Group Tuscan kale, *see* Fine leaved kale, though it can be cut as cut-and-come again leaves for 7–8 months

Brassica rapa Pekinensis Group Loose headed Chinese cabbage, see *Brassica rapa* Chinensis Gp Pak choi

Chenopodium giganteum 'Magentaspreen' Tree Spinach, see *Atriplex hortensis* Orache

---

frost. Yet as soon as day temperatures rise they burst into renewed growth, providing fresh salad very early in the year.

Slower-growing crops sown under cover a little earlier, in early autumn, will provide pickings right through to late spring. I made these sowings in early September in my polytunnel in East Anglia, and in late September to early October in my greenhouse in Southern Ireland. The crops I have found productive for this purpose are the oriental greens, mizuna, mibuna, ordinary and rosette pak choi, komatsuna and several types of mustard, various kales, spinach, corn salad, winter purslane, Sugar Loaf chicory, leaf radish, buck's horn plantain and Texsel greens.

Cut-and-come-again seedling crops give such quick returns (cutting sometimes starts within two weeks of sowing) that it is even worth sowing patches as small as 30cm/12in square. They are ideal 'catch crops' on temporarily vacant pieces of ground before the main crop is sown or planted, and lend themselves to intercropping (see p. 231–4). Because they are small and relatively undemanding, they are very suitable for container growing.

Seedlings like cress, mustard, salad rape, rocket, leaf radish, peas, coriander and fenugreek can be grown in shallow seed trays of light soil or potting compost on a windowsill – though in most cases they will only give one cutting. A quick way to resow is to scrape off the stalks after cutting, sprinkle fresh soil or compost on top, and sow on it. Spent 'grow bags' can be sown with a seedling crop once the main crop is finished; as most of the nutrients will have been exhausted, supplementary feeding may be necessary if you want several cuts. These seedling crops can also be grown on windowsills on an inert base (see Seed sprouting p. 248).

Cultivating seedling crops

Prepare the seedbed in the normal way (see p. 196). It is very important that the soil is weed-free: seedlings are easily smothered by weeds, and once both have germinated weeding is virtually impossible. If necessary, prepare the seedbed in advance, allow the first flush of weeds to germinate, and hoe them off before sowing the seedling crop (see p. 196).

Seedlings can be broadcast, or sown in narrow drills 5–10cm/2–4in apart, or sown in broad drills 7½–15cm/3–6in wide. It can be hard to judge how thickly to sow. Instinct is to sow too thickly, so apply a moderating hand. Allowing for the fact that some seeds will fail to germinate, aim to space seeds about 1cm/½in apart. For a continuous supply, start cutting when the seedlings are an edible size, using sharp scissors or a knife. If you want several cuttings, always cut above the lowest seedling leaves. New growth will develop from this point.

A common fault with cut-and-come-again seedlings, especially spring-sown oriental greens, is failing to make the first cut when the leaves are ready. Left even a few days too long, and the plants start to bolt, become woody, and fail to grow. Sowing little and often is a better course.

Seedling patches must be well watered in dry weather to sustain their rapid rate of growth. Remove any loose leaves or debris, as they will rot and soil the seedlings beneath. Patches that have been growing for several months may need supplementary feeding. I would use a seaweed-based feed.

The lifespan of a seedling patch varies from a few weeks to several months, depending on growing conditions (see the chart on p. 236). Unless cut frequently, many quickly outgrow the true seedling stage, though in most cases the leaves can still be eaten at a later stage, either raw or cooked. Sometimes a patch can be thinned – or virtually 'thins itself' in a kind of survival of the fittest – to allow a few plants to grow to maturity. Sugar Loaf chicory is a good example. A patch which starts as a

ABOVE Baby leaf rocket seedlings thriving on a windowsill.

seedling crop in early spring can be yielding several large hearted plants by winter.

As soon as seedling leaves become tough, the crop should be uprooted. The frequency and number of cuts that can be made depend on the crop and the growing conditions, early spring sowings probably being the most naturally productive. In cool climates this is the best time to leave a few plants to save your own seed (see p. 192). This is only advisable with crops that naturally run to seed at this time of year – not with oriental greens, which would be bolting prematurely. Occasionally gardeners are blessed with a self-sown seedling patch of corn salad, salad rocket, summer or winter purslane, or even weeds like chickweed (*Stellaria media*) – which are at their tastiest at the seedling stage.

Seedling mixtures The traditional French mesclun or Italian misticanza mixes and 'saladini' mixtures of salad seeds make excellent seedling crops. Other mixtures available now include oriental saladini (see p. 81), stir fry and braising mixes, mustard mixes, and mixed green and red lettuce all give rise to instantly varied salads and are fun to grow.

Decorative patterns

There is a lot of scope for creating colourful effects with seedlings. Think of them as a means of embroidering on the ground. Use narrow drills to outline patterns or 'enclose' a single plant – usually a slow-growing brassica. Seedlings can outline squares, rectangles, circles, semi-circles or triangles, or weave across beds in zigzags or wavy lines, overlapping, interweaving or criss-crossing for heightened effects. Alternatively, infill an outline with broadcast seedlings or seedlings sown in wide parallel drills. Once established, adjacent drills merge to give the impression of a dense carpet. You can sow adjoining patches with seedlings of contrasting colours and textures to create a patchwork effect; changing the direction of the rows, from one patch to the next, makes the pattern more striking. Different-coloured varieties – such as green and golden summer purslane, Lollo or Salad Bowl lettuce – grow at the same rate, so are ideal for this treatment.

Seedlings lend themselves to intercropping between rows of longer-term vegetables, most dramatically between coloured plants such as the scarlet-leaved 'Bull's Blood' beet. Use cress, coriander and dill for a light-textured foil; perpetual beet for a bold impact; purple mustard and red lettuce for a red contrast; and 'Red Russian' and 'Tuscan' kales for subtle shades of purple and blue. For more on cut-and-come-again seedling crops and their characteristics, see the chart on p. 236.

Regrowth in mature plants

While many plants resprout at the juvenile stage, a few do so when cut at maturity. In good growing conditions, red, spring and early summer cabbages may produce a second crop of four or five small heads. Making a shallow cross in the stump seems to accelerate the process. Some varieties of lettuce make a second head after the first is cut. I have known this happen with some overwintered greenhouse lettuces and with looser-headed, red-tinged varieties such as the semi-hearting 'Marvel of Four Seasons'. It is most likely to succeed in spring; secondary heads in summer may become bitter.

Far more commonly, plants will produce more leaves, but not a tight head, after the first head or mature leaves are cut. This is the case with the Salad Bowl range of lettuce, Chinese cabbage, pak choi, mizuna and mibuna greens, komatsuna, broad and curly endive, and Sugar Loaf and red chicory. These plants are often grown for use in autumn and early winter, and, mizuna apart, are not considered hardy. What is interesting is that once their large, leafy, frost-vulnerable tops have been removed, the stumps, with whatever leaf has been left, will survive much lower temperatures than would normally be the case. When warm weather returns they start back into growth, providing welcome early salad leaves. If they are planted in late summer/early autumn under cover – whether in polytunnels, frames or cloches – the effect is accentuated. The plants remain in good condition longer, recover earlier and are more productive. They can make a major contribution to filling the spring 'salad gap'.

ABOVE Chilli peppers lend themselves to container growing and will thrive on a well lit kitchen window sill.
ABOVE RIGHT An old metal pot has been put to good use with a crop of mustard and mizuna leaves.

Containers

Why grow in containers For gardeners restricted to patios, courtyards, balconies or roof gardens, containers may be the only means of growing vegetables and herbs. They can also provide extra growing space in small gardens, and an alternative where serious soil problems or contamination are encountered. Containers can be used until the problems are rectified. Where soil sickness has developed in greenhouses, they are a practical option for tomatoes and related crops.

It can be very handy for the kitchen to have salad greens, herbs and other vegetables close at hand, and they can look beautiful. You will have to keep a close eye on them, for watering especially, but pests and diseases are easy to spot early and control, and in many cases – potatoes and tomatoes for example – crops will mature earlier than from the open ground.

Choice of container You can use almost anything as a container provided it is strong enough to withstand the combined weight of damp soil and a heavy crop. Conventional containers include terracotta, plastic and metal flower pots and planters, window boxes, wooden tubs and barrels, hanging baskets and commercial growing bags filled with potting compost. Less conventionally, all sorts of artefacts can be converted into containers, from watering cans, sinks and bath tubs to rubber tyres and chimney pots.

Container size The larger and deeper the

container, the better it can withstand the desiccating effects of sun and wind, the less watering and feeding it will need, and the wider the range of vegetables which can be grown. Small containers are very vulnerable to the elements, dry out very fast and are limiting in what can be grown well.

Size largely determines what can be grown. As a rough guide, seedlings and undemanding shallow-rooting herbs can be grown in a soil depth of 10–15cm/4–6in; plants the size of lettuce require a depth of about 15–20cm/ 6–8in. For large plants like tomatoes and peppers the minimum size would be 25–30cm/10–12in width and depth though larger containers, of at least 35–40cm/14–16in diameter and depth would be needed for vigorous varieties, such as cherry tomatoes. Potatoes grow well in a traditional sack. The underlying rule is make sure your container suits the crop. It can't be overemphasised, that the larger the better. If growing on a roof, however, bear in mind the need to limit overall weight. Where containers will be placed against a wall or fence, opt for those with straight sides.

Siting There is often little option over where containers are sited. A key factor is to avoid wind. It may be necessary to put up some kind of wind barrier on very exposed sites or where winds funnel through nearby buildings. Balconies can suffer badly from wind. Avoid deep shade, and in summer, it may be necessary to avoid full sun, especially for leafy and salad crops. Quite a range of crops tolerate light shade in summer. (See p. 271). Containers can be mounted on castors, which enables them to be moved into the sun in spring, and into the shade in mid summer.

Growing medium Ordinary garden soil on its own is generally unsuitable for containers as it quickly becomes compacted with frequent watering. Use good-quality potting compost, or garden soil mixed with a roughly equal quantity of well-rotted garden compost, worm compost, green waste or potting compost. Smaller quantities of mushroom compost can be added for fertility, and a handful or so of coarse sand or vermiculite can be added to improve drainage. Water retention can be improved by incorporating the coarse-grade seaweed meal made from *Ecklonia maxima*. This is able to absorb several times its own volume of water.

Salad seedlings will do well in potting compost alone, which has enough nutrients for their needs, but crops that take longer to mature will do better in a mix of potting soil and more substantial and richer materials, such as garden soil, garden compost and the other options mentioned above.

Where home-made compost is used, and there is a risk of it containing viable weed seed, a useful tip is to put it at the bottom of the container, covered with a few centimetres of a proprietary, weed-free potting compost. It is advisable to replace the soil in containers every year, as it tends to get stale.

Drainage Successful growing in containers hinges on balancing moisture retention with preventing the soil from becoming waterlogged. Unless the container already has holes in the base, as would be the case with flower pots, it is advisable to drill drainage holes. They should ideally be slanting (so less likely to get blocked), at least 1cm/½in in diameter and about 7½cm/3in apart. Cover drainage holes with upturned crocks and a thick layer of coarse drainage material. I sometimes use charcoal. Grow bags filled with very absorbent compost do not require drainage holes.

Pots can be raised off the ground to improve drainage. Some terracotta pots have built-in 'feet': otherwise improvise feet with tiles, bricks, blocks of wood, tiles and so on.

Sowing and planting Crops such as seedling salads, baby beet, baby carrots, baby turnips and spinach can be sown directly into containers, thinning as necessary. Most of the leafy thinnings would be edible. To make optimum use of precious space more demanding plants are better raised in modules and planted: they can follow an early salad crop for example. Where plant raising facilities are limited, there is a good case for buying in plants. Just make sure they are good quality. It generally makes sense to restrict each container to one type of vegetable, so its requirements can be catered for – though mixing would be feasible in very large containers such a trough.

Watering Containers need to be watered frequently in the absence of rainfall – in hot weather that may mean twice a day – to prevent the surface drying out. Use a can or hose, watering thoroughly until the water filters out through the bottom of the container. Grow bags are a special case, due to their lack of drainage and shallowness. They need to be watered 'little but often'. It is hard to rewet the compost once it has dried out.

It may be worth installing a drip irrigation system for a large group of containers. (see p. 212). Some will work from a water butt or reservoir without the need for mains water.

Mulching the surface of containers conserves moisture and slows down evaporation. Use loose organic material, mulching mats, mulching granules, fine bark chips, even stones or gravel. Loose mulches can be 5cm/2in deep. Moisture evaporates rapidly through the sides of porous clay and plastic pots. Lining the sides with heavy plastic film (such as old fertilizer bags), or folded newspaper of about 5mm/¼in thickness keeps them cooler. With growing bags limit evaporation by planting through small holes or squares cut out of the surface film, rather than cutting the film away completely. A wick and bucket system (see illustration p. 211) can overcome the watering problem in brief absences.

Fertility and feeding Herbs, cut-and-come-again seedlings, and plants that are in containers for less than six weeks are unlikely to require extra feeding. Others, depending on the crop, will benefit from supplementary feeding with a seaweed-based fertilizer or home-made liquid feed. Slow-release organic fertilizers, such as seaweed meal and chicken manure pellets, can also be worked into the surface. The soil in containers is apt to sink during the growing season, and can be topped up with garden compost. Just leave space at the top of the container for watering. Contrary to conventional wisdom, it has been proved that earthworms are beneficial in a container, so don't jettison them. But they will move away if the soil becomes dry.

Support systems Tall or climbing vegetables grown in containers will need some kind of support. Canes or stakes for cordon tomatoes, for example, will need a depth of at least 20cm/8in to be anchored securely. Tepees for climbing beans would require deeper containers. Proprietary plastic and light steel frames are available for grow bags. Otherwise containers are best sited alongside a fence or trellis against which plants can be tied or trained.

OPPOSITE Red-leaved basil is one of many herbs which grows well in a flower pot and is invaluable in salads.

Hanging baskets Although mainly used for flowers, with skill hanging baskets can be used for all sorts of vegetables and herbs, as well as strawberries. Cascading varieties of tomatoes can look spectacular.

The minimum size basket for growing vegetables would be 40cm/16in diameter. Of the various types available, the solid plastic types are easiest to use and are the most moisture retentive. Some have a basal watering reservoir; some are self watering. Wire framed baskets need to be well lined. One option is to have an outer lining of jute or wool fibre, which is both attractive and moisture retentive. Cover this with an inner lining of plastic with holes punched in the lower third. This can be done from outside. Watering a hanging basket thoroughly can be awkward. The task is made easier by sinking a fairly deep pot, of 7½–10cm/3–4 in diameter into the centre of the basket when planting. Direct water into the pot: it will spill out gradually from the top. Water until drips come from the base of the basket.

What to grow? With ingenuity, you can grow almost any vegetable or herb in containers, but it makes sense to concentrate on plants that give good returns from limited space. It is not worth growing slow-maturing vegetables which occupy a lot of space for several months, or moisture-lovers which suffer if checked by drying out, which can easily happen. Brussels sprouts, sprouting broccoli, cauliflower, celeriac, parsnips and swedes fall into these catagories. Large-leaved, top-heavy vegetables and robust climbers – climbing beans, pumpkins for example – are tricky to manage.

As far as possible, choose appropriate dwarf, compact or fast maturing varieties, often listed as 'patio' vegetables. Suitable varieties have been listed throughout in 'Salad Garden' text.

Salad leaves All cut-and-come-again seedlings (see chart p. 236), chrysanthemum greens, red-leaved and Sugar Loaf chicory, endive, lettuce (especially small and Salad Bowl types), mizuna greens, mibuna greens, pak choi (ordinary and rosette), spinach, Swiss chard (in deep containers only).

Root and fruiting crops Baby beet, broad beans (dwarf varieties), dwarf French beans, runner beans (dwarf varieties), carrots (round and early most suitable, maincrop only in deep containers), cucumbers (bush), courgettes (in large containers), sweet and chili peppers, radish, tomatoes, baby turnips. Ornamental kales can be grown in winter containers.

Herbs *Annuals, and perennials treated as annuals:* basil, leaf celery, chervil, coriander, dill, marjoram, mitsuba, summer savory, parsley. *Perennial herbs:* chives, Chinese chives, and *Tulbaghia violacea*, hyssop, mint, rosemary, sage, and tarragon (these require large containers), lemon verbena (if brought under cover in winter). Perennial herbs (apart from lemon verbena and tarragon) tend to lose their vigour when grown in containers, and should be divided and repotted ideally every year. Work generous quantities of vermiculite or perlite into the growing mix. All herbs in containers should be picked regularly to encourage new shoots.

Edible flowers Most of the annual edible flowers can be grown in containers, and add great colour to the displays. The most suitable are pot marigold, (*Calendula officinalis*), nasturtiums, pansies, signet marigold (*Tagetes tenuifolia*).

Blanching

Blanching – literally meaning 'to make white' – is one of the refinements of salad growing. The stems or leaves of certain vegetables are blanched by excluding light to make them crisper, sweeter, whiter and more delicately flavoured. Bitter leaves such as chicory and dandelion are far more palatable when blanched.

Blanched leaves can be beautiful, too. White, pink-tipped blades of 'Red Treviso' chicory, jagged creamy dandelion leaves tinged with yellow and the frothy white leaves of blanched curly endive all look superb on the plate.

Blanching was once a widely practised art: our gardening forbears blanched celery, cabbage, endive, fennel, cos lettuce, cardoons and seakale, as well as the spring shoots or 'chards' of globe artichokes, scorzonera and salsify; and many wild plants. Blanching is now less fashionable. Perhaps it is less necessary; some modern varieties are naturally sweeter, and we may be subconsciously aware that vitamins are lost in blanching. Or are we just lazy? But it's fun to do and the end result is rewarding.

Blanching is often coupled with forcing, where crops are brought into earlier growth in a dark environment, mainly in winter and early spring. Once blanching is completed, plants deteriorate fairly rapidly. So in most cases it is advisable to blanch a few at a time in succession and use them as soon as they are ready.

The essence of blanching is to exclude light, either *in situ* or by moving the plants into a darkened environment. In all methods, high humidity in a close environment means there is a risk of plants rotting. To lessen the risk, foliage should be as dry as possible. Cover plants with cloches several days beforehand if necessary and remove all dead, rotting or diseased leaves.

ABOVE Here endive are being blanched under traditional terracotta blanching pots. The plant in front of the pot has been blanched.

In situ blanching methods

Tying The simplest method of blanching tall or long-leaved plants is to bunch up the leaves and tie them with raffia, string or even elastic bands about two-thirds up the plant. The outer leaves will not be blanched, as they are exposed to light, but the central leaves will be crisp and pale within ten to fifteen days. This is a quick and simple way of blanching mature dandelions, the more upright endives and wild chicories.

Covering Light is excluded by covering the whole plant, leaves often being tied up first to keep them off the ground. Sea kale was traditionally blanched under purpose-made rounded clay pots (see p. 249), and in China, Chinese chives are blanched under narrow, chimney-like clay pots. Alternatives

245

ABOVE The forced, blanched shoots of sea kale are uniquely flavoured, and the plants are very handsome.

include upturned flowerpots with the drainage holes blocked to exclude light, wooden boxes, and cloches, hoops, frames or any framework covered with black polythene film. I have seen rows of endive boxed over with what looked like miniature coffins, and also with low, tent-shaped wooden frames. Whatever you use, allow space for air circulation to keep plants healthy.

Purpose-made blanching caps are used to cover low plants such as curled endive. The job can also be done by simply placing a dinner plate on the plant. This will blanch the central leaves, though the coarser outer leaves will remain green. Soft, black permeable mulching fabrics (see p. 217), folded several times to make them lightproof, are excellent for blanching. Anchor the edges with weights or pins. Straw and hay are more traditional blanching materials, used in a layer 15–20cm/6–8in thick, kept in place with metal hoops, canes or wire netting.

Plants can be forced *in situ* in an old method used for Witloof chicory, dandelion, scorzonera and salsify. In early winter they are allowed to die back, or are cut back to about 4cm/1½in above soil level, and then covered with a ridge of soil, sand or leaves. In spring blanched shoots push through, the covering scraped aside to cut them.

Transplanted blanching methods

Plants are transplanted for blanching for convenience, and when there is a risk of frost damage if they are left in the open.

In frames Traditionally, frames were widely used for blanching, especially for marginally hardy plants such as endives. Dig up mature plants in autumn before the first frosts, and replant them close together in the frame. The foliage must be dry, and plants handled carefully, as any cuts or tears in the leaves invite rots. Water the soil moderately beforehand, so that no further watering is necessary.

Frames can be darkened by covering with matting, boards, black polythene film or carpeting. Alternatively, cover the plants themselves with several layers of soft black fabric or a thick layer of straw, hay or dried leaves. In the past sand or sometimes even soil or ashes were sifted over plants. Keep a watch out for mice: they will be attracted to such cosy corners.

In greenhouses Plants can be forced and blanched by transplanting them into greenhouses and polytunnels, then covering them in any of the ways suggested for *in situ* blanching above. Outdoor plants can also be potted up into large pots, and brought under cover for blanching. It saves space to make a lightproof area under the staging, either by boarding it in with boards, or with black polythene film over low hoops. By the same token a low polytunnel inside a greenhouse can be covered with black film for blanching. In all these cases, replant the plants fairly closely in the soil, if feasible, planting in succession to prolong the cropping period. In spring temperatures can rise dramatically, and remaining plants may deteriorate rapidly or be attacked by aphids. Inspect regularly and if plants have been attacked use them up quickly.

In cellars Cellars, the 'caves' of the French-speaking world, were once widely used for blanching and forcing. Ventilation is good and they maintain a steady temperature of about 5°C/41°F. Plants were either potted into boxes or pots which were put into the dark cellar – no

further covering was necessary – or planted into beds of soil in the cellar. In an old Belgium system a 30cm/12in-wide stack of soil was piled against the cellar wall in layers 10cm/4in or so thick. Dandelion and chicory roots were laid close together on each layer, their necks protruding over the edge. The blanched leaves were cut when ready. The roots were left in the heap to make further, less vigorous but useful secondary growth during the rest of the winter.

Forcing Witloof chicory Roots are lifted and forced under cover in darkness to produce conical, creamy white chicons. One of the easiest systems for gardeners is to pot roots into a large flower pot. At a temperature of 10°C/50°F they will be ready in about three weeks, though commercial growers favour a slightly higher temperature of 13°C/55°F. (See also Witloof chicory, p. 35.)

Forcing chicory in pots (below) To force Witloof chicory indoors, lift the roots in late autumn and trim to within 2½cm/1in of the crown. Pot five or six roots into a large flower pot, covered with an inverted pot of the same size, with the drainage hole blocked to exclude light. If kept at about 10°C/50°F, the white chicons will be ready in about three weeks.

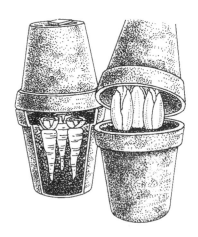

Seed sprouting

Seed sprouting is a highly intensive form of food production. Not only is it possible to sow on Monday and 'harvest' on Wednesday, but the seeds can increase their weight tenfold in the process. No soil or garden is required: just the simplest equipment and a windowsill or somewhere fairly warm to put the seeds.

Sprouted seeds can be used in salads, raw or cooked, and can also be incorporated into soups, stews, omelettes, breads and all sorts of dishes. A word of caution about eating raw legume sprouts, such as beans, peas, alfalfa and fenugreek: they contain toxic substances which could be damaging if eaten regularly in large quantities – that is, more than about 550g/20oz daily. Presoaking, sprouting and cooking all reduce toxin levels, but it is a complex story. Soya and mung beans are the least toxic of the sprouted legumes, French and broad beans the most toxic.

A great many seeds can be sprouted. The following lists some of the most commonly available, but there are many others. Most are used when sprouts are 1½–2½cm/½–1in long as many tend to get bitter if they grow longer. The development of bitterness seems to vary, depending on sprouting conditions and even on the variety of seed used. It is a case of seeing what works best with you. Those that can be left and eaten as young seedlings are indicated. Microgreens or 'microleaves' are essentially sprouted seeds grown and harvested at the next stage of growth. (See p. 253).

The chart opposite lists some of the most easily sprouted seeds in family or type groups, indicating how long they take to sprout and the ideal length for eating as sprouts. Seeds

ABOVE Pea shoots have a delightful, fresh flavour.

can be pre-soaked in water before sprouting, primarily so they sprout faster. Recommended times for pre-soaking vary with the seed.

Legume family Beans, peas and lentils: twelve hours soaking; mung beans twenty-four hours; chick peas and other legumes eight hours. Note that only whole, not split, lentils can be sprouted.

Brassicas Generally eight hours pre-soaking is sufficient. Other easily sprouted brassicas include broccoli, Brussels sprouts, cabbage, cauliflower and mustard.

Grains About twelve hours pre-soaking is recommended. Other easily sprouted grains are oats (*Avena sativa*) and brown unpolished rice (*Oryza sativa*), All are eaten as small sprouts.

Other garden crops For most garden crops 8 hours pre-soaking is sufficient. Other

SEEDS SUITABLE FOR SPROUTING

COMMON NAME	LATIN NAME	AVERAGE NO. OF DAYS TO SPROUT	LENGTH OF SPROUT WHEN EDIBLE
LEGUMES			
Azuki beans	*Phaseolus angularis*	4–5	12–25mm/½–1in
Lima beans	*Phaseolus lunatus*	3–5	12–38mm/½–1½in
Mung beans	*Phaseolus aureus*	3–5	12–75mm/½–3in
Peas	*Pisum sativum*	6–8	37–75mm/1½–3in
Chick peas	*Cicer arietinum*	2–4	5–10mm/¼–½in
Alfalfa (lucerne)	*Medicago sativa*	1–4	Very tiny and 2½–5cm/1–2in
Clover, crimson	*Trifolium incarnatum*	2–5	Very tiny and 2½–5cm/1–2in
Fenugreek	*Trigonella foenum-graecum*	3–5	12–50mm/½–2in
Lentil	*Lens esculenta*	2–4	6–20mm/¼–¾in
BRASSICAS			
Kale	*Brassica oleracea*	3–5	12–25mm/1/2–1in
Radish	*Raphanus sativus*	2–4	12–25mm/1/2–1in
GRAINS & GARDEN CROPS			
Barley	*Hordeum vulgare*	3–5	Very tiny
Rye	*Secale cereale*	3–5	Very tiny or 25–37mm/1–1½in
Wheat	*Triticum vulgare*	3–4	Very tiny
Buckwheat	*Fagopyrum esculentum*	2–4	20–25mm/¾–1in
Sweet corn	*Zea mays*	2–3	6–12mm/¼–½in
Sunflower	*Helianthus annuus*	1–3	12–38mm/½–1½in

The seeds in this chart are a sample of the many that can be sprouted. None included normally requires rinsing more than twice a day. All can be eaten raw, though legumes should not be eaten raw in large quantities. Sprouting times vary with temperature: those given are for the sprouts reaching an edible size; some can be left longer and eaten at a more advanced microgreens or seedling stage.

suitable crops include coriander (*Coriandrum sativum*), leeks (*Allium porrum*), and onion (*Allium* spp.), all of which can also be eaten as seedlings; and pumpkin (*Cucurbita* spp.). With pumpkin and sunflower de-hulled seeds or naturally hull-less varieties sprout best.

The best sources of seeds are health food shops and seed firms. Always buy untreated seed intended for consumption, rather than ordinary garden seed, which may be chemically treated. Remember that seeds for sprouting are viable seeds, and must be stored in dry, cool conditions to maintain their viability until sprouted.

Seed sprouting mixtures are sometimes available. The concept is appealing, but unless they have been carefully blended, germination tends to be uneven.

ABOVE Tiered seed sprouters enable different types of seed to be sprouted at the same time. Each tier is perforated to allow for rinsing and drainage.

microgreens, then conventional seedlings or 'baby leaves' they need to be grown on some kind of substrate or in the ground.

In the germination process, the fats and starches stored in the seed are converted into vitamins, sugars, minerals and proteins. This makes sprouted seeds exceptionally nutritious, notably rich in vitamins and minerals. They are tasty and crisp-textured. However, they develop rapidly and once past their peak they deteriorate from both the nutritional and flavour points of view. For a constant supply, sprout small quantities at regular intervals. Once ready, they can be kept in a fridge for a couple of days in a bowl of water or wrapped in clingfilm; rinse daily to keep them fresh. Bean sprouts should be kept for only about twenty-four hours, ideally at a temperature of about 4°C/39°F, as they are prone to bacterial infection.

Sprouting techniques

There are many ways of sprouting seeds, and I would advise beginners to start with one type of seed and sprout it by several methods to see what suits them best. Success or failure in sprouting turns on the fact that seeds need moisture and warmth to germinate, and in germinating they themselves generate considerable heat. This combination of warmth and moisture provides perfect conditions for moulds to develop. So sprouting seeds rot and go 'sour' unless cooled by regular rinsing with cold water.

Seeds can be sprouted loose in a container, or on a base. When sprouted loose there is no wastage as the entire sprout is used.

Sprouting on a base results in some wastage, as the sprouts normally have to be cut off the base. However sprouts on a

Sprouting uses a lot of seed, so it can be worth saving your own where practicable. Radish is one of the easiest and worthwhile: sprouted radish is deliciously piquant. Allow a few plants to run to seed in spring or summer, and collect the pods when dry (see p. 192). Seed of large mooli radish and winter radish is best for sprouting, as the seeds, like the roots, are large. Sunflower and pumpkin seed can be saved quite easily.

What, in fact, are sprouted seeds? They are seeds that have germinated and grown – usually for twenty-four hours to a few days – until the 'sprouts' are 6–40mm/¼ –1½in long, depending on the species. Up to this point they draw on internal resources. To develop further, and virtually become first

ABOVE An inner jar acts as a weight in sprouting mung beans (see description p. 252).

ABOVE Seeds sprout more evenly in a jar if it is laid on its side. The mesh lid makes rinsing easy.

base remain in good condition longer, and if necessary can be left to develop into small seedlings. Growth is probably somewhat faster in a container. Whatever system is used, there are a few golden rules:

- Use clean equipment.
- Remove cracked, discoloured and unhealthy-looking seed beforehand.
- Keep seeds fresh and cool by rinsing frequently.
- Keep seeds slightly moist – neither swamped with water nor dried out.
- Grow seeds as fast as possible.

Seeds can be sprouted in the dark or the light: it is a matter of choice, though most seeds sprout faster in the dark. Sprouts grown in the dark are white and crisp – typified by Chinese bean sprouts – but less nutritious than the softer, greener spouts which develop in full light. Where sprouts are being grown on to the seedling stage, start them in the dark, but move them into the light once germinated. To sprout in the dark, put the seeds in a drawer or cupboard – an airing cupboard is ideal in winter – or cover the container in aluminium foil. Windowsills can be used for sprouting in the light, but avoid direct sun.

The container method A wide range of purpose-made sprouters is available from seed companies and other suppliers. These include tiered sprouters for sprouting several different seeds simulteously. Whatever container is used, it must be large enough to allow the seeds to expand their volume seven- to tenfold, as happens in some, but not all cases. Ideally they should be self-draining, a feature in most patented seed sprouters.

A cheap and efficient sprouter can be made by drilling holes in the base of a plastic carton – effectively converting it into a sieve. Seeds are then rinsed simply by holding it under a tap, and letting water run through. Jam jars can be covered with plastic mesh, and seeds rinsed by pouring water in and out through the mesh. Muslin is sometimes substituted for mesh: I personally find that it is awkward to use and that the muslin discolours rather unpleasantly. Sprouting seeds grow more evenly in wide, rather than deep, containers such as jars, unless these are laid on their side.

Most seeds sprout faster if pre-soaked beforehand, often simply overnight. It is particularly recommended for beans. However, the step can be skipped: as with so much of seed sprouting, see what you find works best for you.

The basic procedure is to remove damaged seeds, then rinse the seeds with fresh water in a sieve or in a self-draining sprouter. Drain the seeds and put them into the container, in a layer generally no more than 6–13mm/ ¼–½in deep. The larger the seed, the deeper the layer can be. If the container is unlidded, the seeds can be covered with a damp cloth to keep them moist.

For most seeds the optimum temperature for germination is 13–21°C/55–70°F, though temperatures up to 24°C/75°F can be used. In warm weather seeds can be sprouted at room temperature; otherwise put them somewhere warmer. Seeds should always be

germinated quickly, as lingering seeds are the most susceptible to disease.

Rinse the seeds at least twice a day, morning and evening, and more frequently if necessary, until they are ready for use.

My 'patent method' of sprouting mung beans in containers My early attempts at mung bean sprouting failed to produce the long crisp sprouts of Chinese restaurants. A research station in Taiwan revealed one of the keys to success: pressure. Whether grown in traditional Chinese clay sprouting jars, or in the metal bins I saw in a Shanghai bean sprouting workshop, the sprouting seeds are subjected to tremendous pressure as they expand against the sides of the vessel. I have found that this pressure can be replicated by simply putting a weight on the germinating seed. I use a 900g/2lb weight in a 12cm/5in-diameter container, with 1cm/½in of seeds in the bottom. To spread the weight evenly, place it on a saucer, removing both for rinsing. In nine cases out of ten, this system produces excellent results. See illustration p. 251.

Sprouting on a base Seeds can be sprouted on an inert moist base such as paper towelling, cotton wool, flannel or other fabrics – the time-honoured way of growing mustard and cress for eating at the small seedling stage. These materials can all be laid over a foam base to retain moisture. Salad rape, radish, coriander, alfalfa, fenugreek, lentils, peas, Texsel greens and mung beans are among many others that can be sprouted this way. All can be used as sprouts or, slightly later, as microgreens or young seedlings. The seeds quickly root into the base, standing upright and making an attractive dish.

Spread the rinsed seeds evenly in a single layer over the moist base. If necessary, put

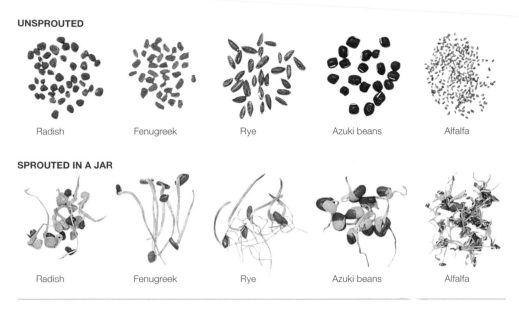

UNSPROUTED

Radish Fenugreek Rye Azuki beans Alfalfa

SPROUTED IN A JAR

Radish Fenugreek Rye Azuki beans Alfalfa

LENTILS

Unsprouted

Sprouted in a jar

Sprouted on a base

MUNG BEANS

Unsprouted

Sprouted on a base

Sprouted in a jar

ABOVE Examples of diffferent types of seed, before sprouting, sprouted on a base and sprouted in a jar.

them somewhere warm to germinate, in either the dark or light. If you intend to use them as young seedlings, start them in the dark (see p. 251). Rinse them daily by running cool water over them, holding the seeds in place with the back of a spoon until they have rooted into the base. If the base is very clean, pull up the seedlings by the roots and eat whole; otherwise, cut them off at the base. If kept moist and cool, seedlings may remain in good condition for two weeks before cutting.

Growing seedlings in soil Any seeds sprouted on a base can also be sown in a seed tray of finely sieved leaf mould or potting compost, which would supply some nutrients. Two or three cuttings of seedlings can be made, making a useful windowsill 'harvest'.

Microgreens

These tiny, tender seedlings, known as microgreens or microleaves, have taken the catering world by storm in the last few years. Harvested at either the seed leaf (cotyledon) stage or when the first true leaves appear, their intense flavours, colours, and textures have won them a prized place in salads, as garnishes, in soups and to add that pizzaz factor to a range of dishes. They are also highly nutritious.

They are an intermediary stage between sprouted seeds and 'baby leaves'. They differ from sprouted seeds in that only the stems and tiny leaves are eaten, not the seeds and roots. 'Baby leaves' would be much larger.

Growing microgreens can be tricky because of the risk of disease – but is certainly worth trying. Almost any vegetable or herb can be grown, but those that mature fastest are the most likely to succeed under domestic conditions. Ones that should be avoided are parsnips, any of the Solanaceous (tomato and pepper) family, and carrots and turnips (whose seedlings quickly develop unpleasant hairiness).

Where to grow Microgreens need moisture, good light and warmth. They are widely grown on benches in greenhouses and polytunnels, but a bright indoor window sill can be used. While the ideal temperature for fast germination is 18°C/64°F or above, many germinate at lower temperatures, the minimum being about 10°C/50°F. Some can be started in a propagator if necessary.

When While some can be sprouted all year round, most do best from spring to autumn – in fact spring and autumn can be optimum times for many. Germination can be very slow in winter: in summer it may be necessary to shade them from intense sun.

Containers Any shallow trays, standard or half size seed trays, modules or punnets can be used. It is essential that they are clean.

Substrate A wide range of materials are used: potting compost, perlite and vermiculite, several layers of paper towel, and purpose-made mats manufactured from jute, various recycled fibres and cellulose. Sowing and potting composts sustain the seedlings longest, and may be the best option for home gardeners, but care has to be taken in watering and harvesting to prevent them becoming soiled.

Sowing Water the substrate gently beforehand (best to use a fine rose on a can) then sow the seed as evenly as possible over the surface. It takes a little experience to judge the right density; not too thick or seedlings will be overcrowded, but not so thinly there will be only small returns! Leave them uncovered.

Watering Water gently to keep them just moist, as overwatering can lead to seedlings damping-off. A mister is ideal. Use a clean source of water – not water from a rain butt.

Harvesting The majority of seedlings are ready within 10–21 days. The fastest growing are salad rocket (7–10 days) and radish (8–12 days). Simply cut the seedlngs with scissors just above the substrate surface. They will be anything from 2½–6cm / 1–2½in high.

Ready to harvest in 12 days or less: broccoli, cabbage, cress, Florence fennel, mizuna, mibuna, mustards (oriental), standard and rosette pak choi, pea shoots, radish, salad rocket.

Ready to harvest in 15–20 days: red amaranth, basil, 'Bull's Blood' beet, Swiss chard, coriander, endive.

OPPOSITE LEFT Coriander microgreens on a base of potting compost covered with paper towelling.
OPPOSITE RIGHT Mizuna, mustard and salad rocket grown on a perlite base.

salad
making

—

Whether it is a simple salad as a side dish, or a salad blended with pasta, potatoes or grains to make a complete meal, the quality of the produce from your garden will transform it to heights unmatched by anything money could buy. This chapter gives a few hints and recipes for creating salads that taste, and look, superb.

Creative salads

The art of salad making has spanned centuries and continents. In Europe it reached extraordinary heights in the 'crowned sallets' of Elizabethan times. These were elaborate constructions. Sometimes a complete head of celery would be the centrepiece, mounted in a pot and surrounded by layer upon layer of sliced meats, eggs, shredded vegetables, nuts and fruits. Or the salad could take the form of a pastry castle with 'towers' and 'ramparts' of carrots, turnips and beetroots, and 'courtyards' planted with herbs and flowers.

One of the most articulate exponents of the art of salad making was the seventeenth-century writer and diarist John Evelyn. His book *Acetaria: a Discourse of Sallets*, which he wrote in 1699, is full of wisdom and observation, most of it as pertinent today as it was 300 years ago. (For the past forty years, it has been within arm's reach of my desk!) John Evelyn's garden at Says Court was organized so that a mixed green salad could be put on the table every day of the year. Here is how he summarized the 'art' of composing a salad:

> *Every Plant should come in to bear its part, without being over-power'd by some Herb of a stronger Taste, so as to endanger the native Sapor and Vertue of the rest: but fall into their places like the Notes in Music, in which there should be nothing harsh or grating, and though admitting some Discords (to distinguish and illustrate the rest), striking in the more sprightly, and sometimes gentler Notes, reconcile all Dissonances and melt them into an agreeable Composition.*

Perhaps the finest examples of contemporary salad making are to be found in the Middle East, in the wonderful mezze tradition, which stretches from Morocco to Afghanistan and from Greece to the Yemen. Mezze can be anything from a simple snack to a banquet of forty to fifty dishes. They are exquisitely prepared and presented salads, served in tiny bowls. Stuffed peppers, courgettes or vine leaves might be cut in slices; crisp raw vegetables set against creamy, fragrant dips; black, purple and green olives contrasted with chopped egg, aubergines served in yogurt, tomatoes in olive oil; and dried lentil and bean salads decorated with cucumber and tomato wedges.

Raw and simple salads

My own feeling is that a great many home-grown salad plants are at their best eaten raw with minimum treatment. Any form of cooking not only destroys the subtleties of flavour, texture and colour, but also the vitamins. Raw salads are quickly and easily prepared.

Crudités

The classic French crudités are the most basic raw salads, made from pristinely fresh vegetables, typically served in delicate mounds with a sprinkling of sea salt. The vegetables can be grated, very finely sliced, diced or cut into matchsticks – a perfect way to treat fennel, celery and Beauty Heart radish. Small vegetables, such as summer radish, spring onions and baby carrots, can be left whole. The idea is to eat them with your fingers as an *hors d'oeuvre*, perhaps dipping them into a vinaigrette, mayonnaise, creamy dressing or dips made from tahini, hummus, or yogurt flavoured with chopped mint or garlic, or vegetable purées such as aubergine (steamed or cooked in light oil until soft).

Blend colours and textures to enhance the effect, and serve them in attractive dishes with, for special occasions, finger bowls of rosewater and scented geranium leaves. Some – radishes and spring onions, for example – are best chilled before serving; keep them in iced water in the refrigerator. Keep any that discolour once cut in water into which lemon juice has been squeezed.

Simple salads

The simple salad is epitomised by the classic green salad of fresh, very crisp lettuce leaves or hearts, tossed in a vinaigrette dressing just before serving. Vary it by adding a few leaves of chicory, endive, purslane, dandelion, spinach, or any other appropriate salad plant. Or make a simple salad with any of these alone, or in simple combinations. Change their nature by using different vinegars and oils in the dressings, and garnishing with herbs, flowers, nuts, sprouted seeds or seedlings.

Simple salads can also be made with non-leafy plants such as tomatoes, dressed just with basil and the lightest of vinaigrettes; lightly dressed bean sprouts on a bed of endive; summer or winter purslane mixed with salad rocket. Almost any salad vegetable, can be treated 'simply'.

Mixed salads and saladini

Mixed salads have many more ingredients and, sometimes, more complex dressings, but they must be subtly balanced and blended so that they have character – not merely nondescript diversity for diversity's sake. Into this category of salads falls 'saladini', the modern incarnation of the sixteenth-, seventeenth- and eighteenth-century salads in which twenty or thirty ingredients were combined.

The term 'saladini' arose from our travels in Europe in the late 1970s. In the northern Italian markets we saw seedlings of lettuce, endive, chicory, salad rocket and corn salad being sold alongside baskets of wild plants. The idea was to buy a few handfuls of each and mix them into a salad at home. These small leaves were called *insalatine*, a diminutive of *insalata*, the Italian word for salad, but my untuned ears misheard it as 'saladini'. We liked the word – it was associated in our minds with the Continental plants we began growing and using in mixed salads on our return – and we adopted it as our own to describe our mixed salads. It is now widely used.

Virtually all the plants covered in this book can be used in saladini. Like John Evelyn with his green salads, it is possible to serve a freshly picked saladini every day of the year. (See the Saladini chart on p. 272). In mixing saladini we always try to balance flavours, contrast textures, and include a few ingredients for their form and colour alone. Chopped herbs and flowers add the finishing touches.

Cooked salads

Many vegetables can be cooked, then incorporated into salad dishes when cool. Of the root vegetables, potatoes, of course, are inedible raw; others, including parsnip, salsify and scorzonera, are generally more palatable cooked. Kohl rabi and Jerusalem artichoke are among those with a markedly different, and I think improved, flavour after cooking.

Many legumes, including green and dried French and runner beans, broad beans and various pulses must be cooked, as they are

259

toxic in varying degrees when raw. To some palates cooked dried beans taste even better when eaten cold.

Among vegetables that can be eaten raw when very young, but are generally better in salads cooked and eaten cold are asparagus, cauliflower, courgettes, calabrese and leeks.

The ideal way of cooking vegetables for salads, to preserve texture and natural crispness, is to roast them in the oven in a little oil.

Salads with hot dressings and 'hot salads'

The best-known hot dressing is the French *aux lardons*: essentially hot bacon pieces and juice mixed with salad leaves, which are eaten immediately. There are permutations on the theme, but this dressing is always used for bitter, sharp and strong-flavoured leaves such as dandelion, endive, wild chicory, spinach and oriental mustards.

The Italian *bagna cauda* is another classic hot dressing or dip. Its key ingredients are garlic, anchovy and oil. Piedmontese in origin, it is used with popular Italian vegetables like cardoons, artichoke, celery and endive.

In China and Japan the term 'hot salad' describes vegetables that are stir-fried for no more than half a minute — just long enough to take the edge off their rawness. Still warm, they are tossed in a dressing and immediately brought to table. Sprouted seeds and any of the oriental greens or mustards can be treated this way. Stir-fry them in a mix of cooking and sesame oil, then use any Asian dressing.

Composé salads

The original French composé salads were mixtures of raw or cooked vegetables. In their modern form the net is cast wider, and they are mixed with, say, a staple such as brown rice, pasta, grains such as buckwheat, lentils, bulgur wheat or quinoa, or alternatively fish, meat, chicken or even cheese, or any combinations of these, dressed and garnished as necessary. Take care when making composé salads: such mixtures, it has to be said, can be dire in the wrong hands.

To prevent pasta and basmati rice from becoming lumpy, moisten with oil or butter as soon as it is cooked and before it has cooled. For preference, use long-grain brown rice, American or Spanish rice, as the grains separate nicely and absorb dressings well.

Other examples of composé salads are the various forms of Salade Niçoise, in which tuna is combined with salad vegetables, combinations of beans and peas with tagliatelle, or tomatoes provençale and pain bagna.

Pickling

Before the advent of deep freezes and year-round availability of almost everything, pickling was one of the most important means of preserving food to enliven dull winter diets. A trawl through old gardening books reveals an extraordinary range of plants that were commonly pickled for salads — globe artichokes, beet, French beans, cucumbers, leeks, mushrooms, onions, purslane, radish seed pods, herbs such as summer savory and tarragon, the buds of broom, elder and nasturtium, and the flowers of chicory, cowslip, elder, scorzonera, salsify, clove-scented pinks and nasturtiums, as well as nasturtium seeds.

There is no longer the same necessity to make pickles, but a few salad plants are worth pickling, because they acquire such a good flavour in the process. Among them are shallots, onions, gherkins, sweet peppers, globe artichokes, small beets and nasturtium seeds. It's fun to make a few old-fashioned pickles such as radish seed pods and glasswort.

In essence pickling implies conservation in a spiced, clear vinegar such as cider, wine, rice vinegar or distilled malt vinegar. In some cases the plants are initially sprinkled with salt or soaked in brine to dehydrate them.

'Quick pickles' are short term pickles. The delicious Asiatic quick pickles are eaten within hours or at most a couple of days. They are widely used for Chinese cabbage, spicy oriental greens, root vegetables and cucumbers. The vegetables are sprinkled with salt, and left, depending on the vegetable, for anything from thirty minutes to overnight. In some cases they are pressed under a weight. They are then rinsed before use.

Quick pickling is a practical mean of softening and tenderising vegetables which can have an abrasive quality raw (such as onions and cabbage) before integrating them into salads. Slice them, sprinkle with salt mixed with a little vinegar and sugar, leave for 15 minutes or longer, and pat dry in paper towelling or cloth. This method could be used for cucumbers too; just sprinkle with a little salt then dress with a little sugar and vinegar.

Salad preparation tips and techniques

Gathering

Collect leaves and flowers early in the day of use. Remove soiled leaves, keep unwashed leaves in the fridge in a closed bag until required. (In my experience unwashed leaves keep fresh longer than they do once washed.)

Cleaning and drying

After gentle washing, swing leaves dry in a collapsible salad basket, centrifugal spinner, or simply pat them dry in muslin cloth or a tea towel.

Blanching

This is recommended for softening and tenderising sharp and bitter leaves, fibrous elements in stems, roots and stringy beans, even mangetout peas and raw spinach to make them slightly more digestible before mixing into salads. Bring a large pan of water to the boil, plunge leaves in for no more than a few seconds, roots for a minute or two. Any longer and they become cooked. Immediately plunge them into cold water, or run cold water through in a strainer. Rapid cooling retains flavour and crispness and prevents discolouration.

Stir-frying

Recommended for preparing mature oriental leaves or fibrous vegetables for use in salads: it preserves flavour and most nutrients, bestowing lovely crisp texture. Ideally use a wok (or deep frying pan). Cut vegetables into 2½–5cm/1–2in lengths. Heat the wok until it starts to smoke, put in roughly one tablespoon of mild cooking oil per handful of greens. When the oil is sizzling hot, add the greens, starting with the thickest pieces. Toss continually for two or three minutes. They need to be tender but still crisp.

Keeping salad fresh

Keep left-over salad leaves in a fridge, lightly dried but still slightly damp, in a plastic or 'ziplock' bag with the air expelled. A piece of kitchen paper in the bag absorbs excess moisture. Wilted lettuce can be crisped up just before use in a bowl of ice cubes.

Salad recipes

A Wise man should gather the Herbs
An Avaricious man fling in ye salt and vinegar,
A Prodigal the Oyle.

This ancient ditty on salad making, quoted with approval by John Evelyn in 1699, is still apt in the twenty-first century. In most cases the simplest and lightest dressing is all that is needed to bring out the natural flavour of a salad. Occasionally more sophisticated treatment is called for to convert it from the mundane into something special. There are no rules. Intuition, imagination, experience and your personal preferences are the cornerstones of the art of salad dressing.

Basic dressing ingredients

Oil and vinegar, often blended with mustard, are the ingredients in a basic dressing. Oil-based dressings keep for at least a week in an airtight container in a cool place; mayonnaise and dressings made with yogurt or cream will keep for a day or two in a refrigerator.

Oils

Olive oil 'Extra virgin' or 'first cold pressing' is the strongest, uniquely flavoured, unrefined olive oil, widely considered the supreme oil for salads. For those who find the flavour too 'heavy' and strong, it can be blended with lighter oils, or use just a few drops in a dressing.

Lighter, neutral oils Sunflower, rape seed, and soya oil are among lighter oils, neutral in flavour. So too are the cheaper refined olive oils, generally labelled 'pure' or 'fine'.

Nut oils Walnut oil has a delightful, distinct, fairly strong flavour. It can be blended with lighter oils. Once opened it will keep in a refrigerator for 4–5 months.

Sesame oil Distinctly flavoured, and perfect in Asian vegetable dressings. Oil made from toasted sesame seed has more depth of flavour.

Vinegars

The lighter wine and cider vinegars are the most suitable for salad dressings. Sherry vinegar has just the right edge for Asian dressings. Balsamic vinegar has a sweet flavour.

Home-made vinegars Make subtly-flavoured herb vinegars by steeping sprigs of, say, tarragon, rosemary, thyme or green basil into wine vinegar in a screw top jar or bottle. Rose-coloured vinegars can be made with a handful of raspberries, sprigs of purple basil or red perilla ('shiso'). All these vinegars are ready after a few weeks and will keep for a year.

Mustards

Mustards are a common component of salad dressings and vary considerably in strength and flavour. Of the well-known mustards, the mild-flavoured Dijon mustard and Meaux mustard are the most suitable for standard salad dressings; others, such as strong-flavoured English mustard, can be used sparingly.

Dressings

Vary the following recipes to your whim to suit the salad.

Vinaigrettes and variations

Basic vinaigrette (French dressing)

For use with green salad, any leafy or crisp raw or cooked salad, thin-leaved kales.

1 part wine vinegar or lemon juice, crushed garlic, salt and pepper, 4 parts light oil.

Mix the vinegar or lemon juice, garlic and seasoning in a bowl or jug. Add the oil slowly, stirring vigorously. A few drops of olive oil can be added to the final vinaigrette for heightened flavour.

Thickened vinaigrette For use with coarser leaves and root vegetables. Stir a little mustard into the oil until it is thickened. Add a tablespoon of yogurt or thin cream to make it richer.

Green vinaigrette For use with tomato, potato, carrot, pasta salads. To a thickened vinaigrette add chopped herbs like basil, chervil, mint or thyme and a final sprinkling of olive oil.

Sauce ravigote For use with cooked root vegetables. Add chopped onions, a few capers, chopped anchovies and gherkins to the green vinaigrette.

Ginger and sesame dressing For Chinese vegetables, bean sprouts and other sprouted seeds, kales, quinoa and roasted vegetables.

150ml sunflower or rapeseed oil, 25ml toasted sesame oil, 1tsp Dijon mustard, 25ml soya sauce, 25ml wine vinegar, large piece of fresh ginger, 1 clove garlic.

Put the Dijon mustard into a bowl, whisk in the vinegar, oils and soya sauce. Peel and chop the garlic very finely and stir in. Grate the ginger on the coarse side of a grater without peeling, then squeeze out the juice by hand into the vinaigrette. Give a final whisk before gently mixing into the salad. Fresh coriander, sweet peppers, blanched chili peppers, sesame seeds are possible additions.

Mayonnaise and variations

Basic mayonnaise For use with cooked vegetables, crudités.

2 egg yolks, 1tsp Dijon mustard, salt and pepper, 300ml/½ pint light oil, 1 tablespoon lemon juice or wine vinegar.

Put the egg yolks, mustard, salt and pepper into a large bowl, and stir to a smooth paste. Add the oil slowly, drop by drop, whisking as you go, until the mixture begins to emulsify. Then whisk in the rest of the oil, stirring continuously. Sprinkle in a few drops of wine vinegar or lemon juice and whisk briskly. Taste, and add more seasoning or vinegar if necessary. Should the mixture curdle, break another egg yolk into a clean bowl with a smidgen of mustard, and slowly whisk the curdled mixture into it. Mixtures that have become too thick can be thinned with a few drops of lemon juice. Mayonnaise can be made by hand, or in a blender or food processor.

Sauce verte (Green mayonnaise)

For use with cooked or raw root vegetables, tomatoes, celeriac. Add finely chopped herbs or a little puréed spinach; alternatively, pound a few sprigs of chervil, tarragon, watercress and a couple of spinach leaves in a mortar and add it to the mayonnaise.

263

Rémoulade For use with celery, celeriac, kohl rabi, potato, other cooked root vegetables including salsfy and scorzonera. Add garlic, chopped shallots, anchovy fillets, capers, gherkin, pitted olives, parsley and chervil to mayonnaise.

Aïoli (Garlic mayonnaise) For celery, celeriac, potato and other cooked root vegetables. *1 egg yolk, scant tsp Dijon mustard, 1–2 cloves, finely chopped garlic and 50 ml each of olive and light oil. Season with salt and pepper.*

Skordalia For use with beetroot, potato, aubergine, courgette. A Greek form of aïoli substituting a well-mashed floury potato for the egg yolk in the mayonnaise to make a lighter dressing. In another version, stale white bread, moistened with water, then squeezed, is substituted for the egg. Before making the mayonnaise pound the bread and garlic together and add ground almonds.

Piquant mayonnaise For use with tomato, beetroot, cooked root vegetables, rice-based salads. Add a little grated horseradish and paprika, or a few drops of hot West Indian sauce.

Blue cheese dressing For use with red chicory and bitter leaves. Stir in blue cheese melted over a saucepan of boiling water.

Other dressings
Tahini (ground sesame seed) sauce
For use with lentil and other grain-based salads, roasted vegetable salads, cooked beetroot
Juice of 1 lemon, 1 clove garlic, peeled and finely chopped, 2 tbsp light tahini, pinch of salt, a little water.
Whisk together (except water) until combined. Thin with water to a thick pouring consistency. Stir in yogurt for cooked beet salad.

Plain yogurt dressing Widespread use, especially chicory, cucumber, sorrel, dandelion, beet, spinach.
300ml/½ pint yogurt, 50ml olive oil, juice of one lemon, 2 crushed garlic cloves, small bunch of finely chopped mint dill or fennel, salt and pepper.
Mix the yogurt and lemon juice, then whisk in the oil, garlic, mint and seasoning until emulsified.

Basic sour cream dressing For use with chicory, sorrel, spinach, dandelion, endive, beetroot, cucumber, watercress, land cress. Mix 300ml/½ pint sour cream with one teaspoon each of fresh fennel or dill and chopped mint, a touch of garlic and salt. This basic dressing lends itself to various additions, for example wine vinegar or lemon juice; chopped onions; hot crispy bacon pieces; thin strips of anchovy; tuna pieces; cooked, sliced mushrooms; roast cumin or coriander seeds; thinly sliced, hot-flavoured brassica leaves; crushed black olives with grated orange zest and garlic. Alternative herbs are celery seed or chopped celery, or a purée of parsley, basil or sorrel with salt and pepper.

Bagna cauda This traditional Piedmontese dressing – literally 'hot bath' – is a rough-and-ready hot sauce into which vegetables are dipped. Widely used for cardoons, it is also excellent for celery, endive, sweet peppers with skins removed after charring, globe artichoke hearts, Witloof and red chicory and any bitter leaves. Alternatively leaves can be finely shredded, and the bagna cauda poured over them. (White truffles are used in the authentic Piedmontese bagna cauda.)
5 tbsp butter or 5 tbsp olive oil, 3 crushed garlic cloves, 4 anchovy fillets, mashed, 225g/½lb mushrooms, chopped.

Put the butter or oil into a heavy pan with the garlic and anchovies. Cook gently over moderate heat until garlic turns yellow. Add the mushrooms and simmer until just tender.

Salads

These recipes are a handful of favourites which can be made with the plants described throughout the book and the dressings above. Precise quantities are only given when essential to the balance of the recipe. Vary ingredients and quantities to suit the salad you are making.

Raw salads

Carrot, Avocado and Wakame seaweed
4-5 peeled and grated carrots, 1 ripe peeled avocado, 10g wakame seaweed, 25g sunflower seeds, soya sauce to taste, vinaigrette dressing.
Cut the wakame into small pieces, cover with warm water and leave for 5 minutes. Put the grated carrots into a bowl, surround with avocado cut into chunks, scatter drained seaweed over the top. Heat a dry pan and gently toast the sunflower seeds, toss with a little soya sauce and scatter the seeds over the top. Dress with the vinaigrette.

Celeriac rémoulade Peel a large celeriac, cut into chunks and blanch in boiling water with vinegar or lemon juice added. Drain and shred the celeriac, dress with a rémoulade and garnish with chopped capers.

Witloof chicory with orange This delicious combination scarcely needs a dressing – just a sprinkling of light vinaigrette. Arrange the spears of Witloof chicons like flower petals on a round plate. Slice a mild, peeled Spanish onion and seedless oranges as thinly as possible and arrange in the centre with whole black olives. Garnish with chopped coriander. Easily adapted to Sugar Loaf chicory and curly-leaved endive.

Witloof chicory with piquant mayonnaise Finely slice Witloof chicons, dress with mayonnaise flavoured with horseradish, add crumbled blue cheese and walnuts. Garnish with chopped parsley, chervil or winter savory.

Dill-pickled cucumber *1 cucumber, 1 onion, 1 tbsp chopped dill, 50g caster sugar, 100ml white wine/cider vinegar, ½ tsp salt.*
Slice the cucumber and onion very thinly. Use a mandolin if you have one. Mix the salt, sugar, dill and vinegar together. Toss everything together in a bowl and leave to marinate for an hour. Irresistible!

Dandelion Tear the fresh green leaves into small pieces and mix with equal quantities of blanched endive or Witloof chicory. Rub the salad bowl with garlic before adding the mixed leaves and toss with a vinaigrette. Garnish with olives. Suitable also for sorrel, salad rocket, young spinach and all types of chicory.

Fennel, avocado and pink grapefruit
Slice a large bulb of fennel thinly; cut a couple of ripe, but not too soft, avocados into strips (acidulate with lemon to prevent discolouration). Remove the pith from two grapefruits and divide them into segments. Arrange the ingredients in circles on a shallow dish, and garnish with watercress and fennel fronds. Sprinkle with a raspberry-flavoured vinaigrette made with walnut oil. Chill before serving.

Glasswort (Marsh samphire) Freshly picked, clean young glasswort can be eaten raw. Wash thoroughly if muddy. Otherwise blanch in hot water for a minute or steam lightly, drain and arrange on a plate. Dress with a vinaigrette made with light oil and lemon juice. Serve with slices of lemon. Eat it with your fingers, slurping the leaves off the stems: they come away surprisingly easily.

Iceplant with raspberry vinegar Arrange iceplant in a dish and toss with a vinaigrette made with raspberry vinegar and walnut oil.

Kale, Avocado and Orange *150g kale, 1 large ripe avocado, 2 oranges, 1 red onion, 50g lightly toasted sunflower and pumpkin seeds, 1 tsp Dijon mustard, 2 tbsp cider or balsamic vinegar, 3 tbsp olive oil, salt.* Wash the kale and slice into ribbons, removing the tough centre stems. Juice half an orange and, setting the rest aside, mix 2tbsp of the juice with Dijon mustard and 1 tsp vinegar, and whisk in the olive oil. Season with a little salt and pour over the kale. Massage the dressing into the kale.

Thinly slice the red onion, sprinkle with a little salt and toss to separate the rings. Toss in a bowl with the remaining balsamic vinegar.

Peel the orange, remove the pith and cut into segments. Dice the avocado and keep until required in the reserved orange juice to prevent discolouration. Just before serving, mix the avocado, onion and orange segments with the kale and sprinkle the seeds on top.

Oriental greens Oriental greens and flexibility go hand in hand. Mix sharp-flavoured mustards, torn or shredded into small pieces, with milder pak choi, chrysanthemum greens and mitsuba stems, or other mild leaves like summer and winter purslane. Dress with a thick vinaigrette or ginger and sesame dressing. Chinese chive flowers are the perfect garnish.

Summer purslane and flowers Arrange young purslane leaves in a flattish bowl and sprinkle with chicory, nasturtium and bergamot flowers and a few rose petals. Add chives, marjoram, and green and purple basil, and decorate with a few sprigs of red currants. Splash with a light vinaigrette made with walnut oil.

Sprouted seeds or kale with ginger and sesame dressing Put sprouted seeds in a large salad bowl, pour on the dressing and toss the sprouts until evenly covered. Chill thoroughly before serving. Unless very young, kale leaves can be steamed or lightly stir-fried first.

Cooked salads

Green beans with lemon and parmesan *450g French beans, topped and tailed, 1 finely sliced red onion, 1 clove garlic, 75ml olive oil, 25ml sunflower oil, lemon zest, 1 tbsp white balsamic or white wine vinegar, 1 tsp Dijon mustard, a large handful of basil, grated parmesan, salt and pepper.* Boil the beans for about four minutes in salted water. Test a bean – it should squeak when you bite it, barely tender. If ready, strain and plunge into cold water. Finely chop the garlic and mix together with the Dijon mustard and vinegar. Whisk in the oils and stir in the lemon zest. Taste, and season. Drain the green beans, add a large handful of basil, sliced red onion and toss together with the vinaigrette. Sprinkle over the parmesan and season to taste.

Italian French bean salad A personal favourite as so simple and tasty. Cook green

French beans until just tender, drain, season, and mix with a vinaigrette and finely chopped onion or shallots. Leave to cool. Serve piled on lettuce leaves, garnished with chopped hard-boiled egg, parmesan and chive flowers. Add chopped fresh coriander, parsley, basil, thyme, marjoram or black olives to taste.

Turkish beetroot salad with yogurt

4 medium-sized beetroots, salt and pepper, 300ml/ ½ pint yogurt, 100 mls tahini, crushed garlic clove, caraway seeds, paprika or sumac to garnish.
Preferably bake the beetroots in foil (or boil) until tender. Cool and rub off the skins carefully. Slice or dice, season with salt and pepper. Beat the yogurt with crushed garlic, a little salt and a few caraway seeds and pour over the beetroot. Garnish with paprika.

Chard with sour cream dressing Wash chard leaves and stems well, drain and cut roughly into fairly thick slices, using the white part as well as the green. Steam for a few minutes until tender. Drain well, put in a dish and season well. Mix with a sour cream dressing and garnish with a pinch of cayenne, chopped chives and dill seed. Suitable also for any of the spinaches.

Chinese artichokes Scrub the tubers (which are normally small). Cook in boiling salted water for a few minutes or fry lightly, or steam until just soft. Cool and serve with a well-flavoured vinaigrette or light creamy dressing, and garnish with chopped green herbs.

Globe artichoke Before cooking, clean them by soaking upside down in cold, salted water for an hour or so. Note that in young plants the top of the stem is also tender and delicious.

Cut back the points of tight heads to make them open up and cook faster. Rub any cut surface with lemon to prevent discolouration. Steam or boil for about twenty minutes, until tender, then drain. Eat slowly, dipped into melted butter or a vinaigrette. Pull off the leafy bracts one by one, dip the base into the dressing and suck it clean. Discard the fibrous 'choke' and keep the succulent, exquisite fleshy base to the last.

Marinated sweet peppers

a mixture of different coloured sweet peppers, fresh coriander, cumin and paprika to taste, olive oil, 3 crushed garlic cloves, salt and pepper.
Put the peppers under the grill at mid-heat. Keep turning until the skin is black and blistered, and the insides well cooked. Remove from the grill and wrap in kitchen paper for ten minutes. The skins will then come off very easily. Cut in half, remove seeds and chop into thin strips. Add salt and pepper, a little coriander, cumin and paprika. Mix the olive oil with the garlic and pour it over the peppers. Leave them to marinate overnight. Serve with chopped parsley and lemon wedges.

Green salad *aux lardons*

equal quantities of red lettuce, spinach, sorrel, endive, dandelion and very young beet tops, pieces of crispy bacon, wine or cider vinegar, pumpkin seeds, croûtons.
Choose small leaves, or tear them if large, and place them in a glass bowl. To make the dressing, cube streaky bacon and cook in a pan until the fat runs; remove the crispy bits and add them to the salad. Add a little vinegar and pumpkin seeds to the fat in the pan, and cook for two minutes. Pour over the salad. Decorate with croûtons. Serve immediately. (Suitable also for any bitter leaves such as chicory.)

267

appendices

—

Note on climate and seasons

Climate In very broad terms, climatic zones are divided into tropical, semi-tropical and temperate – which includes the British Isles, and much of Europe and the USA. The planning charts and other data in *The Salad Garden* are based on my experience in East Anglia, in the British Isles, a 'cool' temperate climate, as opposed to the milder, Mediterranean climate. I have used the term 'temperate' to equate with the conditions there as outlined below (roughly US Zone 8), and the term 'warm climate' for regions with longer, hotter summers, where tender vegetables are easily grown outdoors.

In our East Anglian garden the average annual minimum winter temperature was about −7°C/20°F, and this was rarely maintained for more than a few days. In practice crops like spring cabbage, spinach, Brussels sprouts, kale and corn salad overwintered successfully outside. We expected our first frosts in early October, and could get frost as late as the first week in June. So I rarely planted tender crops outside until late spring/early summer. Average mean temperature in the hottest month (usually July) was about 16°C/60°F. Success with the more tender summer vegetables, like tomatoes in the open, was never guaranteed – hence my extensive use of unheated polytunnels. I hope gardeners in warmer and cooler climates can extrapolate from this. In our present, maritime garden in south-west Ireland we rarely experience frost, can probably sow and plant outside three weeks earlier and enjoy longer autumns and shorter winters – benefits offset by the higher, salt-laden winds.

Seasons To enable the book to be interpreted elsewhere, we have throughout used 'seasons' instead of calendar months. The chart below indicates the equivalent month in each hemisphere. Consider seasons a rough guide to the timing of garden operations. In practice the dividing line between seasons is blurred; weather patterns vary not just from one year to the next, but within climatic zones, and even within a locality. And now the marked effects of climate change and global warming have to be taken into account.

Day length In some plants development is governed by the hours of daylight. 'Long-day' plants flower after the longest day in mid-summer; 'short-day' plants flower before the longest day. Day length-sensitive edible plants, such as onions and oriental brassicas, must be grown in the appropriate period to avoid the stimulus of flowering.

Hardiness Term used in temperate zones for a plant's ability to survive winter outdoors

MONTHS/SEASONS CONVERSION CHART

SEASON	NORHERN HEMISPHERE	SOUTHERN HEMISPHERE
Mid-winter	January	July
Late winter	February	August
Early spring	March	September
Mid-spring	April	October
Late spring	May	November
Early summer	June	December
Mid-summer	July	January
Late summer	August	February
Early autumn	September	March
Mid-autumn	October	April
Late autumn	November	May
Early winter	December	June

without protection. Broadly, 'moderately hardy' plants survive at least -5°C/23°F; fully hardy plants to -15°C/5°F. Half-hardy (tender) plants do not survive frost (temperatures of 0°C/32°F) in the open.

Special situations

Most gardens have shaded, dry or wet areas unsuitable for many crops. Here's a few that with a little help tolerate less favourable conditions.

Light shade (provided they have adequate moisture): angelica, chickweed, chicory (grumolo, red and Sugar Loaf), chives, chrysanthemum greens, endive, garlic mustard, lemon balm, lovage, mizuna greens, Hamburg parsley, Jerusalem artichoke, land cress, marjoram (golden-leaved forms), mint, mitsuba, sweet bergamot, salad rocket, sorrel, sweet cicely, wood sorrel, Alpine strawberries. (Comfrey and good King Henry, although not strictly salad plants, are also shade tolerant).

Light shade in summer only Chinese cabbage, chervil, coriander, lettuce, pak choi, parsley, peas, radish, spinach, Swiss chard.

Dry conditions These require enough moisture initially to get them established, and may need occasional watering: alfalfa (*Lucerne*), basil, buckler-leaved sorrel, February orchid, clary sage, winter purslane, iceplant (*Mesembryanthemum crystallinum*), kohl rabi (more drought tolerant than most brassicas), lavender, leaf amaranth, marjoram, New Zealand spinach, pot marigold, red valerian (*Centranthus ruber*), reflexed stonecrop (*Sedum reflexum*), rosemary, summer purslane, sage, salad burnet, thymes.

Moist conditions (provided they are not waterlogged) golden saxifrage (*Chrysosplenium oppositifolium*), lady's smock (*Cardamine pratensis*), lemon balm, chicory (Grumolo and red), Chinese cabbage, corn salad, Florence fennel, Jerusalem artichoke, land cress, leeks, mint, mitsuba, sweet bergamot, watercress.

Year round saladini chart

The salad-lover wants not just fresh salad all year round, but a variety of plants, epitomized by the mixtures we call 'saladini' (see p. 259). A well-balanced 'saladini' has four main elements. While the backbone is bulky, mild-flavoured leaves, variety is created with smaller quantities of sharp or distinctly flavoured leaves, others with outstanding crispness and texture, and lastly, colourful and decorative elements with herbs and edible flowers as the finishing touches.

The chart on the following page divides some of the most popular plants for saladini into these four categories, indicating the main season in which they are harvested fresh. So a glance down each column indicates the range available for a saladini at any time of year. A few plants fall into several categories, but are listed under their prime characteristic. A few others, which there was not space to include fully, are indicated at the side. Herbs, sprouted seeds, microgreens and most root vegetables have been omitted, as have a few fruiting vegetables, such as most tomatoes and sweet peppers, which are best used on their own rather than in a saladini mix.

Use the chart to plan your own salad garden, so that you will have a supply of varied salad ingredients all year round. The chart is largely based on records kept in my previous garden in Suffolk (see climate note opposite). If you are gardening in a warmer climate, the season for tender vegetables such as tomatoes and cucumbers will be longer,

YEAR-ROUND SALADINI CHART

	WKS	CCA	MID WIN	LATE WIN	EARLY SPR	MID SPR	LATE SPR	EARLY SUM	MID SUM	LATE SUM	EARLY AUT	MID AUT	LATE AUT	EAR WIN
BULKY & MILD														
Lettuce, headed summer	12													
Lettuce, leaf	6	S												
Cabbage, spring	34	sm												
Cabbage, summer	15	sm												
Cabbage, winter	24													
Kales, red Russian*	7	S												
Chinese cabbage (headed)	9	sm												
Chinese cabbage (loose-headed)	8	S/sm												
Pak choi	6½	S/sm												
Winter purslane	11	S/sm												
Summer purslane	8	S/sm												
Corn salad	12	S/sm												
SHARP AND/OR DISTINCTLY FLAVOURED														
Sugar Loaf chicory	13	S/sm												
Curly and broad-leaved endive	12½	S/sm												
Land cress	8	S/sm												
Salad rocket	5½	S/sm												
Sorrel (perennial)		sm												
Oriental bunching onion	4–12													
Small radish	3–4													
CRISP AND/OR DISTINCTLY TEXTURED														
Small cos lettuce	12													
Witloof chicory	24													
Curly and Tuscan kale	18	S												
Rosette pak choi	8	S/sm												
Iceplant	10	sm												
Self-blanching celery	14													
Cucumber	14													
Florence fennel	10	sm												
Manetout peas	10													
DECORATIVE AND/OR COLOURFUL														
Red chicory (headed)	13	sm												
Ornamental cabbage & kale	13	sm												
Mizuna greens	10	S/sm												
Mibuna greens	10	S/sm												
Serrated & frilly leaved mustards	3–4	S												
Small tomatoes	20													
Beauty Heart radish	11													

KEY

CCA = cut-and-come-again
S = cut-and-come-again seedlings
sm = cut-and-come-again when semi-mature/mature
* = also other thin-leaved kales, see ❱ on p. 237

wks = average weeks to maturity

▬▬▬▬ season of availability
▬▬▬▬ season extended under cover

and of course the reverse will apply in cooler climates. To be sure of quality salads all year round, especially in the leaner winter months, I make extensive use of protection or cover. In my case this is unheated polytunnels; it could equally be cloches, frames or protective fleeces.

The chart shows how the season can be extended with the use of protection.

Additional plants

Bulky and mild *All year round:* (S) Texsel greens, (S) komatsuna
Autumn to spring: February orchid

Sharp and/or distinctly flavoured

All year round: spinach, cress, spring onions, leaf radish
Spring: chrysanthemum greens, dandelion, bulb onions, shallots
Summer: chrysanthemum greens, dandelion, mooli radish, (S) oriental mustards,
Winter: chrysanthemum greens, bulb onions, hardy winter radish, shallots

Crisp and/or distinctly textured

All year round: (S) alfalfa
Spring and summer: radish seed pods
Autumn: Chinese and Jerusalem artichokes, radish seed pods, choi
Winter: Chinese and Jerusalem artichokes, trench celery, winter radish

Decorative and/or coloured

All year round: red lettuce, (S) 'Bright Lights' Swiss chard, buck's horn plantain
Spring: Treviso chicory. Flowers: February

orchid, bellis, chives, pansy, pot marigold, oriental greens' flowers
Summer: 'Bull's Blood' beet leaves, red cabbage, (S) red orache, 'Magentaspreen' tree spinach, gold-leaved summer purslane. Flowers: chives, nasturtium, pot marigold, Tagetes, pansy, rose
Autumn: 'Bull's Blood' beet leaves, red cabbage, purple-stemmed pak choi, (S) red orache, 'Magentaspreen' tree spinach. Flowers: as summer
Winter: red cabbage, Treviso chicory, purple stemmed pak choi. Flowers: winter pansy

Where do I start? Suggestions for novice gardeners

If you are new to gardening, the choice of salad crops can be bewildering. I would suggest starting with just one or two from each group, then extending your range as you gain confidence. The following are some of the most easily grown, especially when grown as baby leaves.

Bulky and mild Salad Bowl lettuce, Texsel greens, fine-leaved kales, pak choi, komatsuna and salad rape seedlings.

Sharp/distinctly flavoured Rocket, sorrel, radish, curly endive seedlings.

Crisp or textured 'Little Gem' lettuce, mizuna greens, winter purslane

Decorative Red and green Salad Bowl and Lollo lettuce, winter purslane, mibuna greens, nasturtium and calendula flowers.

Further reading

Note that out of print books can now often be sourced online.

Other books by Joy Larkcom

Grow Your Own Vegetables, Frances Lincoln, revised 2003, 978 0 7112 1963 2 (also available as Kindle edition)

Creative Vegetable Gardening, Mitchell Beazley, revised 2014, 978 1 8453 3924 1

Oriental Vegetables: The Complete Guide for the Gardening Cook, Frances Lincoln ed., revised paperback 2007, 978 0 7112 2612 8

Just Vegetating, A Memoir, Frances Lincoln, 2012, 978 0 7112 2935 8 (part autobiography, part reprints of old articles)

Books on vegetable growing

Bleasdale, J.K.A., and others (eds), *The Complete Know and Grow Vegetables*, Oxford University Press, revised edition 1991, 978 0 1928 6114 6 (the scientific basis of vegetable growing) Kindle edition available.

Evelyn, John, *Acetaria: a Discourse of Sallets*, 1699, Scholar's Choice facsimile 2015, 978 1 2971 0878 5 (original inspiration for salad lovers)

Marshall, Terry, *Organic Tomatoes: the Inside Story*, Harris Associates, 1999

McFadden, Christine, and Michaud, Michael, *Cool Green Leaves and Red Hot Peppers*, Frances Lincoln, 1998, 0 7112 1223 6 (inspirational on growing and cooking for flavour)

Salt, Bernard, *Gardening under Plastic*, B.T. Batsford, 978 0 7112 3170 2 (reissued as Kindle 2015) (covers fleeces, films, cloches and polytunnels)

Vilmorin-Andrieux, English edition edited by William Robinson, *The Vegetable Garden*, 1885, Scholar's Choice reproduction, 2015, 978 1 2983 2703 1 (superb classic) (& other reproductions)

Other aspects of gardening

Appelhof, Mary, *Worms Eat My Garbage*, Worm Woman, Inc updated 2016, 978 0 9972 6141 7 (the definitive guide to worm composting)

Cairney, Edward, *The Sprouters Handbook*, Argyll Publishing, 3rd edition 2011, 978 1 9061 3475 4

Buczacki, Stefan, and Harris, Keith, Collins *Pests, Diseases and Disorders of Garden Plants*, Harper Collins, 2014 4th revised edition, 978 0 0074 8855 1

Henry Doubleday Research Association: *Step by Step leaflets on organic gardening* (those in print available from Kings Seeds – see Seed suppliers p. 726)

McVicar, Jekka, *Jekka's Complete Herb Book* – in association with the Royal Horticultural Society, Kyle Cathie Ltd, 2009, 978 1 8562 6780 9 (very practical)

Phillips, Roger, *Wild Food: A Complete Guide for Foragers*, Pan MacMillan, revised edn, 2016, 9781 4472 4996 2

Powers, Jane *The Living Garden: A Place that Works with Nature*, Frances Lincoln, 2011, 978 0 7112 3026 2 (organic gardening philosophy and practice)

Rose, Francis, *The Wild Flower Key: How to Identify Wild Plants, Trees and Shrubs in Britain and Ireland*, Penguin Books, 2015, 978 0 7232 5175 0

Schwartz, Oded, *The Preserving Book*, Dorling Kindersley, 1996, 978 0 7513 0345 2

Stickland, Sue, *Back Garden Seed Saving*, Eco-logic Books, 2001, 978 1 8992 3315 1 (heritage varieties and seed saving)

Walker, John, *How to Create an Eco Garden: The Practical Guide*, Aquamarine, 2011, 978 1 9031 4189 2 (practical step-by-step techniques)

Walker, John, *Weeds: An Organic, Earth-friendly Guide to Their Identification, Use and Control*, Earth-friendly Books, 2016, 978 0 9932 6834 2

Wilkinson Barash, Cathy, *Edible Flowers*, Fulcrum Publishing, 1998, 978 1 5559 1389 2

Organisations

The following organisations in the UK and Ireland offer extensive resources and information to gardeners.

Garden Organic, Ryton Gardens, Coventry, CV8 3LG UK; tel +44 (0) 2476 308 210; gardenorganic.org.uk

GIY (Grow it Yourself) Ireland, Floor 2, Williamstown Centre, Ardkeen, Waterford, X91 YA2H, Ireland; tel. +00353 (0) 51 584 411; giyinternational.org

Royal Horticultural Society, 80 Vincent Square, London, SW1P 2PE; tel. +44 (0)20 3176 5800; rhs.org.uk

The Organic Centre, Rossinver, Co. Leitrim, Ireland; tel. +353 (0) 71 98 54338; theorganiccentre.ie

Seed suppliers

The mail-order companies below are among those that currently offer a wide or unusual range of salad seed. Many also offer plants and gardening equipment. For up to date information consult their websites. Specific seeds can often now be located via the internet. Many garden centres stock seed.
* = companies which primarily supply professional growers in relatively large quantities.

UK

D.T. Brown Ltd, Western Avenue, Matrix Park, Chorley, Lancs, PR7 7NB; tel. +0044 (0) 845 371 0532; dtbrownseeds.co.uk

Chiltern Seeds, Crowmarsh Battle Barns, 114 Preston Crowmarsh, Wallingford, OX10 6SL; tel. +44(0) 1491 824675; chilternseeds.co.uk (very wide range)

*CN Seeds, Ltd., Pymoor, Ely, Cambs, CV6 2ED; tel, +44(0) 1353 699413; cnseeds.co.uk (Wide range including herbs)

275

Delfland Nurseries Ltd., Benwick Rd., Doggington, March PE15 OTU; tel. +44 (0) 1354 740553; delfland.co.uk/organicplants. co.uk (vegetable plants, biological controls)

Dobies Seeds, Long Rd, Paignton, Devon TQ4 7SX; tel. +44 (0) 844 967 0303; dobies.co.uk

Franchi Seeds of Italy, Phoenix Business Centre, Unit D2, Rosslyn Crescent, Harrow, Middx, HA1 2SP; tel. +44 (0) 208 427 5020; seedsofitaly.com

The Garlic Farm, Mersley Lane, Newchurch, Isle of Wight, P036 ONR; tel. +44 (0) 1983 865378; thegarlicfarm.co.uk (seed garlic)

Johnsons Seeds, Kentford, Suffolk, CB8 7QB; tel. +44 (0) 333 321 3103; johnsons-seeds.com

Kings Seeds Ltd, Monks Farm, Coggeshall Rd, Kelveden, Essex, CO5 9PG; tel. +44 (0) 1376 570000/572456; kingsseeds.com

Marshalls Seeds, Alconbury Hill, Huntingdon, Cambridgeshire, PE28 4HY; tel, +44 (0) 844557 670/ (0)344 557 6799; marshalls-seeds.co.uk

Mr Fothergill's Seeds, Gazeley Road, Kentford, Suffolk, CB8 7QB; tel: +44(0) 3337773936; mr-fothergills.co.uk

Moles Seeds Ltd, Turkey Cock Lane, Stanway, Colchester, Essex, CO3 8PD; tel. +44 (0) 1206 213213; molesseeds.co.uk

Nicky's Seeds, 33 Fairfield Rd, Broadstairs, CT10 2JU; tel. +44 (0) 1843 600972; nickys-nursery.co.uk

Organic Gardening Catalogue, Heritage House, 52-54 Hamm Moor Lane, Addleston, Surrey KT15 2SF; tel. +44 (0) 1932 878570; organiccatalogue.com

Plant World Seeds, St. Marychurch Rd., Newton Abbot, Devon, TQ12 4SE; tel. +44 (0) 1803 872939; plant-world-seeds.com

Poyntzfield Herbs, by Dingwall Ross & Cromarty, Dingwall, IV7 8LX; tel. + 44 (0) 1381 610352; poyntzfieldherbs.co.uk (herbs, some edible wild plants)

Sea Spring Seeds, West Bexington, Dorchester, Dorset, DT2 9DD; tel. +44 (0) 1308 897898 seaspringseeds.co.uk; (specialists, pepper plants)

Simpson's Seeds, The Walled Garden Nursery, Horningsham, Warminster, BA12 7NQ; tel. +44 (0) 1985 845004; simpsonsseeds.co.uk

Suffolk Herbs, see Kings Seeds

Suttons Seeds, Woodview Road, Paignton, Devon, TQ4 7NG; tel. + 44(0) 1803 696300; suttons.co.uk

Tamar Organics, Cartha Martha Farm, Rezare, Launceston, Cornwall, PL15 9NX; tel. 01579 371098; tamarorganics.co.uk

Thompson & Morgan Ltd, Poplar Lane, Ipswich, Suffolk, IP8 3BU; tel. + 44 (0) 844 573 1818; thompson-morgan.com

*Tozer Seeds, Pyrports, Downside Bridge Road, Cobham, Surrey, KT11 3EH; tel + 44 (0) 1932 862 059; tozersseeds.com

Tucker's Seeds, Brewery Meadow, Stonepark, Ashburton, Devon, TQ13 7DG; tel. +44(0) 1364 652233; edwintucker.co.uk

Unwins Seeds Ltd, Alconbury Hill, Huntingdon, Cambridgeshire, PE28 4HY; tel. +44(0)844 573 8400; unwins.co.uk

Ireland

Brown Envelope Seeds, Ardagh, Church Cross, Skibbereen, Co. Cork; tel. +353(0) 28 38184; brownenvelopeseeds.com (open pollinated, February orchid)

Green Vegetable Seeds, Alderwood, Eden Point, Rossinver, Co Leitrim; tel. + 353 (0) 87 353 1420; greenvegetableseeds.com

Seedaholic, Ballintleva, Clogher, Westport, Co. Mayo; +353(0) 98 50666; seedaholic.com

Organic Centre, Rossinver see Organisations.

Shortlist of non UK/Ireland companies supplying salad seed

Many others can be found via the web and gardening press.

Bountiful Gardens, 18001 Shafer Ranch Rd., Wllits, CA 95490, USA; tel. 707 459 6410 bountifulgardens.org

de Nieuwe Tuin, Trompwegel 27, B-9170 de klinge, Belgium; tel. +32 (0) 3 770 78 16 denieuwetuin.be

Diggers Garden Company, PO Box 300, Dromana, Vic 3936, Australia; tel. +61 03 5984 7900; diggers.com.au

Eden Seeds, M.S. 905, Lower Beechmont Queensland 4211, Australia; tel. +61 7 5533 1177; edenseeds.com.au

Ferme de Saine Marthe, BP 70404-49004 Angers Cedex 01, France; tel. +33 891 700 899 fermedesaintemarthe.com

Graines Baumaux, BP 100, F88503 Mirecourt, Cedex, France; graines-baumaux.fr

Johnny's Seeds, Foss Hill Rd, Albion, RR No. 1, Box 2580, ME 04910, USA; tel. +1 877 564 6697; johnnyseeds.com

King's Seeds (NZ) Ltd, 189 Wharawhara Road, RD 2, Katikati, Bay of Plenty, New Zealand; tel.+64 7 549 3409; kingsseeds.co.nz

Kitazawa Seed Co. 201 4th St, No. 206, Oakland, CA 94607; tel. +1 510 595 1188; kitazawaseed.com

Nichols Garden Nursery, 1190 Old Salelm Rd NE, Albany, Oregon 97321 - 4580, USA; tel. +1 800 422 3985; nicholsgardennursery.com

Totally Tomatoes, 334 Stroud St, Randolph, Wisconsin 53956; tel. (800)-345-5977; totallytomato.com

Equipment sources
* = products specifically for organic gardeners (online addresses)

General supplies
*Agralan, Old Brickyard, Ashton Keynes, Wilts, SN6 6QR UK tel: +44 (0) 1285 860015 agralan.co.uk

*Fruit Hill Farm, Colomane, Bantry, Co. Cork, Ireland; tel: + 353 (0) 027 50710; fruithillfarm.com

Ferndale Lodge Gardening Supplies, Woodfield Rd, Paignton, Devon, TQ4 7NF ferndale-lodge.co.uk; tel. +44 (0) 0844 314 1342

Harrod Horticultural, 1–3 Pinbush Road, Lowestoft, Suffolk, NR33 7NL, UK; tel. +44 (0) 333 400 1500; harrodhorticultural.com

Haxnicks, Tildenet Group Ltd, Journal House, Hartcliffe Way, Bristol, BS3 5RJ, UK; tel: +44 (0) 117 9341799; haxnicks.co.uk

LBS Garden Products, Standroyd Mill, Cottontree Lane, Colne, Lancs, BB8 7BW; tel. + 44 (0) 1282 873333; lbsbuyersguide. co.uk

* Organic Gardening Catalogue
(see Seed suppliers)

* Quickcrop Unit 4, Ballymore Industrial Estate, Ballymote, Co. Sligo, F46 YR52, Ireland; tel. +353 (0) 1 524 0884; quickcrop.ie/vegetable-seeds

Two Wests & Elliott, Unit 4, Carrwood Road, Sheepbridge Industrial Estate, Chesterfield, Derbyshire, S41 9RH, UK; tel. +44 (0) 1246 twowests.co.uk

Water Irrigation, Unit E, Stafford Park 18, Telford, TF3 3BN, UK, tel. +44 (0) 8456 899 866 waterirrigation.co.uk (watering equipment)

Polytunnels, plastic films, raised bed hoops
Biobags (Scotland) Ltd, 4 St. Ninians, Monymusk, Inverurie, Aberdeenshire, AB51 7HF, UK; tel. +44 (0) 1467 651 247; biobags.co.uk

First Tunnels, Dixon St., Barrowford, UK, BB89 8PL; tel. +44 (0) 1282 601253; firsttunnels.co.uk

Highbank Polytunnels Ltd, Farmley, Cuffesgrange, Co. Kilkenny, Ireland; tel. +353 (0) 56 7729918; highbank.ie

Keder Greenhouses, Newtown, Offenham, Evesham, Worcs, WR11 8RZ, UK; tel. +44 (0) 1386 49094, +44 (0)1386 49094; kedergreenhouse.co.uk

Knowle Nets, 20 East Road Bridport, Dorset, DT6 4NX, UK; tel: +44 (0) 1308 424342; knowlenets.co.uk

Northern Polytunnels, Mill Green, Waterside Road, Colne, Lancs, BB8 OTA; tel. + 44 (0) 1282 873120; northerntunnels.co.uk

Tenax Spa, Via dell'Industria 3, I-23897 Viganò (LC), Italy; tel. +39 (0) 39 92191; tenax.net/gardening

Biological controls

Defenders, c/o Wyebugs, Occupation Road, Wye, Ashford, Kent, TN25 5EN, UK; tel. +44 (0) 1233 813130; defender.co.uk

Green Gardeners, Chandlers End, Mill Road, Stokesby, Great Yarmouth, Norfolk NR29 3EY; tel. +44 (0) 1493 750061; greengardener.co.uk

Koppert Biological Systems, PO Box 155, 2650 AD Berkel en Rodenrijs, The Netherlands; tel. + 31 (0) 10 5140444; koppert.com (contact for regional supplier)

Nematodes Direct, Holkham House, Well End, Friday Bridge, Cambs, PE14 OHQ; nematodesdirect.co.uk

Nemasys 66 Cathedral Rd, Armagh, N. Ireland, BT 61 8 AE, UK; tel: +44 (0) 28 3752 4800; horticultureireland.com

Photographic acknowledgments

Jason Ingram: 4, 16, 60, 70, 82, 94, 130, 146, 168, 180, 182, 189, 193, 194, 202, 209, 214, 219, 225, 226l, 233, 238, 240, 243, 245, 246, 248, 250, 251, 255, 268

Roger Phillips © Frances Lincoln Ltd: 18, 20b, 21, 23, 24, 26, 28bl, 28br, 28m, 28tl, 31, 34, 36, 42tl, 42br, 45, 46, 48, 49, 50, 53tl, 54, 58, 59tl, 62, 65, 66tl, 66tr, 66b, 69, 74, 77t, 77bl, 77bm, 80, 84, 87, 88, 91, 92, 96, 98, 101, 102, 104tl, 104tml, 109, 112, 114, 115, 118, 122, 123l, 125, 132 (except tr & br), 136, 141, 142, 143, 144l, 145, 148, 153, 157, 158, 160, 161, 163, 165, 167, 224, 253

Joy Larkcom: 12, 13, 15, 184, 186, 231

Richard Johnston: 6, 8, 116, 176, 190, 280, 281

Peter Bauwens: 77br, 127

Thompson and Morgan Ltd: 104bl & tr (white and 'Sunsweet' cucumbers)

Shutterstock.com: JackK 109m; JIANG HONGYAN 20t, 42tr; Jiri Hera 111tl; Johan_R 111br; Julia Tsokur 109mr; Kuttelvaserova Stuchelova 144r; mayakova 128tr; picturepartners 42bl, 59br; Poliuszko 89; Quanthem 56; Stock Up 104tmr; Trong Nguyen 128l; Ungnoi Lookjeab 217; Vic and Julie Pigula 166; wacpan 137

Alamy: Andrea Jones Images 256; Ernie Janes 226r; Keith Leighton 53tr; Rex May 111tr

GAP Gardens: Nicola Browne 173; Nicola Stocken 175

Illustrations

Illustrations by Jane Cradock-Watson, Becky Clarke, Elizabeth Douglass, Nick May and Jim Robins © Frances Lincoln.

Index

Page numbers with an <u>underline</u> indicate the main entry.
Page numbers in **bold** indicate an illustration.

Author's acknowledgements

This extensive revision of *The Salad Garden*, nearly 15 years after the previous edition, has only been possible with the help of friends in the gardening world.

First and foremost, my thanks to Mike Day, formerly head of Vegetable Trials at the National Institute of Agricultural Botany, for the countless hours he spent updating the recommended varieties, bringing his experience to bear on many variety trial results, as well as highlighting recent changes in vegetable growing. Very big thank yous to fellow garden writers and gardeners who generously shared their knowledge with me: Sue Stickland, Sarah Wain of West Dean Gardens, John Walker, Pauline Pears, Mike Michaud of Sea Spring Seeds, (with renewed thanks for the accolade of naming *The Salad Garden* your 'food book of the century' on the Radio 4 Food Programme at the close of the 20th century), and Peter Bauwens of de Niewe Tuin in Belgium. Another special thank you to Karen Austin of Lettercollum Kitchen Project for her culinary wisdom and help in updating the recipes. Thanks to Sally McKenna for her tip on keeping salads fresh.

As ever seedsmen and plant suppliers are a great resource for us garden writers. Thank you to Charles Seddon of CN Seeds, for his expertise on microgreens and less well known vegetables, to Jill Vaughan of Delfland Nurseries, and to Trials Officer Debbie Roe and the many people involved in the Royal Horticultural Society Vegetable variety trials. Thank you, also, to CN Seeds and Mr. Fothergill Seeds for generously supplying seeds used in growing material for the new photography.

Which brings me to a second thankyou to Sue Stickland and Sarah Wain, for their enthusiasm and hard work, often with the odds against them, preparing features for the additional photography for this edition, so ably undertaken by Jason Ingram. And thank you to Peter Bauwens and Richard Johnston, for their exceptional photographic contributions.

Once again, thank you to my husband Don who has to put up with so much while I'm engrossed in writing.

At publishers Frances Lincoln, thank you to designer Sarah Allberrey for her enthusiastic and exceptionally skilful work, to Zena Alkayat for commissioning this new edition, and finally, yes, another special thank you, to Laura Nicolson, who has been the most supportive, constructive, perceptive editor one could wish for: a real joy to work with.

If I have overlooked anyone, forgive me. Please take as read my thanks to the many people involved in work on the earlier editions of *The Salad Garden*.